THEATER OF THE VOID

signale
modern german letters, cultures, and thought

Series Editor: Paul Fleming, Cornell University
Peter Uwe Hohendahl, Founding Editor

Signale: Modern German Letters, Cultures, and Thought publishes new English language books in literary studies, criticism, cultural studies, and intellectual history pertaining to the German-speaking world, as well as translations of important German-language works. Signale construes "modern" in the broadest terms: the series covers topics ranging from the early modern period to the present. Signale books are published under a joint imprint of Cornell University Press and Cornell University Library. Please see http://signale.cornell.edu/.

Theater of the Void

*Plasticity, Hauntology,
and Nuclear Blast*

Teresa Kovacs

A Signale Book

Cornell University Press and Cornell University Library
Ithaca and London

Cornell University Press and Cornell University Library gratefully acknowledge the College of Arts & Sciences, Cornell University, for support of the Signale series.

This project was supported in part by Indiana University's Presidential Arts and Humanities Program and by IU's College Arts and Humanities Institute.

Copyright © 2025 by Teresa Kovacs

All rights reserved. Except for brief quotations in a review, this book, or parts thereof, must not be reproduced in any form without permission in writing from the publisher. For information, address Cornell University Press, Sage House, 512 East State Street, Ithaca, New York 14850.

First published 2025 by Cornell University Press
and Cornell University Library

Library of Congress Cataloging-in-Publication Data

Names: Kovacs, Teresa, author.
Title: Theater of the void : plasticity, hauntology, and nuclear blast / Teresa Kovacs.
Description: Ithaca : Cornell University Press and Cornell University Library, 2025. | Series: Signale: modern German letters, cultures, and thought | "A Signale book" | Includes bibliographical references and index.
Identifiers: LCCN 2024042006 (print) | LCCN 2024042007 (ebook) | ISBN 9781501781438 (hardcover) | ISBN 9781501781421 (paperback) | ISBN 9781501781407 (epub) | ISBN 9781501781414 (pdf)
Subjects: LCSH: Experimental drama, German—20th century—History and criticism. | Experimental theater—Germany—20th century—History and criticism. | Aesthetics.
Classification: LCC PN2654 .K65 2025 (print) | LCC PN2654 (ebook) | DDC 792.0943—dc23/eng/20241009
LC record available at https://lccn.loc.gov/2024042006
LC ebook record available at https://lccn.loc.gov/2024042007

Contents

Preface	vii
Introduction: Theater and the Void	1
1. In a Flash: Change and Futurity in the Theater of the Void	36
2. Falling Out of Time and Space: The Quantum World and the Indifferent Subject in Heiner Müller	71
3. End Times and the End of Time: Silent Murmurs in Elfriede Jelinek	105
4. Darkness, Movement, and Metamorphosis: Radical Possibility in Christoph Schlingensief	138
5. *D-Dramatik* or "Darwin-Type Theater": Unpredictability and Singularity in René Pollesch	170
Conclusion: Theater after the End of the World	201
Bibliography	221
Index	245

Preface

On a rainy day in March 2018, I found shelter at the Geffen Contemporary, one of the smaller locations of the Museum of Contemporary Art in Los Angeles. At first, I was merely grateful to have finally entered a dry space after walking the streets of downtown LA for hours in the pouring rain. However, that first feeling of relief suddenly turned into a much stronger impression, as I found myself in the middle of Adrián Villar Rojas's installation *The Theater of Disappearance*. Immersed in this installation, I forgot that I was in one of the largest metropolitan areas of our world, even though, paradoxically, the installation pushed me back into the very streets from which I had just escaped: it recalled the small stores and restaurants of LA's Little Tokyo, in whose neighborhood the museum is located—but not in their present form. I had the feeling I was taking a walk through the ruins of a long-gone metropolis.

Rojas's work consists of numerous refrigerators full of human debris, including old sneakers, plastic wires, nylon jackets, glass bottles, and artificial limbs. These objects are placed in the middle of meat replicas, fish bones, and dried flowers, so that each individual refrigerator creates a kind of still life that sheds light on the human condition in the twenty-first century. The fridges are surrounded by chunks of stone, wooden boxes containing human skeletons, and columns that reveal layers of stone and glass.

In this eerie landscape, a line by Heiner Müller came to mind: "The landscape might be a dead star where a task force from another age or another space hears a voice and discovers a corpse."[1] Under the influence of Rojas's work, I had the feeling of understanding the sentence anew. In this particular space, I felt like the seeker from another time *and* a contemporary of the corpse; life and death began to merge in a peculiar way.

This experience led me to turn to the theater of Müller in order to look for the ruins and contaminated landscapes that can be found there. And that preoccupation eventually made me realize that contemporary theater is deeply interwoven with the experience of destruction and ruin, exploring as it does what it means to live on a destroyed planet. Thus, the ruinous in this theater is connected not only to the mourning for what has been lost but also to the question of how to survive (and yes, even thrive) in the midst of ruins. Ruinousness is far more than just a metaphor in this investigation. Rather, it is linked to a practice that works toward the possibility of a future and asks how the world can be shaped together; a practice that is aware of the complex relationships between the human and the nonhuman, culture and nature, life and death.

Over the past few years, this impression that we are living in the ruins of our technoscientific age has only intensified. Looking back to the summer of 2019, when I had just arrived in Bloomington, Indiana, to take up my new position in the Department of Germanic Studies, I find the following notes I made at the time: "The outline for this book was made on a hot September morning shortly after I moved to my new home, Bloomington. Everyone here told me that this September had been unusually hot. Everyone also added that this was clearly an effect of global warming, which was going to become

---

1. Müller, *Despoiled Shore Medeamaterial Landscape with Argonauts*, 126.

the pressing issue of our time. It was the same day that the *New York Times* reported on the international climate strikes. The coverage certainly fueled an understanding of our present as an apocalyptic space that could soon turn into a post-apocalyptic one, if no one does anything." A few years, a global pandemic, and two devastating wars later, the impression of a world in ruins has not changed for the better but only intensified. The theater to which I have dedicated this book, a theater that is concerned with finding a future in a time when there seems to be no future, therefore seems even more relevant than in 2019. And yet this book does not simply draw bleak pictures of our present; instead, it traces the exciting and sometimes surprisingly light ways in which theater makers experiment to find life and future in the midst of ruins.

This book, which has occupied me for several years, has been shaped by my experiences along the way and the people who have accompanied me on this journey. *Theater of the Void* is the result of my ongoing reflection on contemporary theater, which always seems to defy description. Over the past fifteen years, I have repeatedly tried to grasp and name the theatrical imaginary of our present, which goes beyond drama and representational theater. It has taken me several years and some fortunate, unexpected encounters in order to find words with which I could describe what I had initially only suspected. Such a lengthy, intensive thought process is only possible with the necessary support. I am therefore infinitely grateful for the generous support of the Austrian Science Fund, of the Indiana University Presidential Arts and Humanities Fellows Program, and of IU's College Arts and Humanities Institute which gave me time to concentrate fully on my research and helped with the production of this book.

However, a book like this never happens in solitude; this book was nourished by all the wonderful constellations in which I found myself as I worked on it. My first thanks go to my home institution, the Department of Germanic Studies at Indiana University. Without the support and trust of my colleagues, I would not have been able to write this book. Fritz Breithaupt, Michel Chaouli, Irit Dekel, Susanne Even, Gergana May, Bill Rasch, Benjamin Robinson,

Johannes Türk, and Marc Weiner have all in their own ways inspired and influenced this book—whether by working with me through specific questions, through their love of words and ideas, or by their dedication to critical thinking. The intellectual life we have cultivated in this department has also played an important role in my work on the book, providing opportunities for exchanges with colleagues, doctoral students, undergraduate students, and visitors such as Wolfram Eilenberger, Arne Höcker, Uwe Wirth, and Burkhardt Wolf. The students in my classes have always inspired me to think further; special thanks go to my students in the courses "Wounded Heroes," "Literature and Climate Change," and "Assembling the Precarious." The discussions in these courses generated many of the sparks that fueled this book. Among the PhD students, my special thanks go to Louise Bassini, Bettina Christner, Maria Fink, David Gould, Helen Gunn, Nina Morais, Lanre Okuseinde, Katherine Pollock, Nicole Rizzo, Katharina Schmid-Schmidsfelden, Ahmed Tahsin Shams, and Cynthia Shin. Their passion for experimental art and all things unconventional has always driven me anew. In addition, in November 2023, we launched a working group for theater and performance in our department, which brings together researchers from different disciplines and has already been an invaluable source of inspiration and energy for me in this short time.

Beyond my own department, I value Indiana University as a lively place for thinking and working together. I am thinking above all of the stimulating group involved in the Cultural Studies Program (special thanks to Tess J. Given, Ray Guins, and Rebekah Sheldon), but also of the many inspiring colleagues and friends who have accompanied me on my journey here in Bloomington, such as Anke Birkenmaier, Alyson Calhoun, Ana Carneiro, Ed Dallis-Comentale, Stephanie DeBoer, Jennifer Goodlander, Joan Hawkins, Kathleen Myers, Roberta Pergher, Mark Roseman, and Sonia Velazquez, as well as my former colleagues Shane Vogel (now at Yale University) and Ilana Gershon (now at Rice University).

And yet—as with all journeys—what has shaped this book cannot be limited to my current home turf. The Department of Germanic Languages and Literatures at the University of Michigan, where I spent two years as a postdoctoral fellow, spoiled me with conversations, friendships, and all kinds of support. I would especially like to recognize Kerstin Barndt, Andreas Gailus, Julia Hell, Johannes von Moltke, Helmut Puff, and Scott Spector, as well as, from the Department of Theatre and Drama, Malcolm Tulip and Tzveta Kassabova. I consider myself incredibly lucky to have been able to share an intellectual space with these colleagues and friends, a space that extended far beyond the campus and included all kinds of feasts.

I am also full of gratitude for everything I learned from the group of scholars with whom I had the privilege to work during my time in Vienna. This is the group involved in the Jelinek Research Center, which, in addition to its director, Pia Janke, is enlivened by so many talented and passionate young scholars (a special thanks to Christian Schenkermayer, Konstanze Fladischer, and Peter Clar) and Jelinek experts such as Inge Arteel, Uta Degner, Ulrike Haß, Brigitte Jirku, Monika Meister, Artur Pełka, Katharina Pewny, and Monika Szczepaniak. The members of this group have fueled and supported my passion for discussing and reading the theater in so many ways. There were also many more colleagues from that time in my life and work who grew close to my heart and to whom I am deeply indebted and grateful. Silke Felber deserves a special thanks, as her support goes way beyond this particular context. We shared an office for years and cultivated a form of collaborative thinking that has inspired me ever since. I consider myself lucky that this connection continues to this day.

In addition to these institutional connections, I must thank the wonderful colleagues and friends with whom I have shared my ideas for the book and who have had a significant influence on my thinking and on this book in particular. Colleagues like Emmanuel Béhague, Claudia Breger, Paul Buchholz, Matthew Cornish, Jack Davis, Leonie Ettinger, Megan Ewing, Peter Höyng, Kristopher Imbrigiotta, Olivia Landry, Richard Langston, Klaus Mladek, Tanja Nusser, Benjamin Lewis Robinson, Anna Senuysal, and Marc Silberman have shared my passion for contemporary theater and critically engaged with my book over the years. I am equally grateful for the constant conversation with Elfriede Jelinek, Jürgen Kuttner, and Kevin Rittberger, who have inspired my work and my thinking in so many ways. In addition, special thanks to Gitta Honegger for her love of words and for providing translations of the passages that I quote from Jelinek's untranslated texts and plays; to Imke Meyer and Regina Kecht, who were crucial in helping me make the move from Europe to the United States; and to Jacqueline Vansant, who read several versions of this book and who believed in me when I was full of doubt—without her, this book would not exist. In addition, I am grateful for the invitations from the Heiner Müller Society (special thanks to Marten Weise who hinted at the explosion), New York University, Rutgers University, the University of Wisconsin–Madison, the University of Cincinnati, the Free University of Berlin, the University of Leeds, the University of Strasbourg, and the Sorbonne, which allowed me to develop (early) ideas related to this book and to clarify my own thoughts and arguments.

I would also like to thank Marie Deer for her friendship and the wonderful editing she did on this manuscript. In addition, I am deeply indebted for all that Paul Fleming and Kizer S. Walker of Cornell University Press have done for me along the way. My thanks also go to the reviewers and the board of the Signale series, who have supported this book and improved it with their valuable comments and suggestions.

Last but not least, I would like to thank the person who has inspired this book and my thinking more than I could ever have wished for. Andrés Guzmán, not only are you my faithful companion in our shared and sincere love and passion for what we need to find out and put into words, but you also challenge me again and again, inspiring me to keep expanding the limits of my thinking. Without you, some of my most important interlocutors would never have made it into this book. I am infinitely grateful that you surround me with thoughts and ideas every day, some of which I can pick up and make my own. There is nothing better in this world than a thinking partnership with you.

Theater of the Void

Introduction

Theater and the Void

We are no less and no more than nobody. As nobodies we are nothing. We are nothing, nada, as nobodies. We are. We are not nothing, even Earth bowed before us, that's not nothing, after all. Somewhere it is not today and not tomorrow, that's where those always live who are nobodies, whom nobody sees, those in-betweeners, and nobody knows where they came from.

—Elfriede Jelinek, *Epilog?*

Epigraph: All translations are my own unless otherwise indicated. Private translation by Gitta Honegger. "Wir sind nicht weniger und nicht mehr als niemand. Als Niemande sind wir nichts. Wir sind nichts mehr als Niemande. Wir sind. Wir sind nicht nichts, sogar die Erde hat doch vorhin das Haupt vor uns geneigt, das ist doch nicht nichts! Irgendwo ist nicht heute und nicht gestern, dort leben die dann immer, die niemand sind, die niemand sieht, die dazwischen, und niemand weiß, woher sie gekommen sind."

Theater and catastrophe are intimately linked. This is particularly true for tragedy, a genre shaped by violent rupture. The songs of the ancient Greek chorus warn heroes and audience alike of the possibly devastating outcomes of human action and ask whether what seems to be a tragic fate can be turned into an opportunity. The chorus tries to lead the tragic hero(ine) in the right direction; it seeks to help the hero(ine) overcome his or her blind actions and it pleads with the hero(ine) to be humble. Given that these pleas usually remain unheard, the chorus then goes on to assume another function, mourning the victims of the catastrophe and the inescapable cascade of unfolding violence. This is famously expressed in Sophocles's *Antigone*, where the chorus responds to the news that Antigone has broken the law and buried her brother with the outcry "Monstrous, a lot. But nothing more monstrous than man."[1]

Theater of the Void turns its attention to the catastrophe, which is commonly perceived as a type of ground zero. My focus, though, is not on the catastrophe itself but rather on the zero point that results from there; this is what guides this book, as it allows me to discuss two interrelated questions. First, what can we see when we use the lens of the ground zeroes of our technoscientific age to approach the highly experimental theatrical settings that began to evolve in the world of German-speaking theater in the 1970s?[2] And second, can there be a zero or a void in theater that is not a mere emptiness but is instead another form of possibility and opportunity? In other words, must the void necessarily be an endpoint, or does it have a future? The first question is motivated by the history

---

1. Sophocles, *Antigone*, 81.
2. In the context of Western, and particularly German-language, theater, it is important to keep in mind that the catastrophes of the late twentieth century cannot be fully disconnected from the cascade of devastating catastrophes that shaped the early twentieth century. On the contrary, the theater of the void is related to the aesthetic experiments that evolved from the experiences of World War I, the Shoah, and the devastations of World War II. For a more general discussion of catastrophe in the twentieth and twenty-first centuries and the relationship between the catastrophe of the Shoah and the catastrophes unleashed later in the twentieth century, see Nancy, *After Fukushima*. In using the term "technoscientific" I follow Karen Barad; I discuss this terminology later in this introduction.

of theater. It allows me to present an alternative framework for contemporary theater that emphasizes its ongoing relationship to the sciences and its involvement in the greatest threats of our present, such as nuclear technology and global warming. The second question is of a theoretical and conceptual nature, as it introduces the catastrophe as possibility: the possibility of a transformation of theatrical form but also, in broader terms, the possibility of social, political, ecological, and planetary change. Subsequently, in thinking about contemporary theater through the void, the book pushes beyond the negative terms—a theater without a linearly unfolding plot, characters, or dialogue—that have so far been used to think of the new theatrical forms. Instead, it offers a terminology that sheds light on the rich fluctuations and action that fill what at first glance seems like mere nothingness.

I approach these questions with a focus on German-language theater; in particular, I pay close attention to the theater of Heiner Müller, Elfriede Jelinek, Christoph Schlingensief, and René Pollesch. This list could easily be expanded with names like Einar Schleef, Dimiter Gotscheff, Heiner Goebbels, and Kathrin Röggla. And turning to the younger generation of directors, playwrights, and performance collectives, we could name Florentina Holzinger, Susanne Kennedy, Thomas Köck, and Kevin Rittberger, to mention only a few. In discussing the void in the context of German-language theater, I do not suggest that the void is limited to this specific language and cultural context. On the contrary, German-language theater is rather a specific version of a more global phenomenon. One tradition that might immediately come to mind for most readers is the theater of the absurd, specifically that of Samuel Beckett, who explored the void under the pressure of our technoscientific age. Existentialist drama can also be related to an exploration of nothingness. While these traditions are the ones most obviously connected to the void and to nothingness, they are by far not the only ones; nor are they—and this is particularly true for existentialist drama—necessarily fitting examples for what I term theater of the void. In fact, we can identify tendencies that point toward a theater of the void in multiple, diverse contexts as soon as we take into consideration that the void is not to be identified with the *content*, but that a theater of the void means the radical transformation of theatrical *form* through the void.[3]

Tendencies in the nineteenth and twentieth century that were involved in the push toward what I call the theater of the void include the incipient attempts to rethink theatrical *form* and aesthetics based on an interest in metamorphosis, transformation, chaos, and nothingness. These attempts allow us to draw a line from the radical revisioning of Greek tragedy by Hölderlin, Nietzsche, and Wagner to the work of avant-gardists and visionaries like Antonin Artaud, Adolphe Appia, Edward Gordon Craig, Erwin Piscator, Friedrich Kiesler, and Tennessee Williams.[4] Alongside this, Bertolt Brecht's work on a theater for the scientific age is crucial to the emergence of the theater of the void in the second half of the twentieth century. Both strands inspired radical theatrical experiments, both inside and outside of the German-language context, that caused similar ruptures and breaks, leading to the forceful explosion of drama in the second half of the twentieth century. The Italian writer and director Carmelo Bene is particularly interesting in this context, because he pushed against the tradition of Western representational theater and experimented with a theater that

---

3. Beckett, of course, rejected the conventional form of dialogue and pushed, in his plays, toward the limits of drama. This is particularly true for his plays from the 1960s onward, even though these had a much smaller impact on the theatrical landscape than did his earlier plays, such as *Waiting for Godot*. Beckett cannot be ignored in the context of the theater of the void. He was, ultimately, an important inspiration for the theater of Müller. See the discussion of Müller's reception of Beckett in Kalb, "Samuel Beckett."

4. I want to thank Nicole Rizzo, currently a graduate student at Indiana University Bloomington, who directed my attention to Tennessee Williams. Williams is particularly interesting in the context of this book because he uses the term "plastic theater" to characterize the new theater that he envisions. Plasticity, for Williams, designates organic change and transformation. He introduced the term in dialogue with the painter Hans Hofmann, who defined the empty space between two objects in a painting as the "plastic space" in order to emphasize that this empty space is not inert but, instead, vital and active (Hofmann, *Search for the Real*, 49). For Williams, not only did plastic theater make use of the empty space that he identified in between the different elements of theater (sound, light, film, etc.), he also defined the position of the playwright himself through this notion. For him, the play*wright* is not simply a "writer" but is the one who—following the etymology of the term—constructs plays from diverse materials. For a succinct discussion of Williams's vision of a "plastic theater," see Kramer, "The Sculptural Drama."

deconstructs language and makes visible the unknown and the unconscious, which Bene himself referred to as the void. Another example is the British playwright Sarah Kane, whose radical theatrical experimentations always evolve from catastrophe—be it war bombings or mass rape—and explore our sociopolitical as well as our inner void. Outside of Europe, we must include Butoh, a Japanese dance form that was created as a response to Hiroshima and Nagasaki. Nonetheless, German-language theater is exemplary because in it, more strongly than in other contexts, the exploration of the void has allowed a radically new theatrical form to evolve that shapes its entire theatrical aesthetics and practice to this day.[5] Furthermore, the German-speaking countries have become an important home for directors, playwrights, and performance collectives from all over the world who are likewise investigating the void and making it the groundless ground of their theater. This is true, for instance, for the U.S.-American director Robert Wilson, the Italian director Romeo Castellucci, the Greek director Dimitris Papaioannou, the Japanese playwright and director Toshiki Okada, and the London-based Otolith Group, just to mention a few.

A Farewell to Postdramatic Theater

Some might find it surprising that this book is dedicated to the question of the transformation of theatrical form in the second half of the twentieth century in German-language theater, since Hans-Thies Lehmann discussed this in depth in his groundbreaking study *Postdramatic Theatre*. Indeed, he not only explained the radical transformation that we find in the context of German-language theater but, more broadly, revealed a shift in theatrical practices in diverse cultural contexts.[6] Lehmann's book has dominated the field since

---

5. Even though I focus on German-language theater in this book, I need to stress that theater can and should not be reduced to a specific language or cultural context, as it is per se transcultural. When I speak of German-language theater, I am aware of this, and I am instead speaking of plays that are produced and artists who produce within the German system. See also Cornish and Savran, "Introduction."

6. However, Lehmann clearly framed those non-European theatrical practices through a German- or European-centered lens. Theatrical practices from the Global

its original publication in German in 1999,[7] as can be seen in the numerous translations of the book as well as the many contributions over the past decades that have been written in dialogue with his paradigm. While some of these contributions focused on single aspects of his study—often by adding further "post-" constructions to it—others speculated about what comes *after* postdramatic theater, arguing for a "new realism" or a "post-postdramatic theater."[8] I neither add another "post-" construction to the already long list nor do I join the choir that dismisses postdramatic theater as compliant with neoliberalism.[9] Instead, I give postdramatic theater a future by showing that we can use a different angle to look at some of the works that have been discussed within this frame, thus revealing a potential in these works that has so far been hidden. As such, I see my work as a continuation of Lehmann's seminal study, but one that simultaneously demands a farewell to this paradigm.

A farewell to Lehmann's postdramatic theater is necessary because of the deadlocks in his study that have started to overshadow current scholarly debates on contemporary theater. In his field-defining work, Lehmann introduced the new paradigm of postdramatic theater to describe experimental works from the 1960s onward that

---

South and Asian theater, with a particular focus on Japanese theater, enter his book through their influence on and reception by European theater makers such as Brecht.

7. A second, similarly influential work is Fischer-Lichte, *The Transformative Power of Performance*, which takes performance art as its starting point and describes the performance as an event in which the focus is not on representation but on presence. Fischer-Lichte's study was highly influential in the context of performance art but offers no approach to understanding new forms of theatrical texts, which is why it is less relevant in the context of this book.

8. See, for example, studies that highlight the ethical dimension (Pewny, *Das Drama des Prekären*) or the transcultural dimension (Heeg, *Das Transkulturelle Theater*; Kovacs and Nonoa, *Postdramatisches Theater als transkulturelles Theater*) or that discuss postdramatic theater in a historical context (see the chapter on "Eastern Directors and Postdramatic Historiography" in Cornish, *Performing Unification*). Eiermann, *Postspektakuläres Theater*; Tigges, *Dramatische Transformationen*; and Balme, "Postfictional Theatre" provide great examples of new "post-" constructions and of the focus on a hybridization of form after postdramatic theater. The scholarly debates around Lehmann's terminology are documented and critically reflected in Janke and Kovacs, *Postdramatik*.

9. In this context, Stegemann, *Kritik des Theaters* and Stegemann, *Lob des Realismus* are central.

could no longer be explained within the framework of "drama."[10] Lehmann's study was crucial for breaking away from the ideal of drama and for liberating theater from a narrow definition that reduced it to literature. In *Postdramatic Theater*, Lehmann approaches theater through performance and sheds light on diverse theatrical practices and formations beyond drama, which he finds in both ancient Greek theater and in contemporary performances. The historical form of drama, he insists, dominated the Western theatrical landscape only from around 1800 to the early twentieth century, while before and after we find forms like *Volkstheater* (popular theater) and medieval and baroque drama, as well as formations like the chorus and the messenger, that go beyond the principles of drama. To emphasize that drama is only one possible form that theater can take, Lehmann differentiates among "predramatic," "dramatic," and "postdramatic" tendencies in European theater.[11]

Lehmann relies on the argument laid out by Peter Szondi in his *Theory of the Modern Drama*, originally published in 1956, for the historicity of form and the interdependence of form and content. While Lehmann convincingly argues for the historicity of drama, his own conception of postdramatic theater is unable to account for *how* theatrical forms will continue to change after the end of drama.[12] This stems from his turn to deconstruction in

---

10. Lehmann borrowed the notion of postdramatic theater from his mentor, Andrzej Wirth, who, in drawing an analogy to postmodernism, introduced the term "postdramatic theater" in 1987 to describe the then new theatrical practices (Wirth, "Realität auf dem Theater," 83). Unlike Wirth, though, Lehmann decisively differentiates "postdramatic" from "postmodern" and makes it clear that postdramatic theater does not necessarily break with modernity. For a discussion of the two terms, see the chapters "Postmodern and Postdramatic" and "Choice of Term" in Lehmann, *Postdramatic Theatre*, 25–27.

11. To better understand the historical dimension, it is helpful to consider Lehmann's first book, *Theater und Mythos* (1991), in which he analyzes ancient Greek tragedy. In the introduction to the book, Lehmann uses the term "postdramatic theater" for the first time, to emphasize the proximity between contemporary theater and Greek tragedy (which he terms "predramatic theater"), neither of which fits our understanding of drama.

12. I do not mean to claim that Lehmann considers postdramatic theater as the end of history. On the contrary, he makes it clear that new forms will appear (Lehmann et al., "Für jeden Text," 33). And yet, his paradigm lacks any concept of

an attempt to overcome Szondi's Hegelianism.[13] According to Lehmann, drama and dialectics are interrelated. "*Drama promises dialectic*," he states, which points to a "finally meaningful perspective—reconciliation in idealist aesthetics, historical progress in Marxist historiography."[14] In his rejection of dialectics, though, Lehmann ultimately deprives the historicity of theatrical forms of any future. And thus, because postdramatic theater was lacking any concept of the future, playwrights, directors, and scholars alike have started to criticize postdramatic theater as nothing but a postmodern ploy that repeats and reproduces neoliberal structures instead of interfering in them.

In this book, I challenge Lehmann's identification of drama with dialectics and his subsequent rejection of dialectics. In other words, I counter his argument that dialectics necessarily implies teleology and totality and argue that when playwrights and directors turned away from drama, they did not necessarily also turn away from dialectics. I make my argument by paying attention to an alternative dialectic at work in contemporary theater, one that Lehmann overlooked because he only considered the dominant materialist tradition of ratio, necessity, and teleology. What I point to, in contrast, is a hidden materialism of the aleatory and of contingency that shapes the theater engaged with the void.[15]

---

change or of future, which is reminiscent—although Lehmann does not seem to have intended it that way—of thinking in terms of the end of history.

13. Problematizing the teleology of history, Lehmann seeks to overcome dialectics through deconstruction, pointing out the dissolution of drama *within* dramatic theater itself. He relies on Menke's reading of Hegel: Menke argues that because for Hegel the reconciliation of beauty and morality (*Schönheit und Sittlichkeit*) is essential, drama stands at the beginning of the end of art within art, as it no longer fulfills this reconciliation. Based on this assumption, Lehmann once again stresses that postdramatic theater does not imply a theater fully disconnected from drama. On the contrary, it should be understood as the "unfolding and blossoming of a potential of disintegration, dismantling and deconstruction within drama itself," a virtuality that "was present, though barely decipherable, in the aesthetics of dramatic theater; it was contemplated in its philosophy, but only, as it were, as a current under the sparkling surface of the 'official' dialectical procedure" (Lehmann, *Postdramatic Theatre*, 44).

14. Lehmann, *Postdramatic Theatre*, 39. Emphasis in the original.

15. I draw here from the discussion of the materialisms of Darwin and Althusser in Malabou, "Whither Materialism." Even though I use the term "contingency"

In discovering the void as an integral part of contemporary theater, I can ultimately bring to the fore theater's involvement with the sciences and technology, which was often believed to have ended with Brecht and his claim to a "theater for the scientific age."[16] Brecht was deeply invested in quantum physics and biology, but reassessed their potential for social and political change and their adoption into the theatrical realm after the experience of Hiroshima and Nagasaki.[17] When I pay attention to how theater and the sciences continue to be intertwined, I stress an alternative scenario for the evolution of a new theatrical form, beyond the rise of mass media, which is the only important point of reference for Lehmann. Theater scholars in the German-speaking world in the second half of the twentieth century have often disavowed the sciences and turned away from them.[18] Only in the past few years have they once again shifted their attention to the sciences, inspired by the rich scholarship in the English-speaking realm[19] and due to the reception of works that bridge philosophy, theory, and scientific research.[20]

---

throughout this book, drawing on Malabou, contingency is not understood here as a total lack of necessity but rather in the sense of what Jean-Luc Nancy calls "fortuity" or the *inopiné* (the unexpected, the sudden), which expresses the emergence of the unforeseen "with an extra nuance of interruption, of emergence, and rearrangement of the expected order of things" (Nancy, "The Existence of the World," 89).

16. The scholarship has broadly ignored this aspect of Brecht's theater. Exceptions include Issbrücker and Hippe, *Brecht und Naturwissenschaften*; and Mairhofer, *Bertolt Brechts Interferenz*. More generally on theater and the sciences, see Case, *Performing Science and the Virtual*.

17. This is the common reading of Brecht's 1947 and 1955 revisions of his play *Life of Galileo*.

18. Theater shares this tendency with continental philosophy, which has been similarly ignorant, in the past decades, about the sciences. See, e.g., Malabou's critique of Derrida in *The Future of Hegel*. For the German-speaking countries, particularly Austria and West Germany, this skepticism about the sciences surely has much to do with the violent break in research in those countries due to National Socialism as well as the continued legacy of scientists conducting research according to Nazi ideology far into the 1970s and the 1980s.

19. See, e.g., Shepherd-Barr, *Cambridge Companion*; and Vanden Heuvel, "Good Vibrations." Even here, however, the attention is mostly on science as the content of theater and not so much on the theatrical form.

20. Exemplary theater makers who clearly reference the sciences include René Pollesch and Kevin Rittberger. Both of them initially engaged with Donna Haraway

The Explosion of Drama, Entering the Void, or: Teetering between Life and Death

In Sophocles's *Antigone*, life and death resonate with each other eerily. Indeed, they are reworked when Antigone rejects the law of her uncle, King Creon, which forbids the burial of her brother Polynices, and fights for her right to bury her brother even if it means her death sentence. In remaining unburied and unmourned, Polynices's body resists being categorized as "dead" and appears instead as "living-dead." Antigone, on the other hand, even though she is still alive and fighting for the right to bury her brother, can no longer be considered living. She is "deadly-living," as her life and future are the deathbed. Complicating notions of life and death, the tragedy reflects on the very conditions of the possibility of non/existence.[21] In so doing, it establishes a dynamic relationality between continuity and discontinuity, between determinism and contingency, and between what was and what might yet be.

When playwright Elfriede Jelinek weaves Sophocles's tragedy into the epilogue of *Kein Licht* (No light), her 2011 play on the nuclear disaster in Fukushima,[22] it is because her theater is likewise invested in the dynamic relationality between life and death. Jelinek's plays have become paradigmatic for a new type of theater that has dominated the stages of city and state theaters in Germany, Austria, and Switzerland since the 1980s. She creates prose-like theatrical texts, devoid of characters and types, dialogues, or staging directions.

---

before including a much wider range of sources, including Darwin, Karen Barad, and particular experiments from the field of quantum physics, such as the double-slit experiment.

21. Throughout this book, I use the slash between words to mark troubled dichotomies and binary distinctions. Following Barad's "agential realism," the slash indicates that the two parts of the dichotomy are neither together *and* apart, nor together *or* apart, but that they are cut together-apart (in one move) (Barad, "Troubling Time/s," 78).

22. Jelinek published the text in 2012 on her website as an epilogue to her play *Kein Licht*, which she wrote in the first six months after the meltdown at the Fukushima Daiichi Nuclear Power Plant on March 11, 2011. This is not the only play in which Jelinek returns to *Antigone*; another example is her "secondary drama" *Abraumhalde* (Slag heap, 2008), which must be staged together with Gotthold Ephraim Lessing's *Nathan der Weise* (*Nathan the Wise*).

Jelinek herself claims that due to the lack of action and conflicts between characters in her plays, many consider them boring. "Nothing is happening," she writes in her poetological statement "Grußwort nach Japan" (Greetings to Japan). Yet, she suggests, it is precisely this lack of characters and of any linearly unfolding action that makes her plays live and thrive. "My plays live somehow," Jelinek states, "but in a different way than if they were imitating people with their deeds and misdeeds."[23] Life, here, is no longer connected to the representation of humans within the dramatic plot but refers, instead, to the text itself, which grows like roots, blurring the boundary between animate and inanimate, matter and form. Jelinek repeatedly uses the metaphor of the rhizome, and particularly the root of the bamboo, to talk about her writing. For her, bamboo resembles something in between life and death, construction and destruction. Even when it is destroyed on the surface, the plant continues to grow underground and can come back to life at any moment.[24]

Jelinek's theater returns to the exploration of the fine line between life and death that characterizes Sophocles's *Antigone*—a return, though, not in the sense of bringing back something that has passed but rather as inventing it anew under changed conditions. In her theater, the collapse of life and death no longer shapes the characters and their fate but moves instead into the very structure of the theatrical text and theater itself, where text and the acting/writing body are eerily entangled and where both are presented to us as infinitely fluctuating between life and death. Jelinek claims that her theater simultaneously *brings to life* and *takes life*; meaning that whenever actors *bring* her texts *to life*, they simultaneously *lose life*, as the theater thrives on their vitality. At the same time, theater means escaping death, even if only for a short moment. Jelinek emphasizes this when she compares writing to tearing tatters out of chaos with the help of a "Charon oar," floating on a death raft. Like the actors, the author, too, gives her life to the text while also

---

23. Jelinek, "Grußwort nach Japan." "daß auch meine Stücke irgendwie leben, aber anders, als wenn sie richtige Menschen und ihre Taten und Untaten imitieren würden."

24. Jelinek, "Grußwort nach Japan."

gaining life while writing.²⁵ This ongoing fluctuation between life and death, between existence and nonexistence, characterizes a theater engaged with the void. It is a theater full of ghosts, the undead, and eerie voices that are disconnected from any origin.

This kind of theater starts to evolve with the radical transformation of theatrical form that we can find in the works of the East German playwright Heiner Müller. In this book, I define Müller's *Bildbeschreibung* (*Description of a Picture/Explosion of a Memory*, 1984) as the most radical rupture involved in the transformation of drama into what I term the "theater of the void."²⁶ *Description of a Picture* brings forth a new theatrical form entirely. It is only a few pages long; has no designated speaker; consists of only one sentence, which spans the several pages; and adopts the genre of ekphrasis only to deprive the audience of any possible subject that might conceive and frame the image for us. The text was so unusual that it made Jelinek reconsider how she writes for theater:²⁷ "After reading Heiner Müller's *Description of a Picture*, I suddenly also noticed my own discomfort with dialogues. One would perhaps have to think of a different kind of 'play score' that no longer functions dialogically.... If I ever do something for the stage again, it will be more along these lines: proselike texts."²⁸ After *Description of a Picture*, Jelinek indeed radically changed her approach to theater. She turned away from Brecht's epic theater, which still remains true to some form of dramatic structure, and started writing proselike plays without dialogue, characters or

---

25. Jelinek, "Es ist sprechen und aus."
26. Although I situate *Description of a Picture* at the beginning of the theater of the void, it is important to note that Müller had already started to develop this kind of theater in the 1970s. This will become clear in chapter 2, in my detailed analysis of his 1979 play *Der Auftrag* (*The Task*).
27. *Description of a Picture* is so unconventional that the editors of Müller's collected works decided to print it in the prose section rather than with his other plays.
28. Jelinek, "Statement für den 'Frauen im Theater-Workshop,'" 98. "Ich habe nach dem Lesen von Heiner Müllers *Bildbeschreibung* plötzlich dieses, auch mein Unbehagen an Dialogen bemerkt. Man müßte vielleicht an eine andere Art von Stückpartituren denken, die nicht mehr dialogisch funktionieren.... Wenn ich je wieder etwas mache für die Bühne, dann eher in dieser Richtung; prosaähnliche Texte."

types, plot, or stage direction; this kind of play has now become paradigmatic for her.[29]

The new theatrical form that Müller introduces arises from speculation over the event of total annihilation while, at the same time, revealing the slow violence that already shapes his present and that usually remains hidden due to a focus on the destruction to come. The first lines of *Description of a Picture* already clearly refer to the technoscientific age. The narrating voice uses the term "mushroom-shaped" when describing the arrangement of trees. This term not only evokes the nuclear bomb but also allows associations with the mushroom as an organism that thrives on radioactive emissions.[30] What unfolds from there are highly unsettling scenes overflowing with sexual desire, which in Müller's work is always also a violent, deadly desire. The speaker introduces us to a man and a woman, within a home that shows evidence of violence, which could also be signs of passion: "The high-backed chair in front has its peculiarity: its four legs are halfway up connected by wire as if to prevent it from collapsing, a second chair lies thrown away behind the tree on the right, its back broken, ... which burden has broken the chair, made the other unstable, a murder perhaps, or a violent copulation, or both in one."[31] *Description of a Picture* is a danse macabre that shows the woman and the man teetering on the edge between life and death. The woman is described as someone who has returned from the dead and is now trapped between her daily murder and her daily resurrection.[32] In this piece, not only does Müller confront us

---

29. For a detailed analysis of the relationship between narration and performance in the context of German-language theater at the beginning of the twenty-first century, see Breger, *An Aesthetics of Narrative Performance*. Even though Breger's book covers a variety of media and does not include Brecht's epic theater or Müller's theatrical experiments, her chapter on "Antinarrative Acts," which discusses the theater of Antonin Artaud, among other things, presents interesting insights into narrative performance.

30. Barad, "No Small Matter," G114; Tsing, *The Mushroom at the End of the World*. *Description of a Picture* is not the only text by Müller to have been shaped by the nuclear blast. Indeed, the devastated and contaminated landscapes that make up his oeuvre all hint at a world destroyed by nuclear war. Marranca captures this when she speaks of Müller's works as a "Baedeker for the nuclear age" ("Despoiled Shores," 17).

31. Müller, *Description of a Picture*, 107–8.

32. Müller, *Description of a Picture*, 108.

with a dream fantasy, but he also addresses the horrors and pleasures of the groundlessness of being. "A protection against the falling rocks that are released by the wanderings of the dead underground which are the secret pulse of the planet the picture is meant to represent, a protection offering some prospect of permanence perhaps when the growth of graveyards will have reached its limits with the small weight of the presumed murderer on the threshold."[33] In this text, where life and death are so radically reworked, hauntings come not only from the past but from the future as well.

All of these highly disconcerting moments culminate in what Müller himself calls the end of the image and of representation: "I think the text is exploding the image. It begins with the image, and the image explodes. At the end there is no image anymore."[34] Consequently, Müller links in the end of the play the mutation of theatrical form with the explosive moment, noting that it must be understood as the "explosion of a memory in a dead dramatic structure."[35] In confronting us with the explosion of the image, Müller ruptures the dramatic form that is stuck in representation, understood in terms of the eye, the gaze, and observation,[36] and introduces a form in which representation is reworked through the ear and, more generally, through all the senses.[37] In so doing, Müller inspires us to investigate the complex entanglement among the im/material, in/visibile, and in/audible. In other words, *Description of a Picture* shows in the most radical way what Müller's theater does in general. It profoundly challenges how we usually conceive of representation, for here theater is no longer understood exclusively as the place for *seeing* (from the Greek *theatron*, derived from Greek *theasthai* = to see, to behold) but instead as a place for *hearing* and *sensing*.[38]

---

33. Müller, *Description of a Picture*, 109.
34. Müller, "Description of a Picture Is," 96.
35. Müller, *Description of a Picture*, 110.
36. Theater is defined through vision and gaze. This intensified with the creation of indoor theaters and the proscenium stage, which began to dominate the Western theatrical landscape in the eighteenth century. See Haß, *Das Drama des Sehens*.
37. On the shift from the visual to the auditory in German theater, see Roesner, "From the Spirit of Music."
38. When I discuss the shift from the eye and the gaze to the ear and all other senses in the context of a radical reworking of theatrical representation, I do not

It is this radical break with conventional forms of representation that makes this kind of theater so timely today, when playwrights and directors are increasingly grappling with the question of how theater might best respond to the challenges of the "Anthropocene."[39] While current debates reestablish an identification of theater with drama and bourgeois representational theater, the theater that began to take shape with Müller does not limit theater to embodiment or the depiction of human-to-human conflict. On the contrary, as a theater that destroys the image and the power of the gaze, Müller's theater is able to grasp social, political, and planetary problems that are entangled with things too small and at the same time too big to appear on stage.[40] In short, his theater manages to engage with things

---

mean to suggest that these other senses are less historically burdened. Scholars like Jonathan Sterne, *The Audible Past*; Jennifer Lynn Stoever, *The Sonic Color Line*; and Dylan Robinson, *Hungry Listening*, who work in the field of sound studies, have pointed out the involvement of sound in racialization and other forms of violence and exclusion. Moreover, there is a rising interest in smell in the arts, the social sciences, and the humanities, revealing its equally complex history and relationship to forms of violence. Important contributions in this field come from Jonathan Reinarz, *Past Scents*; Constance Classen, David Howes, and Anthony Synnott, *Aroma*; and Alain Corbin, *The Foul and the Fragrant*.

39. In this book, I have decided not to use the term "Anthropocene" in speaking of our present but to use the phrase "technoscientific age." I do this to avoid falling into some of the problematic patterns the term reproduces, such as centering on the human. The term "Anthropocene" was popularized by the atmospheric chemist Paul Crutzen in 2000 and quickly became an important concept in the humanities and social sciences as well as a way to critically challenge the destructive impact on the planet of human and particularly capitalist activity. Scholars have offered numerous alternative terms that shift the focus away from the human and instead highlight the particular source of destruction (such as the "Capitalocene" in Moore, *Anthropocene or Capitalocene?*) or focus on world-making and an alternative future (such as the "Chthulucene" in Haraway, *Staying with the Trouble*). An interesting publication on questions of aesthetics in the Anthropocene is Davis and Turpin, *Art in the Anthropocene*. In the context of theater, see Marranca, *Ecologies of Theater*; Kershaw, *Theatre Ecology*; and Chaudhuri and Enelow, *Research Theatre*. For German-language theater, see Malzacher, *Gesellschaftsspiele im Theater*, 41–45 and Raddatz, *Das Drama des Anthropozäns*.

40. I show that the theatrical forms we have seen since the late 1970s offer a means of getting at what theater scholarship has often considered unstageable or unrepresentable, due to questions of scale. This is particularly timely now, when we are confronted with what the philosopher and ecologist Timothy Morton has called "hyperobjects": phenomena like global warming, nuclear weaponry, and neoliberalism

that seem to be beyond our grasp. In so doing, it challenges scale as an analytical tool and asks us to think in terms of topology and seismology.[41] Karen Barad makes this shift from scale to topology in our technoscientific age visible: "It's not that scale doesn't matter; the point is that it isn't simply given and what appears far apart might actually be as close as the object in question; indeed, it may be an inseparable part of it."[42] Being attentive to the possibility that scale might no longer be a stable ground for our understanding of the world, the new theatrical forms that have evolved starting with Müller's *Description of a Picture* confront us with this ever-shifting ground of proximity and distance with which we are currently confronted. *Description of a Picture* is a theater that consciously engages with the groundlessness of being in our technoscientific age, from which it generates the energy to make the theatrical void possible. It is a theater with history and historicity, but no origin.

Müller's theatrical experiments are the violent accident and rupture that lead to the transformation of theatrical form. Starting from Müller, this book traces the kind of theater, invested in groundlessness, in/determinacy, and mutability, that currently dominates the German-language theatrical landscape. Along with Müller, I discuss three other influential theater makers—Elfriede Jelinek, Christoph Schlingensief, and René Pollesch—each of whom has his or her own intricate way of engaging with the void and each of whom has shaped the theatrical practice and aesthetics of the German-speaking

---

that exceed human perception and inherited modes of cognition (*Hyperobjects*, 1). I come back to this in the conclusion.

41. See Barad ("Troubling Time/s," 63), who points out that in the nuclear age something as small as the splitting of the atom has global implications, and vice versa, and thus suggests replacing scale with topology. Topology stresses spatial relations and marks the meeting of abstract and concrete. It has been privileged by a number of theorists, from Blanchot to Deleuze, as a way to emphasize a thinking in terms of relations and reconfigurations of time and space. For Barad, though, the ongoing reconfiguration of space and time is decidedly linked to matter, which allows the more complex constellations that arise between matter and meaning as well as between human and nonhuman to be captured in the theatrical texts I discuss. I discuss the turn to seismology in greater detail in chapter 1.

42. Barad, "Troubling Time/s," 63.

world of the past decades in a singular way. While Müller, Jelinek, and Schlingensief share an ongoing relationship to catastrophe and the tragic mode as a driving force of their theater, Pollesch is an interesting outsider, in whose work catastrophe moves into the background. What Pollesch allows us to see is that, even though catastrophe and the void are intimately linked, there is a possibility for a theater of the void that no longer centers on catastrophe. Thus, including Pollesch as a kind of misfit sets off the theatrical forms of Müller, Jelinek, and Schlingensief and shows that the void can be disentangled from catastrophe. What all four of them share, though, is the fact that they wrestle with issues of representation and scale as they make us work through questions such as what is visible and therefore something, and what is invisible and therefore seemingly nothing. Moreover, all four of them unsettle the distinction between life and death and reveal this fluctuating, in-between state as precisely a great potential for becoming. They do this in constant dialogue with established theatrical figurations and formations and in this way reinvent central concepts such as catharsis, anagnorisis, *Gesamtkunstwerk* (total work of art), and Brecht's *Lehrstücke* (didactic plays) through a new ontology and epistemology of the technoscientific age.

The Void Not as Mere Emptiness but as Potential

This book understands the void not as mere emptiness but as the indeterminate source of and precondition for all that is and might yet be. As a radical opening, it is linked to futurity—but a futurity that implies neither teleology nor a metaphysics of presence. In understanding the void as radical potential, my argument resonates with the heightened interest in *nothing* in theory and philosophy over the past decade. True to the new approach to contemporary theater through the sciences, however, my theoretical framework goes beyond philosophical conceptualizations of the void and includes scientific ones as well. While the bond between theater and philosophy is well established, as theater is conventionally taken to be a form of scenic thought and philosophy a form of "architheater,"[43] theater's relationship to the sciences has thus far received limited scholarly attention; this is particularly true in the German-language context.[44]

Nothing has been theorized by a wide range of philosophers, including Alain Badiou, Timothy Morton, Slavoj Žižek, and others, all of whom understand the void as more than mere emptiness.[45] However, while these works have surely had a great impact on my thinking, my conceptualization of the void is based on two thinkers of the void who have remained less familiar voices in this context, namely Catherine Malabou and Karen Barad. Both of them bridge the gap between philosophy, theory, and the two sciences that are deeply written into the theater of the void: biology and quantum physics. Moreover, they both carve out a position between Hegelian dialectics and deconstruction, the two approaches that resonate with the two dominant models of how theater and drama are understood. Both Malabou and Barad simultaneously draw from and complicate deconstruction, Malabou through the lens of biology and Barad through that of quantum physics.[46] Moreover, Malabou explicitly combines Hegel's dialectics with deconstruction and in so doing reveals a dialectic deprived of any telos, progress, or determination. Instead, she sheds light on a mode of change that is shaped by contingency and in/determinacy, but she also leaves behind Derrida's

---

43. See for example Gabriel and Müller-Schöll, *Das Denken der Bühne*; Lacoue-Labarthe and Nancy, "Dialog über den Dialog"; Lehmann, "Das Denken der Tragödie"; Müller-Schöll, "Denken auf der Bühne"; Puchner, *The Drama of Ideas*; and Rokem, *TheaterDenken*.

44. Exceptions are Case, *Performing Science and the Virtual*, and Roach, *The Player's Passion*. There are numerous studies that link theater and the laboratory, but most of these studies use the laboratory as a metaphor, barely engaging with the sciences and experimentation on a deeper level. See, e.g., Primavesi, "Theater als Labor und Experiment"; and Haas, "Theoretische Bemerkungen zu einer Dramaturgie der nichtmenschlichen Anderen (nach Haraway)."

45. See the notion of zero in Badiou, *Theory of the Subject*; Badiou, *Being and Event*; and Badiou, *Logics of Worlds*; Morton, Boon, and Cazdyn, *Nothing*; and Žižek, *Less Than Nothing*.

46. It is important to note that I am not leaving poststructuralism or deconstruction behind, and nor do Barad and Malabou. Instead, it is a reworked, more material understanding of these theories that guides my analysis.

dictum that there is no outside of the text and replaces thinking in terms of the trace with thinking in terms of plasticity.

Drawing from Althusser's "materialism of the encounter" and Darwin's *On the Origin of Species*, Malabou conceptualizes the void through the notion of plasticity, where plasticity designates the quasi-infinite possibility of structural change constituted by the absence of predetermination. Borrowing a term from Althusser, she speaks of a hidden "materialism of the aleatory" that "starts from nothing."[47] Darwin is an exceptional thinker in the context of such a materialism, as his *On the Origin of Species* makes nothingness the ontological point of departure. Starting from this void, Darwin argues that being mutable, which he calls "plastic," is the most important characteristic of a species.[48] Malabou claims that plasticity in Darwin "designates the quasi-infinite possibility of changes of structure authorized by the living structure itself. This quasi-infinity precisely constitutes the openness or the absence of predetermination which makes an encounter possible."[49] It further indicates "a fundamental connection between the *variability* of individuals within the same species and the *natural selection* between these same individuals."[50] Natural selection, then, "transforms the contingency of the former into a necessity." In other words, it "allows the taking of *oriented*

---

47. Althusser, "The Underground Current," 188. Malabou defines materialism as nontranscendental since form here is no longer connected to an exteriority but rather shaped through the "absence of any outside of the process of transformation." In other words, matter is "what forms itself in producing the conditions of possibility of this formation itself" (Malabou, "Whither Materialism," 48). This immanent dynamic can be understood in two ways. Following dialectical teleology, the process is "governed by an internal tension toward a telos, which necessarily orients and determines every self-development" (49). Here, though, as Malabou points out, along with Althusser, the structure precedes the elements and thus again yields to a transcendental analysis. The materialism of the encounter, on the other hand, is without telos, as "forms are encounters that have taken form" (Malabou, "Whither Materialism," 49).

48. Darwin writes: "It is really surprising to note the endless points in structure and constitution in which the varieties and sub-varieties differ slightly from each other. The whole organization seems to have become *plastic*, and tends to depart in some small degree from that of the parental type" (*On the Origin of Species*, 13; my emphasis).

49. Malabou, "Whither Materialism," 50.

50. Malabou, "Whither Materialism," 50. Emphasis in the original.

form, which obeys the natural exigency of the viability, consistency, and autonomy of individuals."[51] While Darwin's theory of natural selection is often misinterpreted as the "survival of the fittest," Malabou shows that he offers an intriguing model of how form can be taken without teleology or intention. "Natural selection is paradoxically nonanticipatable, a promise of forms never chosen in advance, of differences to come."[52] In a selection process that is unpredictable and without finality, the forms that emerge are "sculpted by the disappearance of the disadvantaged, by the return of eliminated living form to the inorganic."[53] As such, the inanimate "becomes, negatively, the condition of sense or the project of living."[54] We can summarize it in simple terms with the words of the French philosopher and physician Georges Canguilhem, as quoted by Malabou: "Death is a blind sculptor of living forms."[55]

In a similar vein, the intricate relationship between life and death shapes Barad's conceptualization of the void, when they explicitly link the void to a form of haunting. Barad bases their conceptualization of the void on the work done in quantum field theory on the quantum vacuum. In contrast to Newtonian physics, which assumes that the void has neither matter nor energy, quantum field theory posits that, due to quantum indeterminacy, the quantum vacuum cannot be determinately empty. This allows Barad to argue that if the void is not determinately empty, then it is instead the source of all being. "This indeterminacy is responsible not only for the void not being nothing (while not being something), but it may in fact be the source of all that is, a womb that births existence."[56] When the void is not empty but rather an indeterminate potential for non/existence, the void is not a mere background of everything that appears but is a constitutive part of everything that is. Thinking of the void as indeterminacy and as an infinite potential for non/existence, Barad points out that the void is "a threading through of

---

51. Malabou, "Whither Materialism," 50–51. Emphasis in the original.
52. Malabou, "Whither Materialism," 51.
53. Malabou, "Whither Materialism," 52.
54. Malabou, "Whither Materialism," 52–53.
55. Malabou, "Whither Materialism," 52.
56. Barad, "What Is the Measure of Nothingness?," 9.

living with dying and dying with living."⁵⁷ As such, the void is filled with "ghostly non/existences that teeter on the edge of the infinitely fine blade between being and nonbeing."⁵⁸ It is a potentiality that ties itself neither to a telos nor to a metaphysics of presence. Barad acknowledges that this state of non/being is hard to grasp. To help clarify, they provide the analogy of a still drumhead that does not simply mean silence but, following their reading, implies the *"indeterminate murmurings of all possible sounds"* or a *"speaking silence."*⁵⁹ Based on this analogy, Barad suggests that the void is "a quiet cacophony of different frequencies, pitches, tempos, melodies, noises, pentatonic scales, cries, blasts, sirens, sighs, syncopations, quarter tones, allegros, ragas, bebops, hiphops, whimpers, whines, screams ... threaded through the silence, ready to erupt, but simultaneously crosscut by a disruption, dissipating, dispersing the would-be sound into non/being, an indeterminate symphony of voices."⁶⁰ I quote this paragraph because for anyone who is even slightly familiar with Jelinek's theater, Barad's characterization of the void as an "indeterminate symphony of voices" will immediately resonate with the polyphonic texts of the author, which confront us with an overwhelming number of sounds and voices that lack a further specified source or any origin. In fact, one is tempted to adopt Barad's paragraph to describe Jelinek's texts for theater, as it so intricately captures the often-challenging fluctuation between silence and sound and among different rhythms, frequencies, and disruptions that is at the center of Jelinek's theater.

The void, even though consisting of indeterminate possibilities, is not immaterial. On the contrary, as Barad argues of the atom, matter consists of quantum fluctuation and as such is intertwined with the void. These fluctuations produce a haunting that is inscribed into *"even the smallest bit of matter,"* which is *"haunted by, indeed, constituted by, the indeterminate wanderings of an infinity of possible configurings of spacetimematterings in their*

---

57. Barad, "Troubling Time/s," 78.
58. Barad, "On Touching the Stranger Within."
59. Barad, "Troubling Time/s," 77. Emphasis in the original.
60. Barad, "On Touching the Stranger Within."

specificity."⁶¹ Following quantum field theory, Barad suggests that we understand hauntings as "*lively indeterminacies of time-being, materially constitutive of matter itself....* Hauntings, then, are not mere rememberings of a past (assumed to be) left behind (in actuality) but rather the dynamism of ontological indeterminacy of time-being/being-time in its materiality."⁶² Intriguingly, Barad offers here an understanding of hauntology that goes beyond merely a form of subjective human experience and is an integral part of the becoming of the world. Hauntings are more than simply memories of the dead or of past events that linger. Instead, hauntings reorganize past, present, and future in a complex way. In other words, they de-anchor them from the past so that they now can come from the future as well. These hauntings cannot be separated from our existing material conditions, as they are an integral part of the ongoing process of spacetimemattering. In short, matter consists of histories and politics.⁶³

While Malabou and Barad allow us to understand that there is a "blind sculptor" at work in natural selection and the quantum vacuum, we need to ask where there is a void in theater. Theater is a highly intentional creation and follows clear rules and criteria that reproduce norms instead of allowing the unanticipated and singular to happen. As such, it is first and foremost characterized by a lack of void. And yet, the theater makers I discuss in this book address this lack of void and ask how to create an opening that can allow the singular to happen. They are critical about intention and predefined criteria in their working process. We can see this when they reject a mode of theater-making shaped by strong hierarchies that put only a few individuals (mostly the directors or artistic directors of entire institutions) in positions of power and allow them to impose their vision and intention on the rest of the team and the audience. Moreover, they challenge theater in its function of reproducing norms, seeking to make it instead a space where the unanticipated can happen.

---

61. Barad, "No Small Matter," G113. Emphasis in the original.
62. Barad, "No Small Matter," G113. Emphasis in the original.
63. Barad, "No Small Matter," G106–7.

How, though, can theater establish a form of blindness without falling into a too-simplistic analogy of adapting natural laws for the theatrical realm? To answer this, I draw from Malabou, who poses the same question for the social and political realm and who responds to it along the lines proposed by Althusser. Theater has to acknowledge that the theatrical void—similar to the social and political void—"may not exist; if we could be certain of its existence, if we were able to know in advance, the encounter would never take place, and we would fall back into teleology again. The determination of this void of nothingness, of this point of possibility that opens all promise of justice, equality, legitimacy cannot be presupposed and cannot be as blindly and automatically regulated as in nature either. It has to be *made* possible."[64] I adopt Malabou's claim and argue for the realm of theater that the void can only be *made* possible; it is a practice and a task. And it is this very *making possible* of the void that is the concern of the theater makers I discuss in this book. Their works often employ intense ruptures (sometimes clearly, for instance in the form of a nuclear blast) as moments in which great energy is set free, allowing the singular and unanticipated to arise. In other words, the theatrical works I discuss are interested in the failure, the accident, the explosion, and the unqualified, as this is where theater can give form to the "unassignable place" that Malabou describes as a place "without qualities, without privilege, without legacies, without tradition."[65] Only from that place can new forms emerge that are "singular, unpredictable, unseen, regenerating."[66] Understanding that the "unassignable place" is connected to processes of formation and of giving form, this book emphasizes that making possible the unassignable place in theater cannot simply mean making the void its subject; it means that the works must generate their energy from the originary absence of determinate being.

---

64. Malabou, "Whither Materialism," 56. Emphasis in the original.
65. Malabou, "Whither Materialism," 57.
66. Malabou, "Whither Materialism," 57.

Toward a Theater of the Void: Nietzsche and Brecht

Even though the void as a radical potential only enters theater with the explosion of drama and the transformation of theatrical form in Müller, we can sense murmurs of the void in earlier theatrical experiments. Theater is the art form of the mask and therefore intricately linked to the void as the groundless ground of being: the presence of a mask always carries the risk that there is nothing original or essential behind it, but always just another mask that will come to light.[67] While an investigation of the void in diverse historical theatrical formations is indeed promising as such, I want to shed light on a strand of theatrical experiments that are deeply written into the theatrical transformation we can observe in the second half of the twentieth century.

The theater of the void is shaped by two essential attempts to rethink theater in the nineteenth and twentieth centuries that can be summarized under the names of Nietzsche—and with him a line that connects to Hölderlin, Wagner, and the early avant-garde—and Brecht. While Nietzsche and Brecht, as the dramaturg and theater theorist Frank M. Raddatz has pointed out when reflecting upon theater in the Anthropocene, must without a doubt be considered the most influential voices in the reformulation of theater in the German-language theatrical landscape,[68] the particularity of the theater of the void is that within it, these two strands intermingle, intertwining the two seemingly opposite and sometimes even contradictory strands of *how* theater can be reenvisioned.

What is important in the context of the theater of the void is that both Brecht and Nietzsche defined theater in terms of its relationship to the sciences. Nietzsche and, similarly, Hölderlin, Wagner, and the early avant-garde sought to reinvent theater through a turn to the Dionysian, which for Nietzsche is the realm of the unconscious, the unknown, the ritual, the ecstatic, and the orgiastic.[69]

---

67. In this context, see Hamacher, "(The End of Art with the Mask)," who brings to light such a lack of essence in Hegel's discussion of comedy.
68. Raddatz, "Abenteuer Gaia," 102.
69. See Nietzsche, *The Birth of Tragedy*.

Emphasizing the proximity of Western theater to the cult of Dionysus, theater was rediscovered in its cathartic function and became an essential means for the healing of the individual and society through the processes of metamorphosis and transformation. According to Nietzsche, such a healing is only possible through the turn away from reason and logic, which he identifies with Socrates and—in the realm of dramatic writing—Euripides.[70] In his criticism of Socrates, whom he calls the destroyer of Greek tragedy, Nietzsche challenges a scientific worldview based on cognition and the principles of cause and effect. He proposes art, and particularly the rebirth of tragedy, as a cure for scientific man and a supplement to the sciences. Turning away from reason, Nietzsche's theater is filled with the spirits, ghosts, and energies that had been expelled since Socrates. And in a rereading of ancient Greek tragedy that was similar to Nietzsche's, other theater makers started to rediscover elements beyond drama and language bound to signification. Instead, rhythm, sound, and the sensory became central to the theatrical experience, as we can see conceptualized in Wagner's total work of art, the early avant-garde, and Artaud's vision of a theater of cruelty.

Brecht, in stark opposition to Nietzsche, was outspoken in his skepticism of the Dionysian. He compared ecstasy, the orgiastic, and metamorphosis to drugs that lured the audience in and turned them into dangerous masses. What he envisioned instead was—very much in the tradition of Socrates and Euripides—a theater for the scientific age that allowed for distant observation, like a laboratory. Brecht describes this "theater for the scientific age" in several contexts, but most prominently in his *Kleines Organon für das Theater* (*A Short Organum for the Theater*) and his longer theoretical work *Der Messingkauf* (*Buying Brass*), which remained a fragment. In these texts, Brecht explains in great detail the demand for a new mode of acting that does not allow identification or empathy, his principle of alienation (*Verfremdung*), and the use of epic elements that would allow a new theater to arise based on the newest scientific practices and findings. And yet, as Raddatz points out, Brecht's

---

70. Nietzsche, *The Birth of Tragedy*, 60–63.

understanding of the sciences is very much limited to the modern sciences, symbolized by their founding father, Galileo. As Raddatz rightly argues, this way of practicing sciences, and the worldview they created, has become problematic in our present.[71]

The theater of the void is deeply engaged with both of these strands of reinvention, Nietzsche's and Brecht's, and yet also transforms and reinvents them, inspired by the technoscientific age. It is closely related to Brecht's ideas for a dialectical theater that breaks with identification and empathy. At the same time, Nietzsche's turn to Attic tragedy and his interest in its healing function, combined with an emphasis on rhythm, sound, and what lies beyond our cognition, are essential to the theater of the void. Thus, in introducing Nietzschean principles that emphasize what goes beyond cognition into Brecht's political theater, the theater of the void responds to a present in which a new understanding of the sciences is necessary.

In addition to complicating conventional scientific modes of observation and knowledge production through a turn to the senses and to the unknown, the theater of the void is characterized by a rising awareness of the involvement of the sciences in the destruction and devastation of the planet. As Barad argues, our age is not strictly technoscientific but rather "techno-militaro-politico-capitalo-imperialist-racist-colonial" through and through.[72] The theater of the void challenges science's attachment to capitalism, militarism, and imperialism and supplements the sciences through radical sensual experimentations that speak to a complex and entangled world. At the same time, it incorporates the ontological and epistemological shifts brought about by new scientific findings as a means to undo the enclosed system of our technoscientific age. In short, it is a theater formed as a critical response to the entanglement of science, capitalism, militarism, and imperialism that simultaneously engages with the sciences, because they reveal a form of groundlessness of being that promises futurity through introducing the possibility for change into our current, seemingly enclosed

---

71. Raddatz, "Abenteuer Gaia," 106–9.
72. Barad, "Troubling Time/s"; Barad, "No Small Matter."

capitalist system.⁷³ In more general terms, the mutation of theatrical form that began in the 1970s is inseparable from broader questions of change and futurity on a planet that seems to have arrived at an endpoint.

While I identify biology and quantum physics as the two sciences that are crucial to enabling the void to become a source of radical opening in theater, quantum physics also enters this book in connection with the worst possible catastrophe, the one that shaped the late twentieth-century cultural and political imaginary: humanity's complete annihilation due to nuclear technology. The nuclear threat is deeply written into the cultural, political, and economic conscious and unconscious of the second half of the twentieth century. Indeed, it brought to life a new subjectivity, caught between two forms of death—the natural death of an individual and the death of a species by extinction.⁷⁴ Currently, this threat is accompanied by the fears around global warming, a phenomenon that forces us to finally recognize that what we dread is not something that awaits us in the future, but that we are already surrounded by extreme forms of violence shaping the present right now. In this context, using Rob Nixon's phrase, I speak of slow violence in the technoscientific age.⁷⁵ I consider the ambiguity between our speculation about an end to come and the actual violence we are already experiencing in the present to be important, as it allows us to understand the structural similarities between the nuclear threat and global warming. Western societies conceive of both of these as events about which we can only speculate, while at the same time they are already causing major destruction daily. In linking atomic weaponry to the current threat of global warming,⁷⁶ I show that even though they

---

73. See the analysis of our present and a poignant discussion of the loss of future we have experienced since the end of the Cold War in Fisher, *Capitalist Realism*.
74. Schwab, *Radioactive Ghosts*, 26.
75. Nixon (*Slow Violence*) coined the term "slow violence." I discuss this in greater detail in chapter 1.
76. Another link between nuclear threat and global warming is made by the Doomsday Clock, a symbol designed by the *Bulletin of the Atomic Scientists*, which has since 2007 indicated global warming and nuclear annihilation as the two greatest threats to mankind. For a critical discussion of the entanglement of the Doomsday Clock with militarism and colonialism, see Barad, "Troubling Time/s," 57–59. I

were shaped by the possibility of complete extinction due to nuclear technology, the theatrical forms that started to develop in the 1970s are not outdated or limited to the years of the Cold War. On the contrary, the theatrical investigations that began in the 1970s continue to be relevant today.

Organization of the Book

In this book I focus on four individual directors and playwrights who offer insights into a theater that is deeply engaged with the void. My analysis centers on the playwright Heiner Müller from the former German Democratic Republic, the Austrian playwright Elfriede Jelinek, the (West) German director Christoph Schlingensief, and the (West) German director-playwright René Pollesch.[77] Müller's theater marks the beginning of this new kind of theater. His texts transform drama at a moment of heightened energy, fueled by catastrophe. In Müller's own succinct phrasing, we can say that his theater "presumes the catastrophes which mankind is working toward."[78] Like Müller, Jelinek and Schlingensief also create(d) works that confront us with the accident and the intense rupture that make the void, as a potential for becoming, possible. Only in Pollesch does the catastrophe move into the background and give way to a theater that closely examines concrete findings in the realms of biology and quantum physics, in order to generate a similar void in the theatrical space.

The conscious turn to the void is inseparable from the playwrights' and directors' engagement with the sciences. To begin with, it is written into how this kind of theater started to form, namely in response to the threat of the nuclear blast. But it also

---

speak about this in more detail in chapter 1, where I discuss the tension between the "nuclear/climate sublime" and the "nuclear/climate mundane."

77. I use the term director-playwright to mark the particularity of Pollesch's position. Pollesch exclusively directed and staged his own works, which emerged during the rehearsal process. Because he was opposed to the idea of his plays being restaged, they have been rarely published or translated. In Pollesch's conception, the text should not exist separately from the performance.

78. Müller, *Despoiled Shore*, 126.

becomes apparent through the theater makers' interest in scientific research. While Müller and Jelinek are both skeptical of the sciences and barely ever engage with scientific research on a deeper level, their work nevertheless anticipates the radical shifts in our understanding of the world that have been brought forth predominantly by quantum physics and neuroscience.[79] In Schlingensief and Pollesch, on the other hand, we can see an explicit interest in and engagement with both scientific fields, although Schlingensief, unlike Pollesch, approaches them mostly intuitively and anecdotally. Schlingensief is particularly interested in neuroscience and the workings of the brain, which he explored in his theatrical productions throughout his career. This interest began with a talk he attended as a child with his father, a pharmacist, where he learned about the brain and how it overwrites memories.[80] Pollesch was an ardent reader of Haraway and, more recently, Barad, which prompted him to adopt scientific findings in the realms of biology and quantum physics for the theater. It is in his works that we find the most obvious references to the sciences. His plays name and directly engage with specific experiments, scientists, and findings.

My analysis brings together performances, theatrical texts, poetological texts, and comments by authors and directors and reads them with and through the works of Barad and Malabou. Instead of following the current practice of choosing either the theatrical texts or the stagings to analyze, I understand the theatrical text as a possible staging on paper and treat it in the same way that I do a stage performance. I consider this equivalency to be true in general, but even more so for the works I analyze in this book. The directors and playwrights I discuss here cannot be separated from their staging practices. They work as both director and playwright (Müller), they don't work with preexisting texts but instead create the text during rehearsals (Pollesch, Schlingensief), or they cooperate closely with specific directors or ensembles (Jelinek). The decision

---

79. Jelinek occasionally engages with chemistry. This has a biographical explanation: her father was a chemist who survived the Holocaust because he committed to work for the Nazis' weapons industry.

80. Kluge, "Parsifal verlernen."

to focus on both playwrights and directors creates what might look at first glance like an imbalance among the individual chapters. The chapters on Müller and Jelinek only briefly mention actual stagings and focus instead solely on the theatricality of the texts themselves, while the chapters on Schlingensief and Pollesch analyze performances. This apparent imbalance, however, is a necessary one, because only in this way can I emphasize the radicality of Müller's and Jelinek's theater, which is inscribed into the texts themselves and most often gets lost in the stagings. This has to do with the fact that both of these playwrights are convinced that the text must challenge existing theatrical institutions, confronting them with material that is still waiting for its theater to come. Müller emphasizes this on numerous occasions, for instance in a 1974 statement in which he declares: "Theaters are establishments and in need of literature's endeavour to counteract this tendency of conservation. I consider plays which cannot be staged in their original written form a necessity."[81] In a similar vein, he praises Jelinek's plays for resisting the theatrical institution and for confronting the theater with plays that cannot be staged within the existing theatrical institution.[82]

In each chapter, I pay close attention to a specific work or even to one specific scene, from which I go on to discuss more generally the theatrical practice and aesthetics of each director and playwright. Moreover, in order to remain true to the works, which are overwhelming and hard to pin down, I avoid speaking about them in a way that would make them immediately readable. Instead, my analysis first introduces the individual, sometimes seemingly disparate, threads and then only slowly begins to explain how they are interlinked. The chapters are written in such a way that they can be read separately. Thus, the important concepts are not only explained in the introduction and chapter 1; I come back to them whenever necessary in each individual chapter so that the reader can follow the analysis of the works. To help readers orient themselves, I provide cross-references among the chapters and establish connections

---

81. Müller, "I Do Not Believe," 170.
82. Müller, "Bonner Krankheit."

between them when there are specific aspects that return in the context of more than one playwright or director.

The first chapter of this book further develops the concept of the theater of the void and discusses rifts and continuity through the figure of plasticity in greater detail. My theorization of the theater of the void is guided by a close reading of Müller's short, enigmatic speech, "The Wound Woyzeck," which he gave in Darmstadt in 1985 while accepting the German Academy of Language and Poetry's prestigious Georg Büchner Prize. The flash or atomic blast that ends Müller's speech serves as my entry point for engaging with the speculation about total destruction at the hands of atomic weaponry in the context of the formation of the theater of the void and helps me to demonstrate the plasticity of the theater of the void. I point out the importance of the explosion, the accident, and the unpredictable, which are nevertheless never fully disconnected from anticipation and determination and which shape Müller's theater not only thematically but also poetically and dramaturgically. Relying on Malabou, I show that the theatrical form that emerges from this point can best be thought of in terms of destructive plasticity. I emphasize how the future that emerges in the theater of the void is different from that of a theater that follows a conventional understanding of dialectics or deconstruction. This becomes particularly clear when we examine the mode of healing that is addressed in Müller's speech in the context of Woyzeck's "open wound." I show that the theater of the void is shaped by what Malabou calls "regeneration," offering an alternative to models of redemption and salvation or the scar that leaves a trace behind. Finally, I turn to the question of history and historiography that is so important for the theater makers I discuss in this book. While this question is usually linked to the archeological method, I suggest here a turn to seismology. Seismology has in common with archeology the fact that they both defy linear history, as they are both linked to rupture.[83] And yet seismology pushes further, emphasizing the sensory beyond the simple gaze. The seismograph senses ruptures and vibrations that are invisible but not without impact.

---

83. See Foucault, *Archeology of Knowledge*.

Chapters 2 through 5 analyze individual theatrical texts and performances and shed light on the diverse forms that the theater of the void can create, depending on the emphasis placed on the figures of plasticity and hauntology and the importance of quantum physics and biology. Chapter 2, on Müller, undertakes a reading of one of the most puzzling scenes of all of Müller's theatrical texts, what has been called a surrealistic, dreamlike sequence in his play *Der Auftrag* (*The Task*). The scene, which was also published as a separate prose text entitled "Der Mann im Fahrstuhl" (The man in the elevator), lets us experience the journey of an employee who, on his way to a meeting with his boss, seems to fall out of time and space. Time in this narrative no longer moves in a linear fashion that can be measured with a watch but instead is attuned to an unfamiliar rhythm, undecipherable to the narrator. Similarly, the elevator seems to lose its connection to any actual building, as it no longer simply transports the employee from one level to the other. Instead, when the doors open, the employee finds himself on a remote street in the countryside of Peru. Drawing on Barad, I argue that in this short text, we experience a transformation from a world understood through Newtonian physics to one seen through quantum physics. The ending of the story is particularly challenging, as it shows us a subject finding itself in a new and unfamiliar world. With Malabou I argue that what we experience here is a metamorphosis and a new subjectivity created out of an accident or trauma. It is a subject shaped by indifference that can no longer be explained through the drive but only through the radical loss of itself, which subsequently allows a feeling of ease and joy to arise.

In chapter 3, I engage with Jelinek and her theatrical exploration of what it means to live in the end times, or rather, in times when time has ended and become mortal as well as diffracted and dispersed. I focus on her play *Kein Licht*, a text written in response to the 2011 nuclear disaster in Fukushima. Intriguingly, the play intertwines music and radiation in order to explore the material reality of what is invisible. More than any other theatrical work I engage with in this book, Jelinek's play deprives the eye of any visual impression and instead creates a theatrical piece that predominantly addresses our ears. *Kein Licht* is full of noises and voices that reach us but have no origin. A soundscape accompanies the voices of two designated speakers, "A" and "B," who sometimes refer to themselves as first and second violin, as quantum particles, as survivors of a catastrophe, and as a search party. Hence, rather than being the source of any genuine speech, A and B appear merely to be tools or instruments that sense messages coming from other times and places and transform those signals into language. With Barad, I argue that the text allows us to encounter the silent murmurs of the void, the virtual beings that might (have) come into existence. Jelinek not only radically reworks how we think about representation in theater, but she also challenges the notion of catharsis. If the void is far from being empty, then the promise of purgation no longer holds. Instead, her theater invents a catharsis that is radically disconnected from emotions, which gains its most important effect from becoming potentially disaffected.

Chapter 4 then homes in on Schlingensief's work. Here I take up the notion of the wound that is addressed in Müller's speech, as it is key for Schlingensief's theater. Schlingensief staged Wagner's *Parsifal* in Bayreuth in the years 2005 through 2007. From his first encounter with this opera onward, he worked obsessively to challenge the imaginary of redemption that it celebrated and attempted to find a counternarrative. Schlingensief created numerous small artistic initiatives in which he played the opera in strange contexts and to unusual audiences—such as dead and living animals—hoping to get beyond salvation. This search culminated in a short film that Schlingensief created for the salvation scene in his Bayreuth staging, showing the decay of a hare in a time lapse that depicts, as he emphasized, the acceptance of disappearance rather than redemption. Schlingensief returned to this short film in most of his later productions, captivated by the blurriness of the line between life and death in the decomposition process. Based on this short film, I demonstrate how the void predominantly shapes his theater through a turn to cinematographic principles that find their most elaborate expression in the spatial arrangement of a rotating stage, the "Animatograph," which combines the practice of movement and experiments with failure and erroneous vision. Schlingensief was inspired by the workings of the brain and interrogated the interrelation of destruction and construction that he believed he found there; for him, this translated into the repeated claim that memorizing means forgetting. As I show, Schlingensief's theater of the void creates an opening in Wagner's total work of art and transforms it into an art form of metamorphosis without resurrection and sublation.

In chapter 5, I turn to Pollesch, who pushes beyond the catastrophe and reinvents the void outside of a tragic mode. More than any of the other directors and playwrights I discuss here, Pollesch embraces the sciences and returns to Brecht's concept of didactic plays in order to invent it anew for the twenty-first century. I highlight Pollesch's play *Probleme Probleme Probleme* (2019), in which he adapts the double-slit experiment for the stage. The double-slit experiment was crucial to the emergence of quantum physics, as it demonstrated that particles could behave both like particles *and* like waves, depending on the experimental setting. Pollesch relies on this experiment to think toward a queer theater in which any notion of a stable identity is reworked through the ongoing process of becoming. As Barad argues, this process is shaped by the specific arrangement between measured object, measurer, and measuring tool. Here I make a connection to Pollesch's claim that the theater of our time must be a Darwinian theater, a claim that can be found in Pollesch's poetological work *Schnittchenkauf* (Buying canapés)—which is a clear reference to Brecht's poetological fragment *Der Messingkauf*. Drawing on Malabou's reading of Darwin, I show that Darwin's theory of becoming reveals in the realm of biology something similar to what the double-slit experiment brings to the fore in the realm of physics. Pollesch's interest in both, I argue, stems from his attempt to make theater the "unassignable place" where the unexpected and singular can happen.

I conclude the book with a discussion of how the theater of the void resonates with our present and how it might shape theater in the years to come. In this context, I turn to current criticism of theater as an old, outdated art form that is unable to respond to the most pressing issues of our times.[84] I challenge such claims and show

---

84. See Malzacher, *Gesellschaftsspiele*; and Raddatz, *Das Drama des Anthropozäns*.

that the theater of the void offers a theatrical grammar with which to engage with a world out of joint. Basing my discussion on Morton and Amitav Ghosh, I show that the theater of the void introduces a new form of anagnorisis that allows us to experiment with and practice new modes of recognition when recognition is no longer dominantly triggered by a human counterpart but by uncanny encounters with entities that fluctuate between vitality and the inanimate. I close the final chapter with a brief glance into other productions of the past few years that have engaged with the groundlessness of being, as we see in them an even stronger turn to the sciences and a heightened interest in climate change and atomic warfare. I conclude my book by emphasizing that the theater of the void is far from a theater of despair, but instead introduces feelings of ease and joy into our ongoing struggle for change and freedom.

1

IN A FLASH

Change and Futurity in the Theater of the Void

> As doubt grows about the changeability of the world, the desire to contact the dead intensifies.
>
> —Heiner Müller, "Für immer in Hollywood"

> If plasticity means what is vital and supple, it is nonetheless always susceptible to petrifaction. If it expresses what is most essential and primal in life itself, it is no less in alliance with the atomic bomb (Plastikbombe). A living and vital notion, plasticity is also a mortal notion. Sheltering, as long as it is possible, the space liberated by the interplay of the extremes between a living kernel and the nuclear nucleus, existing on the plane of saturation and vacancy, this is what the future requires.
>
> —Catherine Malabou, *The Future of Hegel*

Epigraph: "Wenn der Zweifel an der Veränderbarkeit der Welt wächst, verstärkt sich der Wunsch, mit den Toten Kontakt aufzunehmen."

Heiner Müller ends his short, enigmatic speech "Die Wunde Woyzeck" ("The Wound Woyzeck") with the image of a nuclear blast "that will be the end of all utopias and the beginning of a reality beyond mankind."[1] "The Wound Woyzeck," a public address that Müller gave in Darmstadt in October 1985, on the occasion of receiving the German Academy of Language and Poetry's prestigious Georg Büchner Prize,[2] engages with such mutually contradictory notions as death, destruction, construction, and change. At the core of the speech is the question of futurity, which is anticipated with both hope and fear. At the same time, the speech is characterized by a cool indifference that contradicts the sense that the future is anticipated with the above-mentioned feelings. Within this framework, we experience the ghostly return of historical and literary figures, from German legends (Kriemhild) to Müller's contemporaries (Ulrike Meinhof). These figures confront us with ever-new constellations of violence, unjust rule, and failed revolutions. Simultaneously, the speech punctures the narrow frame of German history through the appearance of the continent of Africa, which interrupts the rest of the speech in a flash and reveals how power relations from the past, such as colonialism, live on, intertwine with the present, and create complex and unequal arrangements.

I take the nuclear blast envisioned by Müller as the starting point for this chapter, which further theorizes the theater of the void. Along with "The Wound Woyzeck," I also consider a few additional texts by Müller that address atomic war and the rise of apocalyptic imaginaries. Even though his Büchner Prize acceptance speech only consists of three paragraphs, it allows us to comprehend the core principles of the theater of the void. As I will show, the speech introduces a subject defined by the possibility of becoming indifferent at any moment and tackles questions of theatrical and subsequently also social, political, and planetary trans/formation in relation to our atomic age. Even though Müller was posing these

---

1. Müller, "The Wound Woyzeck," 111.
2. For a discussion of Müller's acceptance speech and his performance in the context of institutional critique, see Pohlmann, "Heiner Müller's Cooperation." For a broader discussion of Müller's self-representation, see Pohlmann, *The Creation*.

questions as long ago as 1985, explosion as a possibility from which a radically new theatrical, social, and planetary form might arise is eerily timely today, speaking as it does to an experience of the future without a future that also shapes our present.

The nuclear blast is the unanticipated event that changes everything in an instant. However, as I show, in the theater of the void the explosive moment does not simply mean annihilation. On the contrary, it is complex and paradoxical and works in two different ways: it reveals the explosion as a destructive moment embedded in more hidden forms of slow violence *and* it is an opening that carries the potential for change and, as such, introduces a future and even an idea of freedom that can only arise within moments of violence and great rupture. In other words, in the theater of the void there can be a radical break that leads not to complete destruction but to a new kind of possibility. This possibility, though, does not mean that it is a theater committed to reconciliation and salvation. Instead, the theater of the void introduces an alternative possibility that can be thought of in terms of plasticity and regeneration.[3]

Capitalist/Nuclear Enclosure

"The Wound Woyzeck" begins with the words *Immer noch* (still), thus initially confronting us with stagnation: "*Immer noch* rasiert Woyzeck seinen Hauptmann" ("Woyzeck *still is* shaving his Captain").[4] The English translation fails to capture the effect of the German version. Everything that is said stems from the notion of the opening "still is," which introduces the feeling of painful duration in an enclosed system resistant to change. Woyzeck, one of the

---

3. In this book, I use "regeneration," as understood by Malabou, as a form of cloning, meaning a reparation of oneself in replacing oneself (Malabou, "Again: The Wounds of the Spirit"). I discuss this concept in greater detail later in this chapter.
4. Müller, "Die Wunde Woyzeck," 281; Müller, "The Wound Woyzeck," 110. My emphasis.

most fractured and torn characters of German theater, *is still* exploited by the military and medicine while *at the same time* he continues to torture Marie, his lover and the mother of his child. Even more, the abusive system of early capitalism depicted in Georg Büchner's theatrical fragment *Woyzeck* (1836) not only still exists but has become established further and now forms an entire nation, as "the play's population has become a state, surrounded by ghosts."[5]

We can read the first lines of the speech as the anticipation of an erosion or a loss of future, the anticipation of the changes that the political and cultural theorist Mark Fisher describes as having been brought about by the political change in Germany in 1989.[6] Jacques Derrida, in his "hauntology,"[7] argues that the ontology of the present is haunted by a past that is no longer and a future that is yet to come. Fisher, however, expanding on this notion, shows that it is instead the very loss of communism, its disappearance and with that disappearance the understanding that there is no longer any possible alternative to capitalism, that haunts the present. Without this alternative, we are trapped in a present where everything is subsumed under the order of capitalism and where even the imagination of an alternative to capitalism in the future is replaced by the belief that there is no alternative at all. While Müller could only foresee what Fisher describes as living in a "business ontology,"[8] his speech clearly hints at such a loss of future.

However, capitalism does not stand alone in Müller's speech; it is interconnected with the militarism and nationalism that express themselves in the nuclear competition of the Cold War. The atomic age, too, has generated a new form of haunting that can no longer be limited to ghosts coming from the past but also includes hauntings from the future. Müller emphasizes this, repeatedly returning to a quote from Brecht's fragmentary *Fatzer*: "As once ghosts came from

---

5. Müller, "The Wound Woyzeck," 110.
6. Fisher, *Capitalist Realism*, 4.
7. Derrida, *Specters of Marx*.
8. Fisher, *Capitalist Realism*, 17.

the past / So now equally from the future."⁹ For Müller, this sentence captures the intense break and disruption that he experiences in his present, which creates the feeling of suddenly finding oneself in a place of unknown dimensions—in other words, in an *unthinkable* space that is beyond our grasp.¹⁰ We can link the hauntings from the future that Müller explores to what Gabriele Schwab calls the "phantasms of the mutant body" that result from nuclear weapons. As Schwab argues, the nuclear age is characterized by a "double haunting from the past—the spectral ones who have been incinerated in Hiroshima—and a haunting from the future: the spectral ones who have not yet arrived but might be born as mutant children or die in a future nuclear war."¹¹ Müller's theater is characterized by just such hauntings that can no longer be limited to the past but that link past, present, and future in a complex way.¹² This is most clearly expressed in his comment on his 1983 play *Verkommenes Ufer Medeamaterial Landschaft mit Argonauten* (*Despoiled Shore Medeamaterial Landscape with Argonauts*), which "presumes the catastrophes which mankind is working toward" and imagines the landscape as a "dead star where a task force from another age or another space hears a voice and discovers a corpse."¹³ As typical for Müller, he confronts us here with a future catastrophe that is simultaneously expressed in the ruinous landscape of the present and detected by dwellers in ways that hint at the past and at the future.

At the same time, Müller's speech brings to light that nuclear technology is inseparably linked to the feeling of a loss of future. Relying on political and social critic Sabu Kohso, I argue that Müller is aware that nuclear technology is involved, more than anything else, in "indefinitely postponing the end of capitalism, both ontometaphysically

---

9. Brecht, *Fatzer*, 382. "Wie früher Geister kamen aus der Vergangenheit / So jetzt aus der Zukunft ebenso."
10. Müller quotes these lines in numerous texts and interviews. I reference his conversation with Alexander Kluge, "Anti-Oper."
11. Schwab, *Radioactive Ghosts*, 17.
12. Gordon, *Ghostly Matters*, is an important study that should be mentioned here; Gordon reveals the complex temporal relations of hauntings and analyzes the broad social impacts on our present of actions taken in the past.
13. Müller, *Despoiled Shore*, 126.

and technopolitically, as the knottiest apparatus of capture."[14] Kohso shows how nuclear technology, which was initially a military technology, was soon also introduced as an energy resource. This meant a merger not only of the realms of weaponry and energy but also of the military and civilian spheres, offering "the state a dystopian dream of sublime weaponry and to capitalism a utopian dream for sublime energy."[15] In other words, nuclear technology created a bond between the capitalist economy and state sovereignty that "has played a fatal role in the becoming of the contemporary world."[16] Kohso contends that the nuclear disaster in Fukushima brought to light that, like the end of capitalism, it is impossible to even *imagine* the end of nuclear technology. On the contrary, we now understand that not even a catastrophe of the dimensions of Fukushima can cause a radical break but that, instead, both capitalism and nuclear technology have shown the capacity to immediately involve the catastrophe in their systems, even to rely on it. "It is a revelation for us all, showing us the real existence of the nuclear regime that feeds itself by distributing the nexus of nuclear production globally, a regime that not only persisted in this production after the worst disaster but utilized the catastrophic situation in order to maintain its rule."[17] Kohso speaks in this context of the "zombie life of capitalism,"[18] created by infinite disasters that necessitate endless aftercare, which can then be sold as another product of the capitalist market. As Kohso puts it, we live in an "apocalyptic capitalism" that will outlive the end of the world.[19] What nuclear energy stands for, more than anything else,

---

14. Kohso, *Radiation and Revolution*, 88.
15. Kohso, *Radiation and Revolution*, 89.
16. Kohso, *Radiation and Revolution*, 89.
17. Kohso, *Radiation and Revolution*, 93.
18. Kohso, *Radiation and Revolution*, 88.
19. Kohso, *Radiation and Revolution*, 89. Jean-Luc Nancy's analysis of the equivalence between catastrophes gives more insight into the regime of general equivalence introduced by capitalism, which Nancy defines as the catastrophe of our times. Nancy also links this to the catastrophe of meaning that we experience today (Nancy, *After Fukushima*). This reading resonates with Malabou's claim of a war against meaning (Malabou, "From Sorrow to Indifference"), which I address later in the book and which will also become important for my conclusion.

is the capacity for total annihilation, and thus it proves to be the best possible fuel for allowing zombie capitalism to thrive. Müller's plays and writings clearly anticipate this, showing that there is no end to zombie capitalism, because it has made the end of the world into an integral part of its deadly life. And yet, at the same time, his plays explore the other side of the catastrophe and the explosion, emphasizing that they can unleash great energy that creates an opening for a becoming without determination and thus introduces chance and possibility into a seemingly closed system.

The "Nuclear/Climate Sublime" and the "Nuclear/Climate Mundane"

While the anticapitalist stance of German theater and performance in the tradition of Brecht has been exhaustively studied, their engagement with nuclear technology and complicity with capitalism have remained a blind spot in that scholarship.[20] In works on German-language theater, there are only two prominent exceptions, namely Brecht's *Leben des Galilei* (*Life of Galileo*, 1955/56) and Friedrich Dürrenmatt's *Die Physiker* (*The Physicists*, 1962), which have been discussed in the context of science and ethics[21] along with some lesser-known plays, such as Max Frisch's *Die Chinesische Mauer* (*The Chinese Wall*, 1947), Carl Zuckmayer's *Das Kalte Licht* (*The Cold Light*, 1955), Hans Henny Jahnn's *Die Trümmer des Gewissens* (The rubble of conscience, 1961), and Heinar Kipphardt's *In der Sache J. Robert Oppenheimer* (*In the Matter of J. Robert Oppenheimer*, 1964). While in the existing analyses, physics and the sciences more generally have been addressed only in terms of content, I argue that nuclear technology has written itself into German-language theater in a much more

---

20. Outside of the German-language context, there are exceptions, as we see in scholarship on Butoh, the Japanese dance form that was created as a response to Hiroshima and Nagasaki, and Beckett's theater of the absurd. See, e.g., Fraleigh, *Butoh*; Viala, *Butoh*; Schwab, *Radioactive Ghosts*; and Curtin, *Death in Modern Theatre*.

21. See, e.g., Masumoto, "Die Atombombe"; Müller, "Brechts *Leben des Galilei*"; Dorsey, "The Responsibility"; and Morley, "Dürrenmatt's Dialogue with Brecht."

fundamental way. Not only is it to be found on the level of the information and ideas contained in theatrical works but it also shapes the dramaturgy and enters into theater in all its complexity when it is reflected in the radical reworking of categories of time, space, life and death, human and nonhuman, and scale and causality. Thus, nuclear technology does not have to be the explicit topic of a theatrical piece, since we find the nuclear age written into the very dramaturgy and form of such theater.

My analysis unfolds within the tensions of the technoscientific age, shaped by the in-between of the "nuclear/climate sublime" and the "nuclear/climate mundane," concepts that I borrow from the literary scholar Jessica Hurley.[22] The theater that Müller creates is structured by this tension. We can see this better by looking at the author's 1985 conversation with Uwe Wittstock. In this conversation, Müller criticizes a society trapped in thinking about an apocalypse to come and engages directly with the possibility of an atomic war.[23] Here, Müller decidedly rejects what he identifies as a new hype about a possible end of the world fueled by atomic warfare. He claims that the fixation on the end to come renders the violence to which humans and nonhumans are exposed in their everyday lives invisible. Moreover, he links this fascination with the apocalypse to come to the apathetic attitude of a society that denies any responsibility for the world and thinks of freedom in terms of "laziness" toward the world and the social sphere.

What Müller describes here resonates with scholarly works that discuss the implications of atomic weaponry for human as well as planetary life. Atomic weaponry is a radical rupture and break in human warfare because for the first time it makes possible the total annihilation of vast parts of the planet. The historian Gabrielle Hecht speaks of a "nuclear exceptionalism" that has shaped the discourses on nuclear technology in large parts of the Western world.[24]

---

22. In so doing, I offer an alternative to the framings of theater that have been offered so far through the *Wende* of 1989, the rise of mass media, or 9/11. See Cornish, *Performing Unification*; Lehmann, *Postdramatisches Theater*; and Pełka, *Das Spektakel der Gewalt*.
23. Müller, "Der Weltuntergang."
24. Hecht, "The Power of Nuclear Things," 3.

We can see such a position expressed in Derrida's seminal essay "No Apocalypse, Not Now." Derrida claims that nuclear destruction is something that has never occurred before and thus can only be speculated about. While he insists that there are real effects of nuclear weaponry that can be observed, even if they are merely textual, the material side has remained a blind spot in subsequent works by other scholars. Based on such readings, Hurley contends that two "charismatic megaconcepts" have organized the discourse on atomic weaponry, namely the "textuality of the bomb and the nuclear sublime."[25] As a result, in most discussions the "atomic crisis is defined by its pure textuality" and its "absence from the material world."[26] In other words, it is the *unthinkable*, exceptional event.[27] Hurley and others, though, have argued that this is a fatal misperception of nuclear weaponry, hiding the real destruction that has continued under the name of "nuclear testing" since the first nuclear bomb was dropped in New Mexico, on July 16, 1945, on land inhabited by Native Americans.[28] She thus introduces the concept of the "nuclear mundane," which emphasizes the real-world impacts on the environment, infrastructure, bodies, and social life that can be observed and that make visible the existence of a militarized capitalism in which violence is "glorified and prioritized."[29]

From today's perspective, we need to add yet another aspect to the nuclear-capitalist-military regime that shapes how we think about human and planetary life—that is, the aspect of global warming. The threat of global warming shares a great deal with that of nuclear weaponry. Both are discussed in terms of the unthinkable and the exceptional, as an event that has never yet occurred, even

---

25. Hurley, *Infrastructures of Apocalypse*, 7.
26. Hurley, *Infrastructures of Apocalypse*, 5.
27. Here, of course, a link to the philosopher Timothy Morton's "hyperobjects" is possible, connecting the atomic age to broader questions of the capital market and destruction (Morton, *Hyperobjects*).
28. See Lee, "H-Bomb Guinea Pigs!," which shows how that first bomb was dropped on an area of New Mexico that was home to nineteen American Pueblo tribes, two Apache tribes, and some chapters of the Navajo Nation. See also Solnit, *Savage Dreams*, 5; Hurley, *Infrastructures of Apocalypse*, 6–14; and Barad, "Troubling Time/s," 57–59.
29. Hurley, *Infrastructures of Apocalypse*, 10.

while each of them is already a reality that affects everyone, although in unequal ways.³⁰ As with the nuclear threat, where the fixation on the dropping of the bomb as the total annihilation that is yet to come obscures the ongoing violence already unleashed by nuclear weaponry, so too does the focus on the total destruction of the planet that awaits us due to global warming render large parts of the already real devastation invisible.³¹

The tension between what is visible and perceptible and what remains unnoticed can best be captured using what the historian of science Michelle Murphy calls the "regime of perceptibility."³² Thinking of the nuclear threat and global warming in terms of perception allows a link to aesthetics and presents the arts as an exceptional space in which to address the crisis of perceptibility that we are currently experiencing. The theater of the void, characterized by radical experiments with perception and ultimately suggesting a replacing of perception through detection, responds, as I argue later in this chapter, to that potential.

Plasticity: Accident, Wound, Explosion

The tension between the nuclear/climate sublime and the nuclear/climate mundane not only leads to a theater that reflects on the limits and enclosures of our present but also hints toward a possible opening and potential future. While "The Wound Woyzeck" opens with

---

30. The philosopher Brian Massumi argues that our present is shaped by the imagining of a catastrophe to come that has become the predominant mode of warfare at least since 9/11. According to Massumi, it was George W. Bush who shifted from a strategy of "deterrence"—which had been the practice during the Cold War—to "preemption." The logic of preemption, Massumi writes, relies on "the threat [that] has not only not yet fully formed but has *not yet even emerged*. In other words, the threat is still indeterminately in potential" (Massumi, *Ontopower*, 9).

31. Karen Barad links the nuclear regime with global warming along with the fact that the Doomsday Clock, which was introduced during the Cold War to symbolize the likelihood of nuclear war at any given time, now also includes global warming in its considerations. I discussed this in the introduction and will also address it in greater detail in chapter 2.

32. Murphy, *Sick Building Syndrome*, 10.

duration and painful continuity, its third paragraph shifts our attention to a possible transformation. Müller imagines Woyzeck turning into a dog who will return as a wolf. This metamorphosis will allow history to begin anew: "Woyzeck lives where the dog is buried; the dog's name: Woyzeck. We are waiting for his resurrection with fear and/or hope that the dog will return as a wolf. The wolf will come from the South. When the Sun is in its zenith, he will be one with our shadow and in the hour of white heat History will begin."[33] The line evokes questions of subjectivity, as it recalls the figure of noon, which Nietzsche describes as the moment of the shortest shadow and a moment of splitting.[34] At the same time, Müller imagines change here as something that demands or unleashes an enormous amount of energy; an explosive moment that, in its most extreme mode, evokes the nuclear blast. It is here that Malabou's notion of plasticity resonates, as a change that unfolds between life and death and as a place where the future can appear.[35] As such, this very last paragraph marks the other, radical dimension of the speech. It confronts us with the unanticipated accident that changes everything in an instant and that reveals plasticity as the underlying structure of Müller's theater.

The explosion is linked to the gaping wound at the center of Müller's speech. "Woyzeck is the open wound," or, as Müller also puts it in the speech, Woyzeck's wound is "open like a mine pit from which the maggots swarm."[36] The wound here clearly references Theodor Adorno's "Die Wunde Heine" ("Heine the Wound"), a public lecture that Adorno gave in 1956 marking the hundredth anniversary of Heinrich Heine's death. With this speech, Adorno attempted to rehabilitate Heine's status in the German literary canon, which had become tarnished by the Nazis' appropriation of his works. While Müller, too, wondered about the status of a German author who had often been rejected and misunderstood (in Müller's case Georg Büchner), the

---

33. Müller, "The Wound Woyzeck," 111.
34. For a detailed analysis of this aspect in Nietzsche, see Zupančič, *The Shortest Shadow*, 130.
35. Malabou, *The Future of Hegel*, 193.
36. Müller, "The Wound Woyzeck," 110–11. The open wound from which the maggots swarm references Kafka's "Ein Landarzt" ("A Country Doctor") (Müller, "Ich bin ein Neger," 394).

wound in his speech is at the center of his claim to a new dramaturgy, one that forms from the unanticipated violent event. As such, what will be more important for my analysis than the reference to Adorno is another possible allusion that links the wound closely to theater, namely the allusion to Amfortas's "wound that does not heal" from Richard Wagner's final opera, *Parsifal*. This ultimately allows us to make associations with a trajectory of theatrical works that link theater and wound, reaching back to Sophocles's *Philoktetes*—a tragedy with which Müller engaged intensely, as his own versions of it show. The wound instigates an investigation into the relationship between the individual and society, between old and new, between tradition and innovation. In Wagner's opera, for example, the open wound introduces the question of the future for the individual, for a larger group or society, and for theater itself. Müller shares all those interests, but goes further and also includes the planetary scope. He subsequently also comes to a different conclusion. While *Parsifal* ends with the redemption of Amfortas,[37] in Müller, there is no promise of salvation for the wounded subject. It is precisely this lack I am interested in, as it is the break that allows for an opening, for an alternative mode of change, and, subsequently, for freedom to arise.

What kind of change and freedom is envisioned in Müller, then, if it is not a change and freedom that promise redemption? "The Wound Woyzeck" relies on recurring notions of the accident, the unanticipated, and the "may-be": "Somewhere, his body *perhaps* swings itself forward on his hands, shaking with laughter *perhaps*, toward an *unknown future* that *perhaps* will be his crossbreeding with a machine . . . a structure as it *might be* created when lead is smelted at New Year's Eve since the hand is trembling with anticipation of the

---

37. We still need to keep in mind that in Wagner's opera, the healing process is also complicated, as the wound can only be healed by the spear that inflicted it. As such, the ending in Wagner has been read in diverse ways; it is sometimes even questioned whether Wagner's opera ends with redemption. Most radical is Badiou's reading of the opera, arguing that Wagner deprives his opera of an ending and instead explores the "possibilities of an ending" (Badiou, *Five Lessons on Wagner*, 99). Badiou's reading will become important in chapter 4, as Schlingensief's approach to *Parsifal* is attentive to precisely the form of possibility that Badiou thinks that he finds in Wagner.

future."[38] Plasticity allows us to better understand the importance of the expressions of knowing, expecting, uncertainty, and possibility that shape Müller's short text and, more generally, his plays and writings. So far, I have explored the notion of plasticity in connection with the void, as conceptualized by Malabou in her interpretation of Darwin's *On the Origin of Species*. Now, I want to more broadly introduce plasticity—which, as Malabou argues, "is becoming both the dominant formal motif of interpretation and the most productive exegetical and heuristic tool of our time"[39] and thus is more appropriate for our understanding than Derrida's "motor scheme" of writing.[40] Plasticity, as Malabou points out in reference to its etymology (Greek *plassein* = to mold), means "at once the capacity to *receive form* (clay is called 'plastic,' for example) and the capacity to *give form* (as in the plastic arts or in plastic surgery)."[41] While it surely evokes associations with other related words like flexibility and elasticity, plasticity clearly also differs from them. It captures an in-between state. It is between fluid and solid (once formed, it cannot go back to its previous shape; it resists endless polymorphism) as well as referring to something formable and at the same time also formative.

I adopt Malabou's notion of plasticity because it allows me to describe the possibility of change without transcendence that is at work in the theater of Müller and, more broadly, in the theater of the void. Malabou's concept of plasticity is intriguingly situated between determinism and the possibility of change that, in its most radical version, can mean a dramatic break with determinism: plasticity is "at the extremes of a formal necessity (the irreversible character of a formation: determination) and of a remobilization of form (the capacity to form oneself otherwise, to displace, even

---

38. Müller, "The Wound Woyzeck," 110, my emphasis.
39. Malabou, *Plasticity at the Dusk of Writing*, 57.
40. Malabou introduces the notion of the motor scheme as an image for or approach to thought that best captures an historical and intellectual epoch, yet is also able to intervene in it (Malabou, *Plasticity at the Dusk of Writing*).
41. Malabou, *What Should We Do with Our Brain?*, 5. Malabou first introduced plasticity, a term she finds in Hegel's *Phenomenology of Spirit* and *Science of Logic*, in her *The Future of Hegel*, where she argues against anti-Hegelianism and antibiologism as they shaped continental philosophy after Heidegger.

to nullify determination: freedom)."⁴² Plasticity works against the notion of a "pure event," one that arrives fully unexpected. What it reveals instead is a dialectical relationship between anticipation and chance that is not shaped by difference but rather, in a way, by their being threaded through one another and, in so doing, transforming themselves and creating a new form. We can think of it in terms of what Foucault calls the process of "transsubjectivation," which consists of a trajectory *within* the self.⁴³ As such, plasticity offers a concept in which determinism and contingency are not contradictions but are instead at work simultaneously.

And how does this relate to the violent explosions we find in Müller's speech? We must shift our attention to "destructive plasticity," a particular form of plasticity that Malabou is always aware of, but which she only theorizes in more depth in her later works. Starting with her 2008 book *What Should We Do with Our Brain?*, Malabou investigates further what it might mean when there is, next to the positive plasticity that gives and receives form, a negative plasticity.⁴⁴ She reminds us that plasticity also refers to "an explosive substance made of nitroglycerine and nitrocellulose, capable of causing violent explosions."⁴⁵ Interested in this destructive form of plasticity, she dedicates an entire study to it, *The New Wounded*. Here she poses the question: "Might there be a wound of plasticity that, under the effects of a wound, *creates a certain form of being by effacing a previously existing identity?* Might there be, in the brain, a destructive plasticity—the dark double of the positive and constructive plasticity that moulds neuronal connections? Might

---

42. Malabou, *What Should We Do with Our Brain?*, 17. Malabou relies here on Jeannerod, *Le cerveau intime*.
43. Transsubjectivation doesn't mean that a person becomes *different* from what they used to be, nor that the person is able to absorb the other's difference, but instead that the person opens a space within themself, between two forms of themself (Foucault, *The Hermeneutics of the Subject*, 214). Malabou herself makes this reference (Vahanian, "A Conversation," 4).
44. In Malabou's 2004 book *The Future of Hegel*, though, she already refers to plasticity in the sense of the explosive when she speaks about the bomb (185, 189) and, in the last paragraph of the book, specifically about the atomic bomb (193).
45. Malabou, *What Should We Do with Our Brain?*, 5.

such plasticity make form through the annihilation of form?"[46] Starting from this question, she develops a critique of Freud and suggests replacing his concept of sexuality with cerebrality.[47] For her, this shift is important because our new understanding of the brain demands a radical new way of thinking of an event.

Malabou develops her concept of cerebrality based on trauma, posttraumatic disorders, brain injuries, and diseases like Alzheimer's, and shows that in all these cases, the wounds of the brain are so profound that they irrevocably change the self. While in Freud any event can be assimilated into or appropriated by the subject, Malabou argues that plasticity in its destructive version must be understood as a *pure* accident that destroys everything that attaches the subject to himself or herself and to others. "Cerebrality" introduces an event that is "blind to the hermeneutic dimension"; the subject is not able to give any meaning to it, nor does it fit into any affective regime.[48] Malabou here goes beyond Freud's pleasure principle and death drive. What is more, the cerebral event escapes any of the logic of a drive: it has nothing to do with hate or love; it just happens. Accidents of cerebrality are "wounds that cut the thread of history, place history outside itself, suspend its course, and remain hermeneutically 'irrecoverable' even though the psyche remains alive. *The cerebral accident thus reveals the ability of the subject to survive the senselessness of its own accidents.*"[49] As we will see in chapter 2, when I analyze Müller's play *Der Auftrag* in greater detail, Müller's theater is shaped by just such cerebral events, which resist interpretation by the subject and cut the thread of history. Not only does Müller reflect on the danger connected with such a state of indifference, but he also shows it as offering a chance to break away from determinism.

Malabou links this mode of transformation to the notion of metamorphosis. Metamorphosis allows us to better grasp the chance

---

46. Malabou, *The New Wounded*, xv, emphasis in the original.
47. Malabou argues that even though Freud seeks to grasp trauma and its wounds, he ultimately fails to go beyond the pleasure principle. He continues to connect these events to internal sexual causes instead of being able to consider the radicality of the break caused by an accident.
48. Malabou, *The New Wounded*, 9.
49. Malabou, *The New Wounded*, 5, emphasis in the original.

that arises from pure accident. While common Western imaginings think of it in terms of a transformation in form while the substance remains the same, Malabou argues that metamorphosis engages both form *and* being. In her philosophy, it refers to the formation of a form when all other alternatives for change have been exhausted. In other words, it is the formation of the form of flight when flight is impossible and yet would be the only option for escape. In such a transformation, the subject becomes unrecognizable, producing an identity that "does not reflect itself, does not live its own transformation, does not subjectivize its change."[50] And yet, this is precisely where the void is created that allows something unanticipated, singular, and unforeseen to happen.

Malabou speaks about "negative possibility" in order to stress that plasticity implies the possibility of transforming at any moment without being destroyed, and yet becoming radically other. She theorizes here a form of possibility that does not rely on messianic structures[51] nor simply allow for negation to be turned into affirmation. Again, she relies on Freud, but this time on his notion of *Verneinung* (denial or negation), which, she writes, offers a concept for such a possibility. It is a "pure possibility" that is "neither present, nor absent."[52] And yet, in uncoupling negation from repression, she clearly goes beyond Freud:

> To reject what is bad is to put it outside. But this demands that inside and outside be stable, real. Yet it is precisely this that the instances of accident discussed here no longer have. The subject must be able to

---

50. Malabou, *Ontology of the Accident*, 11.
51. Malabou emphasizes that she differs here from Derrida's "messianicity without messianism" as he discusses it in depth in *Specters of Marx*. She criticizes Derrida for remaining trapped in a metaphysics of presence that he seeks to undermine when he speaks of justice, democracy, etc. "to come," meaning that they cannot be known in the present and that they will only be discoverable when they have arrived. They will arrive as a messianic event that can only mean the absolute *arrivant* of something that continues to escape and that can only be a trace. As such, it is formless and invisible. In Malabou, on the other hand, time is plastic and thus works in a different way: the future event does not have a form until it has come to be formed. As such, Malabou puts an emphasis on the creation of change. See also Crockett and Malabou, "Plasticity and the Future"; and Malabou, *The Heidegger Change*.
52. Malabou, *Ontology of the Accident*, 78.

reclaim the good thing when he wishes and to reject the bad thing when he wishes.... Negation enables the subject to stand at the crossroads of two contradictory attitudes: to hide openly, or to dissimulate unknowingly. In contrast to this double attitude, the negative possibility is that which the subject will not or cannot do, with inclusion and exclusion losing all meaning here.[53]

What we can see here is that when we think in terms of a negative possibility, the way that we relate to the past and understand history changes. Whereas Freud's negation yields to the question of what could have been (if it had not been rejected and excluded) and what might thus still have another chance (as it is still waiting and haunting the present), negative possibility "prohibits envisaging precisely the *other possibility*, even if it were an *a posteriori* possibility."[54] Negative possibility "has nothing to do with the tenacious, incurable desire to transform what has taken place, to reengage in the history of the phantasm of another history; it does not match any unconscious tactical strategy of opening, the refusal of what is, in the name of what could have been." On the contrary, "destructive plasticity deploys its work starting from the exhaustion of possibilities, when all virtuality has left long ago."[55] This is important, because the playwrights and directors I discuss in this book are all invested in the question of how past, present, and future relate to each other. And yet, thinking of their theater in terms of plasticity, we understand that this theater inhabited by ghosts is not a naïve attempt to "set things right." On the contrary, the work being done here is more complex than that: it engages with our present in terms of the

---

53. Malabou, *Ontology of the Accident*, 82–83.

54. Malabou, *Ontology of the Accident*, 89, emphasis in the original.

55. Malabou, *Ontology of the Accident*, 89. Barad's agential realism resonates in interesting ways with Malabou's negative possibility, as Barad, too, rejects any thinking of setting things right. And yet, Barad thinks in terms of an opening of the past when they insist that the ongoing reconfigurings of spacetimematterings are the "*continual reopening and unsettling of what might yet be, of what was, and what comes to be*" (Barad, "Quantum Entanglements," 264, emphasis in the original). Unlike Malabou, Barad clearly draws from Benjamin and Derrida, without challenging or breaking with messianic time, but reworks it by giving it a material reality. In other words, in Barad, possibility is not a formless event, but, as for Malabou, it is im/materially formed and created.

possibility of a radical disconnection and rupture that can happen at any moment and that will radically separate us from the past. The past, however, is not simply gone; on the contrary, the erasure does not void our world's material reality of its history and historicity. What seems to be past is not past at all, but can at any time break into our present, reach us, and burst it open. I come back to this in the final section of this chapter when I speak of the theater of the void in terms of seismology.

For Malabou, the possibility of a disconnection evoked with plasticity is key to rejecting any form of essentialism that suggests an identity waiting to unfurl.[56] "The negative possibility, which remains negative until it is exhausted, never becomes real, never becomes unreal either, but remains suspended in the post-traumatic form of a subject who misses nothing—who does not even lack, as Lacan might have written—remains to the end this subjective form that is constituted starting from the absence from the self."[57] Each explosion or accident de-essentializes the subject and thus reveals that there is no such thing as an essence in the first place. The possibility of a form occurring that has nothing to do with an identity waiting to unfurl brings us back to the notion of a freedom that becomes possible because the unexpected can happen at any time and change a determinate path. If total erasure carries the potential for the formation of a new form, explosions are not necessarily negative but can also be creative and constructive: "The explosions in question are clearly understood as energetic discharges, creative bursts that progressively transform nature into freedom. To insist on explosive surges is to say that we are not flexible in the sense that all change of identity is a critical test, which leaves some traces, effaces others, resists its own test, and tolerates no polymorphism. Paradoxically, if we were flexible, in other words, if we didn't explode at each transition, if we didn't destroy ourselves a

---

56. Malabou, *Ontology of the Accident*, 90–91. Here again we see a difference from Barad, who claims, based on the findings of the double-slit experiment, that nothing can be fully erased and that, on the contrary, each attempted erasure also leaves material traces. For a detailed description of the experiment, see Barad, *Meeting the Universe Halfway*, 314.

57. Malabou, *Ontology of the Accident*, 90.

bit, we could not live. Identity resists its own occurrence to the very extent that it forms it."[58]

The theater of the void forms from such energetic discharges, which have a great creative potential. The enormous amount of energy unleashed by the blast that Müller envisions in his speech "The Wound Woyzeck" can be read in terms of such a negative possibility. Müller repeatedly emphasizes that there is potential in the loss of oneself and in becoming radically other. This is clearly expressed in his comment on his play *Mauser*, where he states: "SO THAT SOMETHING CAN ARRIVE SOMETHING HAS TO GO THE FIRST SHAPE OF HOPE IS FEAR THE FIRST APPEARANCE OF THE NEW IS TERROR."[59] To be able to lose oneself, for Müller, is the only way to avoid wrong fantasies of salvation.[60] It is this mode of formation that is key for Müller's plays and that is emphasized at the end of "The Wound Woyzeck." The transformation of Woyzeck into a dog, and the dog into a wolf, is a metamorphosis that engages both form and being and that hints at an understanding of being without essence. A being that is made of (possible) accidents is plural, because it shapes itself anew, again and again, at different times. Thus, as Müller makes clear, the individual speaker is actually a chorus instead.[61] Müller's theater of the void explores this subject that is created from a series of accidents, that destroys any notion of essence, and that precisely for that reason bears great futurity.

Unanticipated Accident and Theatrical Form

Turning now to the explicit question of the transformation of theatrical form, we must take a closer look at the second paragraph of

---

58. Malabou, *What Should We Do with Our Brain?*, 74.
59. Müller, *Mauser*, 106.
60. Wittstock, "Der Weltuntergang ist zu einem modischen Problem geworden," 366.
61. See, for example, his *Hamletmachine*, where one of the speakers is marked as "Ophelia (Chorus / Hamlet)" (Müller, *Hamletmachine*, 54), or his comment on *Despoiled Shore*, where he states that the segments of the text are collective (Müller, *Despoiled Shore*, 126).

Müller's speech. This part comes as a surprise, as if it is something that had just happened to the speech and its author. In this paragraph, Müller shifts his attention from social and political change to questions of theatrical form and transformation, introduced by a short comment on the reception of Büchner's *Woyzeck*: "A text many times raped by the theater, a text that *happened to* a twenty-three-year-old whose eyelids were cut off at his birth by the Weird Sisters, a text *blasted by fever* to orthographic splinters, a structure as it *might be* created when lead is smelted at New Year's Eve since the hand is *trembling with anticipation* of the future."[62] What is going on in this sentence—so abundant in images of violence, in moments of sudden discharge and explosion, and yet also announcing its excitement at the anticipation of an unpredictable future?

Müller's plays are usually read through the prism of Walter Benjamin's historical materialism. This is an obvious connection to make because Müller was an ardent reader of Benjamin, as can be seen from his repeated engagement with Benjamin, primarily with his notions of history.[63] However, I argue that we fail to fully understand Müller's work if we continue to read it exclusively through Benjamin's philosophy, because Benjamin is often—even if wrongly—understood as messianic.[64] Müller radically breaks with the notion of a future as a promise to come, in the sense of a pure event. Instead, in Müller's work, true to plasticity, the future event has to be formed.

---

62. Müller, "The Wound Woyzeck," 110, my emphasis.

63. In particular, Benjamin's "angel of history" appears in Müller's texts in various forms, for example as the "angel of despair" in his play *Der Auftrag*, where "Women / Voice" announces, "I am the Angel of Despair. With my hands I dispense ecstasy, numbness, oblivion, the lust and the torment of bodies. My language is silence, my song the scream" (87). Again, we can see the expression of silence that is the basis for all speech in Müller's work. The scholarship on Müller has engaged with this connection in depth, most comprehensively in Müller-Schöll, *Das Theater des "konstruktiven Defaitismus."*

64. See the account of Benjamin's historical materialism in Breithaupt, "History as the Delayed Integration of Phenomena," which puts a strong emphasis on latency and emptiness instead of reading Benjamin through messianism. Nonetheless, as Breithaupt makes clear, Benjamin's historical materialism remains connected to the idea of an inner kernel that is part of the phenomenon and that is already waiting to be revealed, which differs from the concept of history and historicity revealed through the void.

Müller makes use of the tension inherent in the terrifying, explosive side of plasticity that simultaneously annihilates and gives form. Understanding theater as plastic, Müller is convinced that it must explode and destroy itself to exist and form anew. Therefore, he works on the fine knifepoint between determination and contingency that introduces the blast as a necessary rupture of any limitation through a given form. To better understand this, we can take another look at the quotation just above in which Müller links Büchner's *Woyzeck* to the "Weird Sisters," the Roman Fates who control the "thread of life," and to a cutting away of the eyelids: "a text that happened to a twenty-three-year-old whose eyelids were cut off at his birth by the Weird Sisters."[65] Müller here introduces an image that combines determination and chance by linking the Fates to the violent event of the removal of the eyelids. In so doing, he makes an implicit link to another radical break with common notions of aesthetics and perception, as the removal of the eyelids resonates with Heinrich von Kleist's "Empfindungen vor Friedrichs Seelandschaft" ("Feelings before Friedrich's Seascape"), a text reflecting on Caspar David Friedrich's 1810 painting *Der Mönch am Meer* (*The Monk by the Sea*).

Kleist's text is without a doubt one of the most significant reflections that exists on nothingness or the void in the context of the arts. Here, Kleist claims that Friedrich's painting itself does not offer anything to its observer. Instead, it confronts us with the limitlessness of the void, in which everything that emerges only does so between the viewer and the painting. This relationship between painting and observer, though, is not characterized by distance. Kleist describes the painting as being deprived of its frame. And because there is no clear border, the observer is no longer positioned in front of the painting but is instead part of it. Lacking a frame, the painting challenges conventional modes of perception. It is a work of art that addresses the eye but is no longer perceptible to that eye, as looking at it is "as though his eyelids had been cut off."[66] While the removal of the eyelids violently forces the spectator to see, because he no longer has the ability to close his eyes, at the same time the missing eyelids

---

65. Müller, "The Wound Woyzeck," 110.
66. Kleist, "Feelings before Friedrich's Seascape," 208.

suggest a severe damage of the eyes, as they are no longer protected from light, dirt, etc. According to Kleist, Friedrich's painting stands at the beginning of a radical revisioning of representation and perception. It anticipates a shift from the eye to the senses, from perception to detection. To summarize, we can say that Müller connects Büchner and Kleist, explosion and wound, to make visible the past explosive moments that have radically transformed the theater or art and that reveal their plasticity.

Müller's own attempt to create a new theatrical form or to transform drama relies on the destructive plasticity he observes in Büchner. Accident, explosion, and destruction shape Müller's work. He calls *Description of a Picture* the "explosion of a memory in an extinct dramatic structure";[67] his play *Despoiled Shore Medeamaterial Landscape with Argonauts* unfolds in a devastated landscape full of dirt and trash; and *Grundlings Leben Friedrich von Preußen Lessings Schlaf Traum Schrei* ("Grundling's life Frederick of Prussia Lessing's sleep dream scream," 1977) ends with a projection that imagines the death of human, machine, and animal alike in a mix of atomic blast and earthquake. The fragmented style of the plays emulates the impression of a text blasted into pieces, where the words and sentences seem like parts collected after an explosion. However, while Müller's plays are usually characterized in terms of fragmentation and the destruction of a whole, the texts are not formless, which is stressed through Müller's use of uppercase letters, giving the text a figural structure and connecting the writing to sculpture.

Plasticity allows us to understand that fragment and form are not necessarily opposites, as they are usually conceived in scholarship. As Malabou explains, plasticity refers to "*the spontaneous organization of fragments,*" which she describes, leaning on Lévi-Strauss, as being "endowed with a dithyrambic gift for synthesis."[68] Lévi-Strauss offers an understanding of unity that stresses the "quasi-monstrous ability to perceive the similarity between things which others regard as different."[69] As he describes it, using the example of a wooden storage

---

67. Müller, *Description of a Picture*, 110.
68. Malabou, *Plasticity at the Dusk of Writing*, 7.
69. Lévi-Strauss, *The Way of the Mask*, 8.

box found in British Columbia: "Within the same object sometimes, it is as if one were transported from Egypt to twelfth-century France, from the Sassanids to the merry-go-rounds of suburban amusement parks.... For the animal is represented simultaneously in full face, from the back, and in profile; seen from above and below, from the outside and from within."[70] Müller's plays, along with the plays of Jelinek, Schlingensief, and Pollesch, work with this tension between difference and the monstrous possibility of perceiving similarity between seemingly disparate things. The theater of the void, with its underlying principle of plasticity, offers a third way, between the constitution of a whole in the sense of drama and a theater of disorganization and fragmentation where "synthesis is cancelled."[71] It is a theater that, between the artwork and the audience, allows for the spontaneous organization of the pieces, indeed even synthesizes them. This does not mean that the work is enclosed in something like wholeness but that it remains open to transition, as it creates only brief and temporary moments of synthesis.[72]

Healing in the Theater of the Void

Now, let us return to Müller's critique of resurrection, which introduces questions of healing into our discussion of the explosion and the violent break. In "The Wound Woyzeck," we find two modes addressed—the open wound and the scar. Woyzeck is described as an open wound while, according to the first line of the third paragraph, "the wound Heine begins to scar over, crooked."[73] I contend that in the tension between wound and scar, Müller introduces a new form of healing that becomes important for the theater of the void. This new form is not trapped in a framework either of salvation and sublation, as we find in theatrical models based on a

---

70. Lévi-Strauss, *The Way of the Mask*, 8.
71. Lehmann, *Postdramatic Theatre*, 82.
72. Müller himself speaks in terms of his plays about synthetic fragments. See Weber, "The Pressure of Experience," 17 and 28–29.
73. Müller, "The Wound Woyzeck," 111.

traditional Hegelian dialectics, or of the scar, which dominates readings that follow Lehmann's deconstructive frame.

To better understand this new form, we need to pay attention to a conversation the playwright had with Wolfgang Heise in 1985. There, Müller engages with the question of a possible future and forms of resistance against a closed system of violence and exploitation. During the conversation, the author mentions an early, unpublished version of scene 14 of Brecht's *Life of Galileo*. Müller is captivated by the silence with which Galileo reacts to his daughter's question about the judgment of human failure and the conflicted feelings of longing and fear toward death expressed in this version of the scene. "VIRGINIA: God created man like a shadow. Who can judge him when the sun has set? / *Galileo remains silent*."[74] Müller also points out the following line, "Admirable is the good," which Virginia reads and Galileo does not comment on. Instead, he asks her to repeat the line a little louder.[75] What Müller finds interesting about this unpublished scene is that Brecht here does not judge Galileo, as he then does in his revised version of *Galileo*, after the experience of Hiroshima and Nagasaki.

Müller argues that in these lines we find a possibility for change or, in other words, a concept of the future expressed because Brecht breaks with his usual dialectics. He points out that in this scene, Brecht expresses an understanding of responsibility that goes beyond the individual and that finds an actual alternative position to a society trapped in laziness and awaiting the coming apocalypse ("the opposite of the bourgeois position of 'après moi le déluge'").[76] We can understand this better if we consider the other example Müller gives of Brecht departing from his traditional Marxist dialectics, namely the poem "Als ich in weißem Krankenzimmer der Charité" ("When in my hospital ward..."). This was one of Brecht's last poems, written in Berlin's Charité hospital. For Müller, this poem is the only other text by Brecht that captures a position similar to that of the unpublished scene 14 of *Galileo*:

---

74. Heise, "Ein Gespräch," 497–98.
75. Heise, "Ein Gespräch," 498.
76. Heise, "Ein Gespräch," 498.

> When in my hospital ward at the Charité
> I awoke towards morning
> And heard a blackbird, I saw it all
> More clearly. For some time already
> I had put aside fear of death, since I
> Can nothing lack, if
> I myself am lacking. Now
> I was able to take pleasure also
> In the song of every blackbird after me.[77]

What we encounter here is a subject formed out of destruction, explosion, or trauma, a subject that has lost all relation to his past and yet misses nothing ("da ja nichts / Mir je fehlen kann, vorausgesetzt / Ich selber fehle"); in other words, a cerebral subject. The last two lines of the poem express a healing that neither leaves a scar behind nor promises infinity or eternity. The pleasure or ease the subject feels is no longer dependent on the self but rather on the possibility of repairing itself by replacing itself. The self accepts that it can live without itself as a radical other, as well as accepting a death that does not lead to a superior life. In so doing, it breaks with any solace of salvation that might guarantee an afterlife.

Müller explores such a mode of healing that with Malabou we can describe as regeneration. Regeneration, according to Malabou, is a form of cloning. It involves a repairing of oneself by replacing oneself. This mode of healing is modeled on stem cell research and the capacity of some animals for self-regeneration, a capacity that is

---

77. Brecht, "When in my hospital ward . . . ," 1071. The German original reads:

> Als ich in weißem Krankenzimmer der Charité
> Aufwachte gegen Morgen zu
> Und eine Amsel hörte, wußte ich
> Es besser. Schon seit geraumer Zeit
> Hatte ich keine Todesfurcht mehr, da ja nichts
> Mir je fehlen kann, vorausgesetzt
> Ich selber fehle. Jetzt
> Gelang es mir, mich zu freuen
> Alles Amselgesanges nach mir auch.

Brecht, "Als ich in weißem Krankenzimmer der Charité," 300.

almost extinct in humans and other mammals with the exception of some forms of regeneration of the liver, the epidermis, and the blood vessels. Malabou speaks of the "paradigm of the salamander," explaining that when a limb of a salamander is cut off, it grows back without leaving a scar. This form of self-regeneration or regrowth relies on the capacity of cells to transdifferentiate, meaning that cells can not only generate the kind of tissue that they come from but can also transform into other types of cells and generate a tissue that is different from their initial form.[78] Thus, regeneration is a mode of healing that allows the possibility of a return by replacing oneself in order to survive.

Malabou's model is situated between Hegel's dialectics and Derrida's deconstruction.[79] She returns to Hegel, who in *Phenomenology of Spirit* writes that "the wounds of the spirit heal, and leave no scars behind,"[80] and then she goes on to discuss the differences between healing in Hegel and Derrida. According to Malabou's interpretation, in Hegel's dialectical plasticity the wound without a scar implies sublation, resurrection, and a transformation into a superior life and regeneration of presence. This becomes clear when Hegel compares the spirit to the phoenix, the bird that is reborn from its own ashes as "exalted, glorified, a purer spirit."[81] In Derrida's deconstruction, on the other hand, "the process of recovery ... is understood through the text as tissue. To read, to understand, is to make wounds everywhere, first cuts, gashes, in the textile or web and the flesh. The text always reconstitutes itself, but it keeps imprints or traits of all readings and all acts of the spirit.... The regeneration of living tissue coincides with the process of scarring and the inscription of the memory of the wound."[82] In short, all presence consists in

---

78. Malabou, "Again: The Wounds of the Spirit," 30–34. For example, nerve cells can transdifferentiate themselves into skin cells in order to help skin to regenerate from within.
79. This is a move that Derrida himself prepared for in his later works, with his rising interest in the undeconstructible, outlined under the names of justice and democracy. Malabou shows that Derrida's neglect of science meant that he was not able to make this transformation himself.
80. Hegel, *Phenomenology of Spirit*, 407.
81. Hegel, *Lectures on the Philosophy of History*, 76.
82. Malabou, "Again: The Wounds of the Spirit," 30.

its own erasure, as the movement of *différance* always already displaces metaphysical understandings of totality, stability, and the subject. But what regeneration does instead is to capture a mode of healing that neither implies the return of the same nor stems from the other. It does not lead to a superior life, eternity, or the reinstallment of presence, nor does it leave a scar behind. It creates a third possibility, a healing without a scar that is yet a "finite survival, a momentary resource":[83] "The therapeutic and ontological work of plasticity disturbs the dialectical work of auto-reparation of the absolute, as well as the motifs of writing and of textuality in general. Reparation here comes neither from the same nor from the other. Because of this complexity, it appears not only as the supplement of the supplement, a simple replacement for writing. It no longer belongs to the era of metaphysics, but it likewise announces a change of system of the supplement itself."[84]

In Malabou, regeneration suggests a mode of healing by erasing writing. It is a deprogramming or a "de-writing." This is where the great potential of regeneration becomes visible, as it changes difference and inscription and shows that it is possible to modify a given structure and to break away from the text.[85] Drawing further from Malabou, we understand that Müller finds in Brecht a form of healing that is true to plasticity. Interestingly, Müller makes reference to Brecht's poem in the context of two other conversations as well. In both of them, he emphasizes the poem's exceptional position as a text that expresses a form of change linked to accepting destruction and death in a way that allows a feeling of ease to arise. Müller comes closest to being able to express what I call regeneration in his 1988 conversation with Frank Raddatz, in which he calls the poem Brecht's most extreme and most utopian position, because it is the ultimate formula for ease, pleasure, and even joy that do not depend on religion or belief in any afterlife.[86]

---

83. Malabou, "Again: The Wounds of the Spirit," 34.
84. Malabou, "Again: The Wounds of the Spirit," 36.
85. Malabou, "Again: The Wounds of the Spirit," 36.
86. In Müller's words, "The real goal is to reach this position of enjoyment without religion or a belief in the hereafter" ("Diese Position des Genießens zu er-

I consider Müller's interest in this position that was formulated by Brecht to be key to a better understanding of the theater of the void. Müller takes inspiration from Brecht and carves out a position between the return of the same and the reliance on the other. What I consider so important about this position is that it insists on responsibility and the fact that we can do something to change determinism, without falling into the romantic notion of an original substance that is waiting to unfurl. Instead, what this position emphasizes is the great potential and opportunity that lies in the wound itself. In other words, healing in Müller relies on catastrophe and explosion. It is a form of healing that comes from within and that demands from us that we replace ourselves so that we can regenerate in order to survive, even if not infinitely.

Explosion of the Image, Theater of Voices, or: Historiography as Seismology

The emphasis on explosion and the unexpected accident allows radical dramaturgical changes that can best be seen in Müller's *Description of a Picture* but that also apply to the theater of the void more generally. To better understand these changes, we must return to Müller's claim that *Description of a Picture* explodes the image so that at the end, there is no image anymore.[87] What does this mean for theater, as the place for seeing, if it is deprived of the image? How is theater reworked when its visual dimension diminishes?

I argue that in the theater of the void, the image *has* to explode so that all kinds of noises, sounds, and sensual impressions, which usually remain unnoticed in favor of the dominance of the gaze, can surface. In other words, representation is no longer predominantly defined by the eye; instead, the ear and other senses come to the fore.

---

reichen, ohne Religion oder Jenseitsglauben, ist das eigentliche Ziel") (Raddatz, "Ich wünsche mir Brecht," 327).

87. Müller, "Description of a Picture Is," 96.

And, what is more, representation yields to the shared experience of detection, which no longer relies on human cognition.

To better understand the radical break caused when representation is no longer linked to the eye, we can turn to Roland Barthes's essay "Diderot, Brecht, Eisenstein," in which he discusses representation in terms of eye versus ear. Barthes argues that the affinity between mathematics and acoustics was established in ancient Greece but was then repressed by another affinity, that of geometry and theater. This second affinity, according to Barthes, has predominantly shaped the arts, with the exception of music. Theater, Barthes writes, is the practice "which calculates the place of things *as they are observed*." He concludes: "The stage is the line which stands across the path of the optic pencil, tracing at once the point at which it is brought to a stop and, as it were, the threshold of its ramification. Thus is founded—against music (against the text)—representation."[88] Representation, Barthes argues, is thus defined not by imitation but by the existence of the position of the observer. Its foundation is the "sovereignty of the act of cutting out [*découpage*] and the unity of the subject of that action."[89] Subsequently, Barthes raises the question of how art could cease to be significant, readable, representational, or metaphysical. In other words, he wonders when music will replace the gaze.

While Barthes points out that the new theater invented by Brecht in the twentieth century remains committed to the gaze in its emphasis on tableaux and the gesture, I argue that the theater of the void that emerges with Müller breaks with geometry and instead introduces music and the sonic at its center. This might, at first glance, seem like a contradiction. Müller has repeatedly taken up the metaphor of the landscape to describe his theater, a concept connected more closely than others to the gaze and to framing through a subject.[90] He has also stressed the importance of space in his

---

88. Barthes, "Diderot, Brecht, Eisenstein," 69. Emphasis in the original.
89. Barthes, "Diderot, Brecht, Eisenstein," 69–70.
90. Landscape as a concept originated in the visual arts and was only later adopted to speak about real, physical surroundings. In Müller's context, the landscape is closely connected to Gertrude Stein's "landscape play." Stein created this as an alternative writing practice, in which she claimed, unlike in conventional theater, the

theater. After all, he was also a painter before he decided to give up the visual arts, in 1949, to focus solely on his writing. His theater can therefore not be separated from the visual arts, as Wolfgang Storch claims.[91] But on second glance, we understand that this connection of Müller's theater to the visual arts is actually one of destruction and explosion of the image, as shown not least by his *Description of a Picture*. Using Barthes's terms, we can argue that Müller breaks with geometry and reinvents representation through another possible tradition, that of music and the ear. And then, in the words of the philosopher and neuroscientist Antonio Damasio, we can go even further and describe the theater of the void as a theater of sensing. Sensing, here, hints at a form of detection that is *not* perception, that is "*not* constructing a 'pattern' based on something else to create a 'representation' of that something else and produce an 'image' in mind." Although this form of sensing is no longer limited to human cognition, it is not the opposite of cognition. On the contrary, it is "the most elementary variety of cognition."[92]

When we pay attention to the importance of sensing that replaces the image, we start to understand the radicality of the transformation that the theater of the void introduces into theater. When theater no longer takes geometry as the foundation of its representation but is instead reinvented through the ear, then a form of cognition becomes central that no longer privileges human consciousness but instead redraws the line between human and nonhuman life, bringing them together as living organisms with the capacity to detect and sense the murmurs of the void, to borrow a phrase once again from Barad.

---

text would not contrast with the atmospherically spreading theatrical elements of the performance. Her landscape plays were not intended to interrupt the other elements of the theater but were instead supposed to fit into them as an equal partner. This could only succeed, Stein thought, when the texts no longer focused on meaning, identification, dialogue, and psychology. For Stein, landscape is a complex, ongoing process. It is not about moving or the linear succession of time but about the relation of objects and subjects (Stein, *Lectures in America*, 114–15). Accordingly, we need to recognize that landscape in the context of theater breaks with geometry and introduces music as its underlying principle.

91. Storch, "Die Bildenden Künste," 113.
92. Damasio, *Feeling and Knowing*, 13.

In this kind of theater, the concept of history must necessarily also change. I argue that Müller's theater anticipates the shift to "deep history" that we can currently observe. Deep history reevaluates the relationships among history, biology, and human cognition and no longer promotes a thinking in terms of a succession from evolution through prehistory to recorded history. Instead, deep history implies that "human behavior is seen as the product not just of recorded history, ten thousand years recent, but of deep history, the combined genetic and cultural changes that created humanity over hundreds of [thousands of] years."[93] Because it is attentive to this deep history, Müller's theater is usually linked to archeology, which we see in his own comment at the end of his play *Anatomie Titus Fall of Rome* (1985), where he speaks of the "theater as the midwife of archeology."[94] However, as the theater scholar Nikolaus Müller-Schöll points out, the phrase is disconcerting because it combines the idea of the emergence and creation of something new with the search for origins and the revealing of historical layers.[95] Drawing on Benjamin, Müller-Schöll interprets the phrase about midwifery, which is followed by the claim that "the actuality of art is tomorrow,"[96] as art hinting at a radically absent future. In a poststructuralist, deconstructivist tradition, Müller-Schöll subsequently claims that Müller's archeology is an *Ab-Bau*, a de-construction that must be understood as the work on the ground or, and here he quotes Müller again, the work of a surveyor. But approaching Müller through the void, we must also challenge this reading. The future is not the "event to come" that is never fully realized. Instead, Müller has a conception of the future as that which takes form when it comes to be formed. In other words, Müller's work is not exactly that of the surveyor but rather the work of the seismograph.

It is the seismograph that is at the center of Alexander Kluge's eulogy for Müller. Kluge quotes a conversation he once had with Müller in which he asked him whether he was a surveyor or a

---

93. Wilson, *In Search of Nature*, ix–x.
94. Müller, *Anatomie Titus*, 225.
95. Müller-Schöll, "Arbeit am Gelände," 57.
96. Müller, *Anatomie Titus*, 225.

prophet. Müller answered that of the two, he was more of a surveyor, but that in fact, he was a seismograph. In commenting on this, Kluge summarizes Müller's theater as follows: "He is a seismograph who measures meticulously. And he measures as precisely as does a quantum physicist."[97] And while the seismograph often functions as a mere metaphor for artistic intuition and genius, I actually suggest taking it seriously here. The seismograph hints at an alternative mode of sensing. As the cultural theorist Karin Harrasser argues, it is a machine that is specifically sensitive to vibrations, one that evokes the metaphors of recording and sensing, which can be better grasped when read together with Siegfried Kracauer's comments on history. Harrasser conceptualizes "doing history as a seismograph" along the lines of Kracauer's *History: The Last Things before the Last*, in which he presents an approach to history that, Harrasser argues, has to be captured as an attitude rather than a distinct method. She writes that such a doing of history and historiography unfolds on three levels. First of all, history is an "attitude toward the present," that is, it inspires a constant movement between what is now and what has been that causes a break and alienates us from the present, factual world. Secondly, it is an "antiquarian interest" that demands an ongoing conversation with the dead and an openness to waiting and listening for the voices of the dead that might reach us. This attitude testifies to the contingency of what is kept in archives. Thirdly, history is a "passion for the non-fixed," which shows that Kracauer is interested in the nonlinear process of the history of ideas, which consists of ruptures and misunderstandings rather than a success story.[98]

Using Kracauer's terms, we can understand that the seismograph refers to an "active passivity" in which one must "drift along, and take in, with all [the] senses strained, the various messages that happen to reach" one.[99] Or, as Harrasser puts it, to "conceive of doing history as a seismographic operation has many advantages, as it establishes a relation to the past that shakes and concusses the present,

---

97. Kluge, "It Is an Error," 7.
98. Harrasser, "Violence and the Care for Images."
99. Kracauer, *History*, 84.

that raises awareness for the non-individual and the more-than-human. It defamiliarizes the matter-of-factness of the contemporary world and, not least, it forces us to conceive of the past as something we have not come to terms with."[100] Instead of seeing them as a way of rectifying things from the past, I suggest reading the noises that reach us as ruptures that discharge great energy, enabling explosion and introducing futurity.

Müller's theater establishes an attitude toward the present in which we must become sensitive to the sounds and voices that might reach, intervene in, and explode our present and thus allow change to happen. This becomes clear when we think of Müller's theater as a kind of message in a bottle, meaning that it depends on a medium that enables those noises to be heard, as well as marking the fact that the sounds we register in this theater cannot be localized. Hence, the speakers mentioned in this theater and the bodies that appear on stage greatly differ from conventional dramatic characters. It is not their subjectivity or biography that is of interest but their function. They are tools: a medium that receives, makes audible, and records noises and voices from different times and spaces.

But how does a theater disconnect body from voice in order to mark the body as a sensory tool and medium rather than as the authentic source of speech? We must pay attention to the importance of deictic terms in Müller's theater. Deictic terms are terms that generate or make reference to the specific position and perspective of the speaker and/or viewer. They refer to their own perspective and are related to an audience. Pronouns like "this" and "that" and adverbs like "there," "then," "here," "now," and "whence" are deictic words, which include the vantage point of the speaker or viewer in their meaning. Moreover, all utterances that include information about the perspective of the speech are deictic. Deixis refers to the body of the speaker; it is "utterance in carnal form."[101]

The bodily presence onstage that is evoked by the deictic terms that Müller uses is different from that in the dialogic drama. Even though Müller often does not mention any character or speaker, the

---

100. Harrasser, "Violence and the Care for Images."
101. Bryson, *Vision and Painting*, 88.

plays nevertheless still relate to a body as the source of speech through the deictic forms. What is confounding about Müller's plays is the fact that although he uses deictic terms, he simultaneously eliminates any markers of actual communication or explication. And yet deixis relies on such markers. We can see this in a simple example: the message "I love you" is only understandable when both a speaker and an addressee are present. When either the speaker or the addressee or both is/are absent, for example if we find this message as a message in a bottle, the temporal and spatial reference remains unclear and we can no longer frame the sentence adequately.[102]

In Müller's plays, voices refer back to a speaker who simultaneously remains indefinite, since all concrete markers that could contextualize the expressions are missing. Without the possibility of relating the utterance to a body, whoever is making the speech on stage will always be perceived as inauthentic. The performers are merely borrowing the speech, just as the speech is borrowing them. They are a form of messenger. As soon as we understand that the performers are sensory tools and not characters, we can interpret Müller's claim that the basis of his theater is renewed silence. Müller speaks about silence in one of his most important poetological texts, his letter to the director Dimiter Gotscheff, which he ends with the words: "When the discotheques are abandoned and the academies deserted, the silence of the theater will be heard again, which is the foundation of its language."[103] Müller criticizes the fact that in theater, silence is misunderstood and barely ever realized. He in-

---

102. Müller himself compares his writing to a message in a bottle: "I can only produce texts for messages in bottles anymore, messages that I put in a bottle, and then I throw the bottle into the water in the hope that it will be fished out at some point, whether by a Martian or a Puerto Rican or whatever. And who will then try to draw information, from this text in this bottle, that he may be able to use in his life" ("Ich kann nur noch Texte für Flaschenpost herstellen, die ich in eine Flasche stecke, und dann werfe ich die Flasche ins Wasser mit der Hoffnung, dass sie irgendwann aufgefischt wird, ob von einem Marsmenschen oder von einem Puertoricaner oder was immer. Und der versucht dann, aus diesem Text in dieser Flasche Informationen zu beziehen, die er vielleicht verwenden kann für sein Leben") (Müller, "Ich bin ein Neger," 399–400).

103. Müller, "Brief an den Regisseur," 269. "Wenn die Diskotheken verlassen und die Akademien verödet sind, wird das Schweigen des Theaters wieder gehört werden, das der Grund seiner Sprache ist."

sists, however, that silence is not merely a gap, not emptiness. On the contrary, silence is the basis from which all speech emerges: "Before the word there is always silence, and silence is the condition for speaking."[104] While silence is usually interpreted in a messianic tradition as an "event to come,"[105] I argue that in Müller, silence is not the formless event; it must be understood in terms of the void that is shaped by the figures of haunting and plasticity. It is the groundless ground from which form emerges, filled with all the possible sounds that have been, are, and might yet be.

---

104. Müller, "Am Anfang war," 296. "Vor dem Wort ist immer das Schweigen, und das Schweigen ist die Voraussetzung für Sprechen."
105. For example in Müller-Schöll, ". . . die Wolken still."

2

Falling Out of Time and Space

The Quantum World and the Indifferent Subject in Heiner Müller

> I realize that for quite a while something has been wrong: with my watch, with the elevator, with time.
> —Heiner Müller, The Task

Heiner Müller's revolutionary play *Der Auftrag* (*The Task*, 1979) centers on the failing mission of three emissaries of the French Revolution—the Black former slave Sasportas; the farmer Galloudec; and the bourgeois Debuisson, a son of slaveowners—who were sent to Jamaica to spark a slave revolt against the colonizers of the island, the British Crown.[1] At the beginning of the play, the

---

1. *Der Auftrag* draws from Anna Seghers's novella *Das Licht am Galgen* (*The Light on the Gallows*, 1961), but clearly reinvents it based on Müller's interest in the complex relationship between time and space, his ever-stronger interest in the intersection of race and colonialism, and his questioning of the established concepts of a revolution. One of the most obvious changes is that while in Seghers we find a Jewish revolutionary, Müller introduces a Black revolutionary, inspired by thinkers like

revolt has already failed; this is key for the dramaturgy that unfolds. Instead of recounting the chronological account of a revolution, the play is shaped by a complex temporality that allows different times to go through each other. And it is by means of this temporality that the play reflects and comments on the possibility of a successful revolution. *The Task* thematizes the mistaken conceptualization of a revolution as a teleological event. What Müller develops instead, by introducing a vast revolutionary topology in which linear time gives way to diverse temporalities, is an alternative model of change and futurity that relies on the void as the indeterminate source of everything that is and might yet be.

The thinking of time in terms of linearity is immediately disrupted and replaced by a more complex temporality when *The Task* opens with a letter that links different times and places. We only have access to the letter, which was written by Galloudec on his deathbed in Cuba, through a sailor who had promised the dying Galloudec to make sure that the letter reached the revolutionary Antoine. In the letter, Galloudec reports what happened to him and the two other emissaries after they heard that Napoleon had come to power in France: Debuisson betrayed the revolution, Sasportas was executed by the British, and Galloudec was captured in Cuba, where he wrote his letter. When the letter finally arrives in Paris, though, Antoine has long since turned his back on the revolutionary cause. While the letter is a rather conventional and well-established way of complicating dramatic time, Müller goes further, ultimately making it impossible to bring time into any certain chronological order. This first becomes evident when the three emissaries suddenly appear as ghosts, surrounding Antoine, who has turned the scene into an orgiastic feast. While even ghosts are not unusual on the stage—we need only think of Shakespeare's *Hamlet*—the scene shows Antoine in the middle of intercourse when an angel of despair, a figure evocative of Benjamin's angel of history, appears[2] to relate past, present, and future in an intricate way. Benjamin's angel turns his

---

Frantz Fanon. Fanon's *Black Skin, White Mask*, in particular, is an important intertext for Müller's play.

2. Müller, *The Task*, 87.

head to the past to silently observe the debris that is piling up behind him as a single catastrophe, while he himself is simultaneously being blown toward the future.[3] Müller's angel, though, speaks in a prophetic tone of hope that comes from battle and destruction: "My hope is the last gasp. My hope is the first battle."[4] In these words, he evokes change in the form of destructive plasticity, which begins to fully unfold in the short, puzzling narrative "Der Mann im Fahrstuhl" (The man in the elevator),[5] a text that interrupts the rest of the play and confronts us with a world in which time and space are out of joint.

The Task is incredibly heterogeneous, consisting of diverse parts that include a play within the play and several narrative passages. And yet we can still identify three essential constellations that shape the play: Antoine's receipt of the letter; the beginning of the revolutionary work by the three emissaries in Jamaica; and the separation of the revolutionary collective after its members are informed of Napoleon's ascension to power.[6] At first glance, "Der Mann im Fahrstuhl" does not fit into any of these constellations. We are confronted with a first-person narrator who finds himself in an elevator on the way to a meeting with his boss to receive an important assignment. While he is on his way there, however, he loses his ability to make sense of time and space. Rather than arriving at his boss's office, the employee instead finds himself on a rural street in Peru. As the translator Carl Weber argues in his introduction to the play, the short prose text is "the most Kafkaesque text ever published by Müller"; Müller himself claims that it is "based on the

---

3. Benjamin, *Über den Begriff der Geschichte*.
4. Müller, *The Task*, 87.
5. Müller also published "Der Mann im Fahrstuhl" as a separate prose text. It is regularly staged both as part of *The Task* as well as on its own as an individual piece. This is particularly due to the successful adaptation of the prose text in 1987 by the composer and director Heiner Goebbels, in collaboration with the author. Müller has regularly inserted prose-like texts into his plays that he has also published separately; in addition to "Der Mann im Fahrstuhl," these include "Erzählung des Arbeiters Franz K.," "Nachtstück," "Befreiung des Prometheus," and "Herakles 2 oder die Hydra."
6. See Klein, "Der Auftrag," 190.

protocol of a dream."⁷ Scholars have pointed out the centrality of the short narration and discussed "Der Mann im Fahrstuhl" as a metaphor that abolishes dramatic time in order to bring to light the complex temporal-spatial constellation that is inherent in the question of revolution.⁸ I agree that the text is evocative of Kafka, and I follow those readings inasmuch as I, too, contend that in *The Task*, Müller is less interested in any particular historical event of revolution or counterrevolution than he is in the broader systemic question of endurance and change.⁹ And yet, I also go beyond these readings, suggesting that "Der Mann im Fahrstuhl" should be read in terms of a *metamorphosis* rather than as a *metaphor*.

The short narrative functions as an unanticipated accident that unleashes great energy. It stages a situation in which flight is not possible and yet flight would in fact be the only way out. Without there being any possibility of fleeing, the dramatic form itself transforms to offer a form of flight or metamorphosis. It is here, in the revelation of the futurity that is inherent in Müller's theater, that an alternative mode of change beyond teleology is offered.¹⁰ Borrowing from Müller's *Description of a Picture*, "Der Mann im Fahrstuhl" can be seen as "the gap in the process" and the "perhaps saving ERROR" that interrupts the play.¹¹ In other words, the short narrative allows the unanticipated to happen and hence shows that it is possible to break away from fate. In the process, we find, within the failed revolution, a successful one, one that takes place in the formation of a new theatrical form.

---

7. Weber, introduction to *The Task*, 83. The text is particularly reminiscent of Kafka's "Eine Kaiserliche Botschaft" ("An Imperial Message") from *Ein Landarzt* (*The Country Doctor*), as well as of *Der Verschollene* (*Amerika: The Missing Person*).

8. Klein, "Der Auftrag," 192.

9. As is typical for Müller, the entire play is characterized by a complex arrangement of diverse times and places that hint at hidden connections between different revolutionary moments throughout history. Thus, for instance, the references to Napoleon in the play also hint at Stalin. Moreover, the boss in "Der Mann im Fahrstuhl," who is addressed by the narrator as "Number One," has been interpreted as a reference to Stalin as well as to the former GDR leader Erich Honecker (cf. Weber, introduction to *The Task*; Schütte, "Brückenschlag," 478).

10. For a more detailed discussion of metamorphosis and its importance in the context of destructive plasticity, see chapter 1.

11. Müller, *Description of a Picture*, 109.

Interpreting the short narrative in this way sheds new light on the entire piece. Scholars have thoroughly discussed such diverse aspects of the play as historicity and the possibility of change or revolution,[12] Müller's interest in colonialism and the question of solidarity with the Global South,[13] and his reinvention of Brecht's didactic plays, particularly *Die Maßnahme (The Measures Taken)*.[14] And yet, the theoretical framework for this scholarship is predominantly informed by Benjamin and his short essay *Über den Begriff der Geschichte (On the Concept of History)*, or by psychoanalysis. And while these readings rely on a form of messianism,[15] or on the subsequent appropriation of the event through the subject, I show that Müller's play breaks with both and instead reveals a subjectivity in which hermeneutic interpretation might no longer be possible for the subject. As soon as we become attentive to this, we start to understand that not only does *The Task* reenvision Brecht's *The Measures Taken* but that it is equally connected to the break with Brecht's usual dialectics that can be found in the unpublished scene 14 of Brecht's *Life of Galileo* and in his poem "When in my hospital ward...."[16]

On the following pages, I first introduce the short story "Der Mann im Fahrstuhl" in greater detail and point out its main moves and ruptures; I then go on to discuss how the narrative bursts open the Newtonian understanding of space and time and positions the first-person narrator in a quantum world instead, where scale is

---

12. Cf. Lehmann, "Dramatische Form"; Schulz, *Heiner Müller*, 159–66; Hörnigk, "Zu Heiner Müllers Stück"; Müller-Schöll, *Das Theater des "konstruktiven Defaitismus,"* 561–76; Raddatz, *Dämonen unterm Roten Stern*; Bathrick, *The Powers of Speech*, 144–50.

13. Here, the focus is on Müller's interest in Fanon and the ontology of *négritude* that Müller adapted from Aimé Césaire and Léopold Sédar Senghor. Cf. Schulz, *Heiner Müller*, 165; Lehmann "Dramatische Form und Revolution in Georg Büchners *Dantons Tod* und Heiner Müllers *Der Auftrag*"; Teraoka, "Der Auftrag und Die Maßnahme."

14. Cf. Müller-Schöll, *Das Theater*, 561–76; Teraoka, "Der Auftrag und Die Maßnahme."

15. As already noted in chapter 1, scholars have convincingly argued that Benjamin must not necessarily be understood through messianism. And yet the readings of Müller predominantly read Benjamin through this lens.

16. I discuss both references in greater detail in chapter 1.

replaced by topology and the ongoing becoming of spacetimematterings. Furthermore, I uncover the new subjectivity anticipated in this play and show that Müller shifts from the figure of difference or Freudian repression to that of metamorphosis and transdifferentiation. I discuss this in the context of the final paragraphs of "Der Mann im Fahrstuhl," where Müller imagines a meeting between the narrator and his doppelgänger, only one of whom will survive. This, I argue, hints at a subject that emerges from the very erasure of form. In other words, I show that Müller imagines the encounter of the self as becoming a radical other, who cannot be recognized by the subject.

The Man in the Elevator

"Der Mann im Fahrstuhl" follows a play within the play in which the two emissaries Sasportas and Galloudec take on the roles of the French revolutionaries Danton and Robespierre, while the third emissary, Debuisson, sits on a throne and takes on the position of a king for whom the other two perform. The play within the play, which Müller calls "Das Theater der Revolution" ("The Theater of the Revolution"),[17] ends with a fight between the two revolutionaries in which they rip off each other's theatrical masks, followed by the dethroning of Debuisson, in whose place the former slave Sasportas is subsequently positioned and crowned.[18] Finding himself in this new position, Sasportas announces that "the Theater of the white Revolution is over"[19] and sentences Debuisson, the son of slaveowners, to

---

17. Müller, *The Task*, 91.
18. The figure of Sasportas introduces questions of materialism and race into the play that open up broader discussions of Blackness and German-language theater. While such a discussion goes beyond the scope of this book, I want to point out further readings that speak to this question. For an analysis of race and Blackness particular in German-language theater, see Layne and Tonger-Erk, *Staging Blackness*, as well as Partridge, *Blackness as a Universal Claim*, which also includes a discussion of performances that address racialized minorities. Furthermore, Layne, "Space Is Place" is of interest in this context, as it focuses on experiments with Afrofuturism in German-language theater and thus allows a link between my discussion of futurity and Afrofuturism.
19. Müller, *The Task*, 93.

death: "Because your skin is white. Because your thoughts are white under your white skin. Because your eyes have seen the beauty of our sisters. Because your hands have touched the naked bodies of our sisters. Because your thoughts have eaten their breasts their bodies their genitals. Because you are a property owner, a master. Therefore we sentence you to death, Victor Debuisson. The snakes shall eat your shit, the crocodiles your ass, the piranhas your testicles. *Debuisson screams....* Now nothing belongs to you anymore. Now you can die. Bury him."[20]

This verdict, which is clearly inspired by Fanon's *Black Skin, White Masks*,[21] is immediately followed by the prose piece "Der Mann im Fahrstuhl," which arrives as a surprise and breaks into this violent climax of the play within the play without being introduced or explained. The only separation between the play within the play and the short narration that follows it is one blank line. There are no stage directions, no information about a possible speaker, and no other texts that might frame what follows. Instead, we are thrown into action that is already ongoing: "I am standing among men who are strangers to me, in an old elevator with a metal cage that rattles during the ascent."[22] While "Das Theater der Revolution" ends in a chaotic scene of intense bodily movement and strong affects, "Der Mann im Fahrstuhl" is characterized by descriptive passages, indifference, and coolness. This even applies to the parts where the first-person narrator speaks about strong emotions like fear and panic, as the tone of the narration doesn't reflect the end time scenario in which the narrator finds himself but instead seems disconnected from any strong emotion throughout the story.

The "I" that stands at the very beginning of the text remains vague throughout the entire narration. Even more, this "I" seems shaped by strong contradictions that do not allow us to grasp or get a better understanding of it. It is a subject formed by possibilities that are never fully settled, while at the same time this subject

---

20. Müller, *The Task*, 93.
21. For an analysis of Müller through Fanon, see Lehmann, "Dramatische Form"; Teraoka, "Der Auftrag und Die Maßnahme."
22. Müller, *The Task*, 93.

seems entirely determined by its position within an enclosed, hierarchical system, occupied by its function as an employee: "I am dressed *like* an office clerk *or* a worker on a Sunday.... I have been summoned to the Boss (in my thoughts I call him Number One), his office is on the fourth floor *or* was it the twentieth."[23] The narrator feels trapped in a double sense. On the one hand, it is the narrator's inability to understand the situation in which he finds himself that creates the highly uncomfortable atmosphere. This enters the text through speculations and the repeated use of the conjunction "or," both of which emphasize that what we are encountering here is a subject shaped by possibilities and uncertainties. On the other hand, this sense of possibility and uncertainty is accompanied by hints at a closed system that is fully determined and from which the "I" cannot break away. The narrator is fully dedicated to his seemingly omnipotent boss. He experiences himself in a torture-like situation when he describes his shirt as a noose around his neck which could tighten at any moment and the elevator he is standing in as his prison.

In a way that is similar to the vagueness of the narrator, the plot that unfolds is also characterized by uncertainty. We can neither get a firm grasp on the boss and his relationship with the narrator nor can we understand time and space. The narrator is insecure about his exact function and position; he doesn't know where to locate his boss's office, nor does he recognize the men who are standing next to him in the elevator at first and should be his coworkers. The narrator is occupied with questions about his appearance. Worried about the impression he is making, he looks for a mirror, but it is nowhere to be found: "I would like to have a mirror so that I could also control the fit of my tie with my eyes."[24] Ultimately, the narration suggests that the eyes have lost their ability to perceive their own body as well as the outside world, while the ear is introduced as an organ that cannot be closed down but forces us to be connected to the world and to take in all kinds of noises and voices ("They [the other men in the elevator] talk softly about something

---

23. Müller, *The Task*, 93–94. My emphasis.
24. Müller, *The Task*, 94.

I understand nothing of. Nevertheless, their conversation must have distracted me.")[25]

What the narration presents to us is an out-of-joint world in which any basis for knowledge has faded. As such, instead of facts, we are confronted with speculations by the narrator about what might (have) happen/ed. This even concerns the very task itself that stands at the center of the narration and drives the entire narrative. There is no guarantee of its existence, as the narrator only assumes that the boss is awaiting him with a task: "I suppose it concerns a task that is to be assigned to me."[26] Here too we encounter a great discrepancy. Even though the existence of the task remains vague, the narrator is convinced of its heightened urgency. Not only that, but he imagines the suicide of his boss in case of a failure. He is convinced that the task concerns "the last possible action to prevent the destruction whose start I am now experiencing."[27]

While the narration leaves us wondering about and searching for an actual meaning, the only certainty that we do gain, after a while, is the sense of a world that is not only out of joint but facing an apocalypse. The entire sequence is dominated by notions of death, destruction, estrangement, loss of future, and loss of orientation. Yet there is also another rupture, which divides the short narration into two parts, when the elevator suddenly comes to a halt and allows the narrator to exit. When the doors open, he is no longer in an unspecified building but finds himself instead on a village street in Peru. Paradoxically, it is while experiencing this greatest sense of foreignness and seeing himself as a stranger and invader in a foreign country that the narrator for the first time gains a sense of location. And while fear and panic dominate the experience of this other place at first, these feelings ultimately give way to a sentiment of ease. Even hope is expressed. And yet this ease and hope are still bound to death and destruction, as the story ends with the anticipation of the

---

25. Müller, *The Task*, 94. See also chapter 3 on Jelinek, where the ear plays an even more dominant role.
26. Müller, *The Task*, 94.
27. Müller, *The Task*, 95.

encounter with the other, the narrator's doppelgänger, in which only one of the two will survive.

For my analysis, I focus on two crucial elements or culmination points of the story. The first is the short sentence "The time factor is crucial."[28] The second is the expression of the pain and violence that result from the uncertainty experienced by the narrator, which Müller interestingly places within parentheses: "(the Or cuts like a knife through my negligent brain)."[29] The first moment allows me to shed light on time as a structural category linked to our technoscientific age, which at the same time can be undone and reconfigured in the quantum age. I show how Müller's narrative radically breaks with stable categories of time and space and instead forces us into the troubled topology of our quantum world. The cut into the brain, on the other hand, anticipates the break that follows only a few lines later in the story, in which the narrator is suddenly positioned on a remote country street in Peru. In describing the "Or" as a cut, Müller evokes an aesthetics of injury that characterizes modern and postmodern art in general[30] and German-language theater specifically. But how can we understand the cut implemented here? In the previous chapter, I discussed the importance for Müller of Kleist's reflection on the effect of Friedrich's painting *The Monk by the Sea*, where Kleist claims that the painting forces a form of perception "as though his eyelids had been cut off."[31] Moreover, the cut is reminiscent of the filmic cut, thus opening theater toward the cinematic.[32] Central

---

28. Müller, *The Task*, 94.
29. Müller, *The Task*, 95.
30. See Fleishman, *An Aesthetics of Injury*, analyzing what Fleishman calls the narrative wound from Baudelaire to Jelinek. His main argument is that in modernism, art seeks not only to depict but also to inflict wounds. Even though Fleishman's study presents an intriguing reading of the wound, however, it is only of limited importance for the present study, as Fleishman applies a theoretical framework that relies on the "motor scheme" of writing, as opposed to my framework, which replaces writing with plasticity (see the introduction to this book). Moreover, he excludes theater and theatrical texts from his discussion, which otherwise ranges from novels to film. Including theater would further complicate the relationship between text and body that Fleishman lays out.
31. Kleist, "Feelings before Friedrich's Seascape," 208.
32. Müller here is very close to Schlingensief, whose work centrally focuses on the abandonment of the cinematic cut and its replacement with a practice of

to the short passage is the fact that Müller once again replaces the eye, which is what shaped previous artistic works that sought to challenge conventional forms of representation, with a cut directly into the brain.[33] As I will show in the following pages, this shift from the eye to the brain is important because it hints at a different quality of the cut. It is not a figure of difference and deferral, as the cut through the eye suggests; something else is happening in Müller, something that suggests the ongoing re-formation of the subject and the replacement of thinking within the paradigm of the tissue, as in deconstruction, with thinking that uses the paradigm of the salamander (plasticity).[34] As such, it subsequently hints at another form of becoming that leaves the cut behind and is based instead on metamorphosis and transformation.

Undoing Time: "Der Mann im Fahrstuhl" and the Quantum Age

The category of time plays a prominent role in "Der Mann im Fahrstuhl." While time at first is discussed in terms of punctuality and thus seems to be linked to politeness and propriety in the workplace in a way that is similar to the narrator's overall concerns about his appearance, it quickly becomes clear, when the measurability of time itself becomes an issue, that time matters as a more essential category:

FIVE MINUTES TOO EARLY WOULD BE / WHAT I'D CALL TRUE PUNCTUALITY. The last time I looked at my wrist watch the hands

---

movement and transformation. See chapter 4, where I discuss this question in greater detail.

33. In the context of the eye, *Un chien andalou* (1929), directed by Luis Buñuel and Salvador Dalí, is another essential artistic work in this tradition. We can further think of Georges Bataille's *Story of the Eye* (1928) and Jelinek's *Lust* (1989), where the trope of the eye and the cut is specifically connected to eroticism and pornography. Müller's shift to the brain allows us to think about an alternative trajectory that evokes, among others, Mary Shelley's *Frankenstein* (1818), as well as Gottfried Benn's *Gehirne* (1916).

34. For a detailed discussion of these paradigms, see chapter 1.

pointed at ten. I remember my feeling of relief: fifteen minutes remain until the hour of my appointment with the Boss. The next time I looked it was only five minutes later. As I look again at my watch, between the eighth and the ninth floor, the hands point at exactly fourteen minutes and forty-five seconds after the hour of ten: there goes my punctuality, *time doesn't work to my advantage anymore.* Quickly I assess my situation: at the next stop I can step out of the elevator and run down the stairway, three steps a time, to the fourth floor. If it is the wrong floor it, of course, will mean a *loss of time* which probably can't be made up. I can ride on to the twentieth floor and, if the Boss's office isn't located there, ride down again to the fourth floor, provided the elevator doesn't go out of order, or I can run down the stairs (three steps at a time) and break my leg in doing so, or my neck, just because I am in a hurry. . . .

A quick glance at my watch informs me irrefutably of the fact *that for a long while it has been too late even for basic punctuality*, though our elevator, as I notice on second glance, hasn't even arrived yet at the twelfth floor: the short hand is pointing to ten, the long hand at fifty, the seconds long since haven't mattered. *Something seems to be wrong with my watch* but there is *no time left now for a time check*: without having noticed where the other gentlemen stepped off I am alone in the elevator. With a horror that grips the roots of my hair I see on my watch which I cannot turn my eyes from any longer *the hands circling the dial with increasing speed so that between two bats of an eyelid ever more hours have passed. I realize that for quite a while something has been wrong: with my watch, with the elevator, with time.*[35]

I quote this rather long paragraph here because that is necessary for understanding what the short narrative looks like and how time is slowly revealed as a crucial factor in the narration, one that goes far beyond punctuality and stands at the core of theatrical transformation and of Müller's theory of revolution and change. From the beginning, the narrator is concerned about arriving on time for the meeting with his boss. The watch and its weird lapses occupy his thoughts as he imagines a range of possibilities for what is happening to time, ranging from being ahead of time to losing time and then running out of time. We can read this as an ironic comment on the cliché of timeliness as a "German" virtue, evoking as it does the popular saying that "five minutes ahead of time is punctual for

---

35. Müller, *The Task*, 94. My emphasis.

Falling Out of Time and Space   83

a German." The possibility of time running late, running out, and becoming out of joint, though, concerns something more essential than that.

To grasp the function of time in this narrative, we need to keep reading and consider the fact that the narrator introduces the sciences, particularly physics, as a possible way to comprehend what is happening to time and space throughout the narration, regretting that he studied poetry instead of physics and is now at a loss because he lacks a fitting model for understanding what is happening to time during his ride in the elevator:

> I plunge into wild speculations: the force of gravity abates, a disturbance, a kind of stutter of the globe's rotation, like a cramp in the calf during a soccer game. I regret that *I know too little about physics to resolve in pure science the screaming contradiction between the velocity of the elevator and the lapse of time my watch indicates.* Why didn't I pay attention in school. Or read the wrong books: *Poetry instead of Physics.* The time is out of joint and somewhere on the fourth or twentieth floor (the Or cuts like a knife through my negligent brain) probably in a spacious and richly carpeted room, behind his desk which probably is placed at the far end of the room, facing the entrance, the Boss (whom in my thoughts I call Number One) is waiting with my task for me the loser.[36]

What should we make of this reference to physics? While we could of course treat it as a rather humorous comment on the supposed opposition of art and science, I suggest that we take it seriously—perhaps even more seriously than Müller himself—and ask how reading this scene through physics might help us to understand it differently. As will become clear in the following pages, including physics in our considerations allows us to move beyond labeling "Der Mann im Fahrstuhl" as a surreal dream text and to see it instead as an anticipation of the temporalities that shape the strange topology of our technoscientific age, attuned as it is to the atomic clock.

The wristwatch that plays such a central role in the narration can be read as a clock that symbolizes the rhythm of the atomic age. As

---

36. Müller, *The Task*, 94–95. My emphasis.

Barad has pointed out, clocks are interlinked in more than one way with the quantum age. Barad discusses the clocks of Hiroshima, Nagasaki, Fukushima, and the Trinity test site as symbols for how time comes to a halt due to the enormous amount of energy unleashed by an atomic explosion, alongside other clocks like the atomic clock and the symbolic Doomsday Clock that are examples for how, in the nuclear age, our lives and bodies have become attuned to the rhythm of the atom.[37]

The narrator's obsession with every second passing by can be read as a hint toward the atomic clock. By calling into question the development of atomic clocks and the need for such a precise time measurement, Barad reveals an important link between time and capitalism, militarism, and imperialism. They argue that atomic clocks have allowed the world to become synchronized in a way that it never was before.[38] Based on this understanding that the atomic clock is a tool for synchronization, they then go further and argue that it is militarism and global capitalism that have been the driving forces of this development, because their "mechanical guts," such as GPS, telecommunications, and high-speed internet transfer, rely on the precise and globally synchronized measurement of time: "Globalism is tied not only to the militarization of space but also of time. The latest atomic clock [is] so precise that it won't lose or gain a single second in 15 billion years—roughly the age of our universe."[39] Barad subsequently links the temporal regime dictated by the atomic clock to colonial practices, thus positioning their reading within indigenous and postcolonial critique. Drawing on the work of the indigenous studies scholar Daniel Wildcat and the philosopher Vine Deloria, Barad problematizes the conception of time as determinate and singular, a conception that in turn dictates a norm that some people are "on time" while others are "ahead of time" or "running late."[40]

---

37. Barad, "Troubling Time/s," 62.
38. The first atomic clock was released in 1949. Barad thus speaks of atomic clocks in terms of "postwar gadgets" that are "tuned to resonance and precision" ("Troubling Time/s," 59).
39. Barad, "Troubling Time/s," 60, 59.
40. Barad, "Troubling Time/s," 60.

It is important to keep in mind that the development of the atomic clock did not invent, but only intensified, a conceptualization of time as having direction, which has been challenged by thinkers throughout the twentieth century.[41] In hinting at the fact that atomic time paradoxically promotes a conception of time that quantum theory then undermines and undoes, Barad references Benjamin and his radical challenges to history as thought of in terms of time and space. But Barad goes even further, revealing time and space as being diffracted. Diffraction is not simply a category of difference but rather a "difference within." This difference is neither exclusive (here *or* there) nor additive (here *and* there); it means being "*indeterminately here-there*" in a way that applies to space, time, and matter.[42] Temporal diffraction thus means that "temporalities are specifically entangled and threaded through one another such that there is no determinate answer to the question: What time is it?"[43] What becomes obvious here is that Barad's temporal and spatial diffraction is closely related to Malabou's figure of plasticity, as it, too, stresses transdifferentiation rather than difference, a distinction that will be crucial for my reading of the second part of the narration.

To better understand the importance of the clock as a symbol of synchronization in our techno-militaro-politico-capitalo-imperialist-racist-colonial regime and how it affects Müller's theater, we need to keep in mind that "Der Mann im Fahrstuhl" is not the only text in which the clock is so central. Indeed, we find a surprisingly similar scene in *Die Hamletmaschine* (*Hamletmachine*, 1977). The second part of this play, entitled "DAS EUROPA DER FRAUEN" ("THE EUROPE OF WOMEN"), begins with a conventional introduction of place, character, and time. But while the information given for the first two categories actually follows the conventions of drama— "Enormous room. Ophelia."—the specification of time is rather disconcerting: "Her heart is a clock."[44] Instead of designating a specific point in time, Müller forces us here to think of time in relationship

---

41. See the discussion of different concepts of time in Schade, "Hold Your Breath Against Time."
42. Barad, "Troubling Time/s," 65.
43. Barad, "Troubling Time/s," 68.
44. Müller, *Hamletmachine*, 54.

to the body. Ophelia's body is synchronized to the beat of the clock. The small scene that follows describes resistance to this rhythm, which is perceived as a prison: "I smash the tools of my captivity, the chair, the table, the bed. I destroy the battlefield that was my home."[45] In both "Der Mann im Fahrstuhl" and *Hamletmachine*, we find the motif of the prison as well as a moment of resistance to the synchronization with clock time. Similarly to "Der Mann im Fahrstuhl," where the narrator leaves his prison only to find himself on a country street in Peru, and where he takes off the clothes that mark his former function as an employee, Ophelia too gets rid of her clothes, digs out the clock that used to be her heart, and walks into the street clothed in her blood.[46] Both of these texts, then, present forms of resistance shaped by violent scenes of destruction, and we are once again reminded that for Müller change is inseparable from struggle and sometimes takes on such extreme dimensions as the total annihilation of form.[47]

Along with the pressure of following the rhythm of clock time, the narrator experiences himself as living in the end times, as time and space appear to be attuned to the apocalypse to come. Even though atomic war is never explicitly mentioned, the sense of end times that is evoked seems to be inseparably interwoven with the nuclear age and, specifically, with the possibility of a nuclear war. The narrator not only starts the journey to meet his boss from a basement in which he passes empty concrete rooms with signs about air raid precautions, but he is also convinced that the task that is going to be assigned to him by his boss is of the utmost importance and urgency—so critical that it concerns the last possible act against total destruction: "Perhaps the world is falling apart and my task,

---

45. Müller, *Hamletmachine*, 54.
46. Müller, *Hamletmachine*, 55.
47. While feminist readings of *Hamletmachine* interpret this passage as female resistance to the totalizing time of patriarchy that denies "female time" (cf. Biesenbach and Schößler, "Zur Rezeption des Medea-Mythos in der zeitgenössischen Literatur," 41), reading the passage together with "Der Mann im Fahrstuhl" shows that the issue is even more complex than that and cannot be reduced to a juxtaposition of male vs. female time. Instead, it deals with the synchronization of time in our technoscientific age as something that is universal and concerns everyone, and yet does not affect everyone in the same way.

so important that the Boss wanted personally to assign it to me, has already become meaningless because of my negligence, NOT OPERATIVE in the administrative language I've learned so well (useless language!), ON FILE where no one will check anymore because the task concerned precisely the last possible action to prevent the destruction whose start I am now experiencing, locked up in this crazed elevator with my crazed wrist watch."[48]

The narrator's conviction that his failure to receive and fulfill the task might lead to an enormous change that will render everything that came before meaningless is reminiscent of the beginning of *The Task*, when Antoine has abandoned his revolutionary work and is instead supporting Napoleon and the new republic. In the short prose piece in the elevator, though, the possibility of a radical change and rupture connects the revolution with the possibility of total destruction by nuclear war, thus eerily speaking to Müller's contemporaries. As such, the line "FIVE MINUTES TOO EARLY WOULD BE / WHAT I CALL TRUE PUNCTUALITY," which I quoted earlier, goes beyond punctuality and is connected to the feeling of end times, evoking the warning that it is "five minutes to midnight."[49] It hints at a shortage of time, or at time pressure, and emphasizes the need to act in view of a possible catastrophe. The leaps in time that the narrator experiences in the course of the story can therefore be read not only as a reference to the reworking of time (and space) in quantum theory but also as associated with the end of time, symbolized by the Doomsday Clock.

The Doomsday Clock was introduced in 1947 by the *Bulletin of the Atomic Scientists* as a way to make visible the world's proximity

---

48. Müller, *The Task*, 95.

49. We find this same kind of clock time in another of Müller's plays, *Die Schlacht* (*The Battle*, 1974), in the small scene entitled "KLEINBÜRGERHOCHZEIT" ("PETTY BOURGEOIS WEDDING"). Müller wrote this play as an answer to Brecht's *Furcht und Elend im Dritten Reich* (*Fear and Misery of the Third Reich*). Irritated by Brecht and his conventional dialectical analysis of the Nazi regime, Müller claimed that a linear plot could no longer represent reality. Here, too, Müller tries to find a way to break with linear time and allow his audience to experience time as diffracted. In the play, the father uses the phrase "it is five minutes to twelve" to announce that the war is almost over and thus it is time to follow Hitler's suicide. The father, though, turns away from this idea after he has killed his wife and daughter.

to a global catastrophe, based on the calculations and assumptions of a board of scientists and political analysts. While up until 2007 these assumptions were based solely on the likelihood of an atomic war, since that year the board has also taken climate change into consideration. The clock was first set at seven minutes to midnight. Since that initial setting, it has been changed twenty-four times—with its earliest setting (the farthest from midnight) coming in 1991, in reaction to the end of the Cold War, as marked by the dissolution of the Soviet Union. Meanwhile, until quite recently, the closest it had come to midnight was in 1953, when it was set at two minutes to midnight due to the United States' first tests of thermonuclear devices, followed by similar tests in the Soviet Union. But in 2018, the two-minutes-to-midnight mark was reached again. Currently, the hands of the clock are closer to midnight than ever before: ninety seconds.[50] Müller's play was written in 1979, at a time when—after the nuclear conflict had seemed to ease throughout the 1960s and early 1970s—the threat posed by nuclear weaponry was once again rising. Thus, in 1974, when India tested its first nuclear device, the Doomsday Clock was changed from twelve minutes to midnight to a setting of nine minutes to midnight. This setting was revised once again in 1981, after the 1979 invasion of Afghanistan by the Soviet Union and the 1980 election of Ronald Reagan had yet again intensified fears of a possible nuclear war. Barad stresses the strangeness of this specific clock, which is linked to a "false sense of globalism assuming homogeneity of times and spaces" and which obscures the "uneven distribution of nuclear and climate crises' resources and precarity." It is "time synchronized to the future of no Future" that is "fixated on its own dissolution."[51] As such, it has an anesthetizing effect, rather than representing a rupture that might change time. This connects to Müller's criticism of the fascination, during the Cold War years, with the apocalypse to come.[52] While Müller's narrator is trapped in a time that is reminiscent of the Doomsday Clock and that attunes him to the apocalypse, the narration at the same

---

50. This new time was first set in 2023 and reaffirmed in 2024.
51. Barad, "Troubling Time/s," 58.
52. See chapter 1 for a discussion of this in greater detail.

time clearly breaks with this kind of thinking of living in end times. The form of the play interrupts any linearity, introducing a model of change that is able to bring chronological time to an end and instead presents time as diffracted and dispersed.

"Der Mann im Fahrstuhl" intensifies the radical undoing of time that we experience throughout *The Task*. The revolutionary play within the play already confronts us with an overwhelming number of present and historical locations and markers that can be better grasped in terms of topology than scale. Jamaica, the Russian Revolution, and the French Revolution are not independent places and events but instead coexist with, intermingle with, and reconfigure each other. The short prose narration, though, undoes Newtonian time within only a few sentences when it catapults the narrator onto a street in Peru and thereby creates a constellation in which it becomes clear that space and time can no longer be measured in terms of scale, distance, and geometry.

We need to keep all of this in mind when we think of the narrator in "Der Mann im Fahrstuhl" and his inability to read time. We can understand how directed, linear time becomes brittle in terms of a dream structure. I suggest reading "Der Mann im Fahrstuhl" as a text shaped by the radical rethinking of time in the quantum age, a text that is attuned to the new temporalities of its present. As such, it rethinks how change and revolution might happen. No longer is revolution bound to a conception of time as a succession from one moment to the other. In particular, this text shows that the conception of history as time and the conception of time as progressing from one moment to the other creates a prisonlike situation that causes panic and despair in the narrator. When Müller focuses on this conception of time and links it to our atomic age, he reveals the complex entanglement of linear time, colonialism, militarism, and imperialism. *The Task* shows that any revolution must fail if the revolutionaries adopt this specific conception of time as their own rather than challenging it. The play, though, does not limit this experience of time to the colonizers; what it emphasizes instead is that the understanding of time as unfolding linearly has long become internal to the revolutionaries of the Global South as well, and to the colonized more generally, as shown by the fact that the conception of revolution as a teleological event drives all three emissaries in the play. Thus, Müller does not fall into an overly simplistic turn to the Global South as a space of hope but instead critically questions its embeddedness in a world attuned to the atomic clock.

Along with his critique of this conception of time and revolution, Müller presents change as multilayered, involving coexisting moments that include multiple times and spaces. *The Task* is shaped by a temporality that no longer thinks of the past as passé and the future as this single moment ahead of us but that allows us instead to grasp the complex spacetimematterings that continue to (re)configure the past, present, and future. Again, I borrow this term from Barad, who speaks of spacetimemattering to emphasize that, in their interpretation of quantum physics, space, time, and matter cannot be separated. Instead, spacetimemattering comes into being as an iterative process of (re)making the complex coconstitution of space, time, and matter. In Barad's words, "*spacetimemattering* is a dynamic ongoing reconfiguring of a field of relationalities among 'moments,' 'places,' and things' (in their inseparability), where *scale is iteratively (re)made in intra-action.*"[53]

Müller's *The Task* shares with quantum physics the break with Newtonian physics. It challenges the universality and homogeneity of space, time, and matter, assuming instead that "every bit of matter, every moment in time, every location . . . , is diffractively/differentially constituted; or more precisely, *every 'morsel' of spacetimemattering is diffractively/differentially constituted.*"[54] This dynamism—that Barad calls *différancing* and that I link to a threading through in the form of a transdifferentiation—reaches its peak when, in "Der Mann im Fahrstuhl," the doors of the elevator open and the protagonist is suddenly able to exit, but instead of stepping out onto one of the floors of the office building he finds himself "without any task on a village street in Peru."[55] While the elevator is usually limited to vertical movement, here it evokes a horizontal one. We can read this as a

---

53. Barad, "No Small Matter," G111. Emphasis in the original.
54. Barad, "No Small Matter," G109–10. Emphasis in the original.
55. Müller, *The Task*, 95.

Falling Out of Time and Space   91

reversion and a nod toward the railway, which is deeply linked to the topic of revolution,[56] but we must also keep in mind that even while the story offers us the concrete geographical marker of Peru, it deprives us of any hints when it comes to the category of time. The world the narrator experiences when he exits the elevator could be in the past, present, or future. The narrator perceives the landscape as destroyed and animated by figures that could be either the undead or cyborgs.

Metamorphosis, or: Encountering the Indifferent Other

The longer the narrator is stuck in the elevator and the more frantic he becomes in his attempt to meet his boss, the more the elevator feels to him like a prison. He imagines ways out of it only to realize that flight is impossible and that he cannot run away from his desperate situation. This is when the doors of the elevator suddenly open and the narrator finds himself in unfamiliar surroundings on a street in Peru:

> I step from the elevator at the next stop and I stand without any task on a village street in Peru, the now useless tie still ridiculously fastened beneath my chin. Caked mud with vehicle tracks. On both sides of the street a barren plain with occasional grass plots and patches of gray shrubbery reaches hazily for the horizon where mountains float in the mist. Left of the street a kind of barracks, it looks deserted, the windows black holes with the remnants of panes. Two gigantic natives stand in front of a billboard advertising products of a foreign civilization.[57]

---

56. When the elevator was first patented by Otis Tufts in 1859, it was promoted as a "vertical railway." Railways played such a central role in the October Revolution that the literary critic China Miéville, for example, speaks of it as a "revolution of trains" (*October*, 319). The railway also functioned as a central metaphor for Marx, who described revolutions as the railways of history. This was questioned by Benjamin, who argued that we should instead understand the revolution as people's attempt to find a brake and bring the train to a halt (cf. Schütte, "Brückenschlag, Familienalbum und Traum/a-Material," 479).

57. Müller, *The Task*, 60. This passage is reminiscent of the description of a landscape at the beginning of Müller's short text *Description of a Picture*. I will come back to that text later in this chapter.

Not only is this leap in space and time legible within the strange topology of the quantum world, but at the same time it hints at the re-forming of a subject based not on difference but on the process of transsubjectivation, or metamorphosis. This metamorphosis is the result of the negative, destructive side of plasticity. In other words, Müller here stages the formation of a subject through explosion, when there is no way out and when flight, which is the only possible solution, is impossible. Relying on Malabou, who emphasizes that we must allow for the impossibility of flight "in situations in which an extreme tension, a pain or malaise push a person towards an outside that does not exist,"[58] we can then read the exit onto the village street in Peru differently. The narrator is not simply escaping into another country—the changed landscape must be understood as the formation of the form of flight itself, as the narrator is becoming a stranger to himself precisely because he could not flee.

It becomes clear that Peru is not the easy exit for the European when we take a closer look at how Peru is depicted here. The place seems desolate, abandoned, and inhabited only by a few creatures whose humanity is surely questionable. And yet, however strange and foreign this landscape is, it bears signs of capitalism and capitalist production. This is evoked not only by the billboard promoting products unknown to the narrator but also by the description of the landscape as shaped by piles of detritus. The text here makes us understand that there is no end and no alternative to capitalism, as it seems to be the only structure that is alive and functioning in the otherwise devastated setting.[59] What becomes obvious is that even though the narrator finds himself in what appears to be a completely alien environment, capitalism has long since left its mark there and is the underlying structure from which there is no escape. Keeping this in mind, we understand that Müller's turn to the Global South does not involve the problematic romanticization of that space but instead reveals with its cold gaze that the absolute Other does not exist.

---

58. Malabou, *Ontology of the Accident*, 10.
59. See the discussion in chapter 1 of the analysis of "zombie capitalism" in Kohso, *Radiation and Revolution*.

Falling Out of Time and Space 93

The metamorphosis and the formation of an alterity in which the Other is absolutely lacking ultimately leads to a changed perspective, as desperation yields to chance and thus to the possibility of freedom. While the narrator's experience in Peru is still unfolding on the fine line between determinism and possibility, his confrontation with his new surroundings introduces a sense of ease, of pleasure, and of joy that was missing in the first part. These feelings are first mentioned after the narrator realizes that there is no going back. "I think about going back, I haven't been noticed yet. Never would I have thought during my desperate ascent to the Boss that I would feel homesick for the elevator that was my prison."[60] True to plasticity, once transformed, the narrator cannot go back. Whereas before he only fantasized about the possible suicide of his boss, now he is convinced of his death. "Destiny didn't even grant me, the employee of a deceased Boss, the favor of dying on duty, my cause is a lost cause, my task enclosed in his brain that won't relinquish a thing anymore this side of death until the vaults of eternity, whose combinations the sages of the world toil to decode, are opened."[61]

Realizing that he no longer has any task or assignment to fulfill, the narrator first loosens his tie and then removes it entirely. What unfolds from here is the employee's reevaluation of what is of importance. The tie that has caused him "such profuse perspiration"[62] on his way to the boss is now something that produces anxiety because it might make him appear suspicious and mark him as other. In the course of the story, though, after numerous seemingly dangerous encounters between the narrator and the dwellers of Peru go by without any actual harm happening to him, he gains full awareness that the task that was to be assigned to him is lost forever. This time, everything he feared before is not simply directed into a new anxiety. Instead, the tie, his clothes, and everything else lose their importance. They become, in fact, completely meaningless to the narrator: "No science in this world is going to drag my

---

60. Müller, *The Task*, 95.
61. Müller, *The Task*, 95.
62. Müller, *The Task*, 95.

lost task from the brain tissue of the deceased [his boss]. It will be buried with him, the state funeral, which is probably taking place this very moment, doesn't warrant resurrection. Something like serenity grows within me, I sling my jacket over my shoulder and unbutton the collar of my shirt: my walk has become a stroll."[63]

The walk that becomes a stroll adds to the feeling of serenity that shapes the narrator's five following encounters: with a dog carrying a charred arm in its mouth; with some young men who are threatening someone, but not threatening the narrator; with a woman exposing her breasts; with two children trying to repair a hybrid between a steam engine and a train; and finally with his own double, "with my face made of snow."[64]

Dog,[65] men, woman, children, and self unfold a scene of non/human encounters from which Müller develops his thinking about chance and change, which is also tied to a reflection on the relationship between the individual, society, and the planet. Although this relationship must necessarily be a strained one for Müller, it can be productive, as the text suggests.[66] The loss of the task and the encounter with the doppelgänger, which only one of the two will survive, is commonly read as a resignation.[67] What I am arguing, however, is that this is where Müller introduces a form of ease, joy, and pleasure that he finds in Brecht's unpublished scene from *Life of Galileo* and in the poem "When in my hospital ward...."

To better understand why I suggest reading the end of the narration in such a way, look more closely with me at the last paragraph:

> Where the street recedes into the plain a woman stands poised as if she had been waiting for me. I stretch my arms out for her, how long since they've touched a woman, and I hear a male voice say THIS WOMAN IS THE WIFE OF A MAN. It sounds final and I keep walking. When I

---

63. Müller, *The Task*, 96.
64. Müller, *The Task*, 96.
65. The dog appears throughout Müller's essays and plays. It can stand for fascism, particularly for blind obedience, as for example in *Die Schlacht* and *Germania Tod in Berlin*, but it is also connected to revolt and insurrection, as for example in *The Wound Woyzeck*.
66. See Müller's comments in Poulet, "Es lebe der Widerspruch!," 755.
67. Cf. Schütte, "Brückenschlag, Familienalbum und Traum/a-Material," 479.

look back the woman stretches her arms out for me and bares her breasts. On a railway embankment overgrown with grass two boys are tinkering with a hybrid of a steam engine and a locomotive that stands on a broken track. As a European I see at first glance that their labor is wasted: this vehicle is never going to move, but I don't tell the children, to work is to hope, and I keep walking into the landscape that has no other work but to wait for the disappearance of man. Now I know my own destination. I cast off my clothes, outward appearances don't matter anymore. Eventually THE OTHER ONE, the antipode, the doppelgänger, will meet me, he with my face of snow. One of us will survive.[68]

What stands out in this last paragraph is that the narrator could act, but decides not to. The scene with the woman returns to the motif of the female seducer that was introduced in the first part of the play. There, a character named FirstLove confronts Debuisson with his betrayal of her because of his love for the revolution. "You don't have to be afraid, little Victor. Not of me. Not of your first love. The one you have betrayed with the Revolution, your blood-smeared second love."[69] FirstLove returns at the end of *The Task* as the allegorical figure of Treason, trying to seduce Debuisson with a gesture similar to that of the woman on the street in Peru.

It is worth lingering over this other seduction scene that ends *The Task*. Debuisson at first doesn't want to give into Treason, begging Sasportas to kill him so that he won't betray him and the revolution. "Kill me before I betray you. I am afraid, Sasportas, of the shame to be happy in this world."[70] It is astonishing that Müller introduces the notion of happiness here, which hints at the importance of ease and joy in how Müller conceives of chance and change. Debuisson's pleas remain unheard. He is left behind by the other two emissaries, who decide not to kill him.[71] Seduced by Treason, Debuisson continues to fight his desire—in a very Freudian way, by pushing his eyes into their sockets—but ultimately gives in to it: "Treason smiling showed

---

68. Müller, *The Task*, 96.
69. Müller, *The Task*, 90.
70. Müller, *The Task*, 100.
71. Here, Müller clearly contradicts Brecht's *The Measures Taken*, which approves the killing of the young revolutionary because of his betrayal of the revolutionary cause.

her breasts and silently spread her legs wide open, her beauty hit Debuisson like an axe. He forgot the storm of the Bastille, the Hungermarch of the Eighty-thousand, the end of the Gironde, their Last Supper, a corpse at the banquet, Saint Just, the Black Angel, Danton, the Voice of Revolution, Marat hunched over the dagger, Robespierre's broken jaw, his scream when the executioner ripped off the bandage, his last pitying look at the exultant mob."[72] Indulged by Treason, Debuisson loses all his memories except for one, about "a sandstorm off the coast of Las Palmas" in which "crickets were blown with the sand onto the ship and stayed for the passage across the Atlantic." In this memory, "Debuisson ducked against the sandstorm, rubbed the sand from his eyes, covered his ears against the song of the crickets."[73] This very last memory counteracts Debuisson's earlier attempt to blind himself. The sandstorm does not damage his eyes; he simply rubs the sand off them and covers his ears against the song of the crickets, which can be linked to Odysseus's temptation by the song of the sirens. In short, Debuisson at the end of the play has become the cerebral subject who is no longer explainable through the logic of the drive.[74] It is this acceptance of what it entails to be a plastic subject that yields to the ease and joy that is expressed in the very last line of the play. "Then Treason threw herself upon him like a heaven, the bliss of the labia a dawn."[75] Müller reveals the great potential for change and freedom that lies in the process of forgetting[76] and in the explosion of the self, which allows us to become a radical other when there is nowhere to flee.

Reading the final lines of the play in this way helps us to better understand why treason and betrayal, as Müller has pointed out

---

72. Müller, *The Task*, 100–101.
73. Müller, *The Task*, 101.
74. For a lengthier discussion of this aspect, see chapter 1.
75. Müller, *The Task*, 101.
76. The opportunity that lies in forgetting is, of course, already expressed in Nietzsche, for example in the early text "Der Wanderer und sein Schatten" in Nietzsche, *Menschliches, Allzumenschliches*. But see also the chapter on "Wounded Attachments" in Brown, *States of Injury*. Brown builds on Nietzsche to ask how forgetting a history of victimhood might allow for an emancipatory democratic project.

in the context of several conversations,[77] are not necessarily bad things in the author's eyes. On the contrary, and this is what the end of *The Task* suggests, they can be viewed as productive if they mean the possibility of re-forming oneself and allowing an old form to explode—like the false understanding of revolution that links it to colonialism, imperialism, and linear time.[78] Following this reading, the ultimate failure of the revolution that dominates the part of the play that follows "Der Mann im Fahrstuhl" and that Debuisson comments on with the words "The world will be what it was, a home for masters and slaves"[79] should not be misunderstood as a final verdict that revolution is not possible. On the contrary, what Müller rejects is the concept of revolution rooted in the French Revolution. As such, the loss of the task after the successful counterrevolution in France does not necessarily mean the end of revolution but rather the destruction of one possible form of revolution, which also means the possibility of its transformation.

We can experience this shift through the figure of Sasportas, who, in the second part, rejects all ties between the revolution in the Global South and the French Revolution: "What is Paris to these men, a distant stone pile that was for a short time the metropolis of their hope."[80] The historian André Combes argues that in Sasportas

---

77. Treason occupied Müller throughout his literary production, but became more important after 1989 and Müller's engagement with his own privileged position in the GDR. See, for example, Müller's 1995 comments in Werner, "Verwaltungsakte produzieren keine Erfahrungen": "Betrayal is not only a negative thing, it also has a liberating quality: one frees oneself or tries to free oneself from this nightmare of dead ancestors." ("Verrat ist nicht nur etwas Negatives, er hat ja auch einen Befreiungsaspekt: Man befreit sich oder man versucht sich zu befreien von diesem Alp toter Geschlechter") (727).

78. It becomes palpable how critical Müller was of a revolution that does not radically change the deeper structure and the relations between people in the conversation that followed his Büchner Prize acceptance speech, *The Wound Woyzeck*, in which he expressed skepticism about any hope for real change in the Global South or Eastern Europe as long as the fundamental power structure remained untouched ("Ich bin ein Neger," 391–92).

79. Müller, *The Task*, 96.
80. Müller, *The Task*, 97.

we see a nomadization of the revolution[81] in which tasks no longer play a role, because they will always produce a center and its periphery, but in which the revolution can freely move and circulate, as expressed through the homelessness of revolution and slave: "The home of slaves is the rebellion."[82] I draw from Combes's insightful analysis of Müller's reinvention of the revolution as fought by subjects who are not yet acknowledged as historical subjects but rather "no-one," as the last paragraph suggests, with its reference to Odysseus, and I read it as the unassignable place or the social and political void, as envisioned by Malabou—the void from which, as she suggests, the unpredictable, unseen, and regenerating can evolve.[83]

With the final scene of *The Task* in mind, we also start to better understand the end of "Der Mann im Fahrstuhl." Unlike Debuisson, who first battles not to give in to Treason, the narrator of "Der Mann im Fahrstuhl" immediately accepts the warning by the man in Peru that the woman belongs to someone else (is that man Debuisson?) and easily passes by her without succumbing, in fact without even feeling sexual desire. While the scene evokes associations with Orpheus and Eurydice, it runs precisely counter to that myth. Müller's narrator can turn his head without it meaning the painful, final loss of the woman. The woman remains in her pose of seduction, unanswered by the narrator.

The encounter with the boys who are trying to fix the hybrid between a steam engine and a locomotive works in a similar way. The narrator does not give in to his impulses and decides not to crash their hopes by telling them that the repair is impossible, but he simply passes by and allows them to continue their work: "This vehicle

---

81. Combes, "Gegen 'die Aushöhlung von Geschichtsbewußtsein durch einen platten Begriff von Aktualität'," 144.
82. Müller, *The Task*, 100.
83. Malabou, "Whither Materialism?," 57. Today, the Sasportas figure in Müller's play opens up potential parallels between the materialism of joy in the theater of the void and discussions of Black joy as a theory, method, and political device to counteract histories of systemic racism, white supremacy, and anti-Blackness. Discussing this in greater detail would go beyond the scope of this book, but I do want to mention Moten, *In the Break*, which I find particularly intriguing as a way to think about Müller's Sasportas figure and the connections among the void, opportunity, freedom, and race.

is never going to move, but I don't tell the children, to work is to hope."[84] From there, the narrator comes to terms with the fact that the landscape has no other work to offer and—if one wants to apply the phrase that "work is hope" here as well—then also no other hope than to wait for humankind to disappear; the narrator accepts that his life will not lead to redemption or salvation, but he feels ease knowing about his finitude.

It is at this point that the narrator ultimately gets rid of the rest of his clothes and states with certainty that eventually the other with "his face of snow" will come toward him and that only one of them will survive. The literary scholar Uwe Schütte applies the relationship between the narrator and his doppelgänger in "Der Mann im Fahrstuhl" to the relationship between that text and the rest of the play: "Together, the drama and the prose stage a game of repetition as difference, comprehensible through the figure of the antipode."[85] While I, too, see the encounter with the doppelgänger mirrored in the relationship between the short prose text and the rest of the play, I deviate from Schütte's reading when he understands the meeting with the doppelgänger as an encounter in terms of difference and as a meeting with the repressed and thus deadly self. I argue that the doppelgänger is not in fact the repressed self. Instead, what Müller is showing us here is the process of metamorphosis and of transsubjectivation, a self born out of death and explosion.

This negative, explosive form of plasticity is evoked when the doppelgänger is envisioned as the other with "my face of snow,"[86] which suggests coolness and indifference. Malabou sees coolness and indifference as characteristic of the new subjectivity. As she shows, neurobiology allows us to understand that the subject can be severely injured, losing all its capacity for wonder and for being affected, and yet still be alive.[87] It is a subject destroyed,

---

84. Müller, *The Task*, 100.
85. "Drama und Prosa inszenieren miteinander ein Spiel der Wiederholung in der Differenz, faßbar in der Figur des Antipoden." Schütte, "Brückenschlag, Familienalbum und Traum/a-Material," 479.
86. Müller, *The Task*, 96.
87. Malabou, "From Sorrow to Indifference." Malabou is drawing here from the works by the neurobiologist Antonio Damasio, who sheds light on the radical

yet still existing. This new subject, born out of trauma, loses all its connections to its former existence; it becomes a new person, a stranger to itself. As such, it is questionable whether the doppelgänger with the face of snow will even recognize the narrator when they meet.

Next to this negative form of plasticity, the narration also introduces plasticity as a progressive possibility that allows the subject to rebel against and change determinism. This is expressed through the emphasis on the importance of knowing in one of the very last lines before the narrator takes off his clothes and anticipates the meeting with his antipode: "Now I *know* my own destination."[88] As Malabou argues, the possibility of actively shaping our neuronal and, similarly, our social and political destinies relies on a political consciousness of the consequences that plasticity can have for social life and the self.[89] She writes that "securing a true plasticity of the brain means insisting on knowing what it can do and not simply what it can tolerate. By the verb *to do or to make* we don't mean just 'doing' math or piano but making its history, becoming the subject of its history."[90] The narrator of "Der Mann im Fahrstuhl" arrives at this kind of consciousness at the end of the narration when he gains insight into the *making* of history, which allows him to finally let go of everything that came before (which is symbolized by his subsequently taking off all his clothes). It is here that he begins to fully embrace plasticity, finding in it the possibility of rebelling, struggling, and changing fate, knowing that this also carries the risk of exploding at any moment.

---

changes brought about by severe brain lesions, including trauma. Based on his studies, she speaks of a subject acting without emotion or in "cold blood" (Malabou, *Self and Emotional Life*, 11).

88. Müller, *The Task*, 96. My emphasis.

89. See also Pitts-Taylor, "The Plastic Brain," which gives an overview of different possible conceptualizations of the plastic brain and shows that only Malabou's concept also provides an account of power relations involved in thinking of the subject as neuronal.

90. Malabou, *What Should We Do with Our Brain?*, 13.

Coda: Finding a Radical New Dramaturgy

"Der Mann im Fahrstuhl" can be read as the rupture that allows the creation of a new form from within. What I am implying here is not a simple cause-and-effect relation, in the sense that everything in *The Task* that comes after the break is radically different from what came before. Instead, we have to understand the narration itself as the transformation of drama into a radically different theatrical topology, which eventually replaces any dramatic structure entirely, as we see in Müller's text *Description of a Picture*.

Müller himself considered *Description of a Picture* to be the "ground zero, or endpoint" of his literary production.[91] The text was written for the theater, yet it challenges the conventions in such a way that scholars hesitate to call it a theatrical text. *Description of a Picture* has many similarities with "Der Mann im Fahrstuhl." It is so similar, in fact, that I suggest reading it as a continuation of the short narrative, even though it decidedly goes further, lacking any subject position through whom the description is presented and consisting of only one sentence but that spans several pages. What the two texts share is the importance of the explosion and the accident, the examination of the eye as no longer the central organ of perception, and the dominance of subjunctive and potential structures (again present through the repeated use of "or" and "maybe") that position everything in between determination and potential, formation and dissolution, novelty and anticipation.

In their radicality, Müller's texts have often been considered unstageable; put another way, and as the author himself repeatedly claimed, they are texts that are still waiting for their theater to arrive.[92] Müller confronts us with an impossible theater that cannot be realized within the present conventions of the theatrical institution. Indeed, when we consider how Müller's plays have been staged, we can see that most productions—even the ones where

---

91. Edelmann, "Solange wir an unsere Zukunft glauben, brauchen wir uns vor unserer Vergangenheit nicht zu fürchten," 457.

92. See Müller, "I Do Not Believe in a Harmony between Theatre and Literature," and Müller, "Bonner Krankheit."

Müller himself functioned as the director—differ from the radical theater that Müller develops with his texts; the stagings have in fact been rather conventional. So far only a few directors (and these are directors whose aesthetic can also be discussed within the theater of the void) have found convincing ways of enabling Müller's theatrical void on the stage; sometimes, this has meant transforming the pieces into mere *Hörstücke* (audio plays). The most prominent of these directors are Robert Wilson, Dimiter Gotscheff, and Heiner Goebbels.[93] Each of these three has not only staged numerous works by Müller but also collaborated closely with him. The fact that this collaboration fostered an ongoing dialogue, which was the inspiration for a joint search for a theater of the void, becomes most palpable in Müller's letter to Gotscheff in which Müller emphasizes that it was Gotscheff who allowed him to experience the silence in theater that comes before the words.[94] Wilson, Gotscheff, and Goebbels all have in common that they challenge the proscenium stage, working instead with stages characterized by a reduction of visual elements and with ruptures and breaks. These ruptures also shape their approach to language, which they treat as material and not as a linguistic meaning. The morphing of language into sound and rhythm is most obvious in the works of Goebbels, who is also a composer and who has dedicated his career to transforming theater and music theater by bringing them together

---

93. Wilson's theater has received a great deal of scholarly attention. For a general overview of his work, see Holmberg, *The Theatre of Robert Wilson*; for the collaboration between Müller and Wilson, see David Bathrick, "Robert Wilson"; for a discussion of nothingness in Wilson's theater, see García and Guillén, "The Silent Utopia." For an analysis of Gotscheff's theatrical aesthetics, see the excellent chapter dedicated to the director in Dreyer, *Theater der Zäsur*, in which the author engages with the return of tragedy in theater since the 1960s. Dreyer reads Gotscheff's theater through notions of emptiness and hauntings, which allows an immediate link to the theater of the void. Goebbels himself repeatedly reflects theoretically on theater, most prominently in *Aesthetics of Absence*. His "aesthetics of absence" (*Aesthetics of Absence*, 1–7) is closely related to the theater of the void. However, his notion of "absence" fosters too strong of an opposition to "presence," whereas my theorization of the void intricately links absence and presence, as, within the void, existence and nonexistence, presence and absence are in constant fluctuation.

94. See the end of chapter 1 for more detail.

and allowing the art forms to intertwine.[95] His production of "Der Mann im Fahrstuhl," which premiered in 1987 at the Artrock Festival in Frankfurt am Main and also included Müller himself as a performer, was a staged concert that transposed Müller's theatrical form into musical structures. According to Goebbels, it was the English translation of Müller's text, lying in front of him upside down, that made him aware of the importance of the "I," which he then used as a rhythmic pattern. The same is true for the repeated conjunctions "and," "but," and "or," which Goebbels emphasized by having an actor shouting them out loud whenever they appeared in the text.[96] In addition to stage adaptations of Müller's works, Goebbels also created numerous audio plays and other auditory artworks based on Müller's plays, for instance *Die Befreiung des Prometheus* (1975), *Wolokolamsker Chaussee I–V* (1989), *Shadow/Landscape with Argonauts* (1990), and *Herakles 2* (1992). The fact that Müller's texts have served as such inspiring sources for Goebbels's sonic experiments is a reflection of the destruction of the image and the shift toward the ear in the theater of the void.

Müller's *Description of a Picture*, even though it is often categorized as prose, must be considered a text for theater. It stands at the end of the metamorphosis that started with "Der Mann im Fahrstuhl" in *The Task* and has demonstrated, more than any other text, that plasticity is an underlying structure of theater that makes it possible for any given theatrical form to explode and form anew. As such, *Description of a Picture* is a singular text, marking as it does one of the biggest shifts in what a text for theater looks like and what dramaturgy it follows. The works that I discuss in the following chapters are all linked to this transformation. None of them is thinkable without Müller's consciousness of the consequences of plasticity. This is most evident in Jelinek, who explicitly refers to Müller's *Description of a Picture* and indeed, inspired by this text,

---

95. Goebbels's most notorious work, *Stifters Dinge* (*Stifter's Things*, 2007), is a piece without human actors that unfolds a slowly changing environment consisting of evaporating water, piled-up pianos, and other objects. Even though it does not use a text by Müller, this piece must be considered in close dialogue with Müller's theatrical texts because it emphasizes emptiness, metamorphosis, and transformation.

96. See Goebbels, "Text als Landschaft," 34–35.

radically changed how she wrote for the theater.[97] Müller, however, also runs through Schlingensief and Pollesch, albeit in those cases without any concrete marker linking their theater to *Description of a Picture*, but with numerous references to other aspects of Müller's theatrical work.

---

97. See the introduction to this book, where I discuss *Description of a Picture* in more detail.

3

END TIMES AND THE END OF TIME

Silent Murmurs in Elfriede Jelinek

> The body can mistake our tones for something else and
> then even incorporate them into the bones, so they say.
> So then at some point we'll have become our tones!
> Maybe our bodies have already stored what we produced
> as tones in the skeleton and we just haven't noticed it.
> We absorbed it unwittingly.
> —ELFRIEDE JELINEK, *KEIN LICHT*

Epigraph: Private translation by Gitta Honegger. "Der Körper kann unsere Töne mit etwas anderem verwechseln und dann sogar in die Knochen einbauen, so sagt man. Wir werden dann irgendwann unsere Töne geworden sein! Unsere Körper haben das, was wir als Töne erzeugt haben, vielleicht schon in ihr Skelett eingelagert, und wir haben davon nichts gemerkt. Wir haben es aufgenommen, ohne es zu merken."

Elfriede Jelinek wrote *Kein Licht* (No light)[1] in reaction to the nuclear disaster in Fukushima that followed the earthquake and tsunami that hit Japan on March 11, 2011.[2] However, the audience is not presented with a dramatization of the event. Instead, the play leads us into a buzz of voices, cries, shrieks, and murmurings that teeter on the knife-edge between life and death, materiality and immateriality. The text is overwhelming in the abundance of possible threads and topics introduced by its voices, whose location is impossible to pinpoint. Laughter and tears move in and out of each other in this play. So do screams and silence. In this play, language is mixed in with all kinds of other sounds so that the words uttered are no longer the center of attention but only one sonic element among others. As a result, *Kein Licht* allows us to observe how a theatrical text pushes against its own limitations of being perceived

---

1. The play premiered on September 29, 2011, at the Schauspiel Köln (directed by Karin Beier). It was published in November 2011 in the theater journal *Theater heute* and appeared one month later on Jelinek's website. I will be quoting here from the version published on the website.

2. The nuclear meltdown of three reactors at the Fukushima Daiichi nuclear power plant was the peak in a devastating series of catastrophes that included a magnitude 9.1 earthquake and a thirty-nine-meter-high tsunami. Jelinek's play is an attempt to grasp the terrifying events that transformed more than 3,500 square miles of northeastern Japan into contaminated ground. After the earthquake and tsunami, 15,899 people died, 6,157 more were injured, and 2,529 went missing (Kohso, *Radiation and Revolution*, 21). Sabu Kohso provides an in-depth analysis of the disaster in Fukushima that traces the relationship between nuclear power, capitalism, and the nation-state. See also Barad, "Troubling Time/s," which sheds light on the entanglement of nuclear physics, militarism, colonialism, and imperialism and, specifically, reveals the connection between the bombings of Nagasaki and Hiroshima in 1945 and the U.S.-based "Atoms for Peace" program, promoting the development of nuclear energy in Japan after World War II, which ultimately served as a way for the United States to expand its nuclear arsenal during the Cold War (Barad, "Troubling Time/s," 73–74). For an even more detailed analysis of the push for nuclear energy development in Japan by the United States after their bombings in Hiroshima and Nagasaki, see Brown, "Marie Curie's Fingerprint," G38–40. Brown argues that the development of civilian nuclear power reactors like Chernobyl would never have happened without the Cold War. Given that oil was a much cheaper energy source, the investment in expensive and risky nuclear power plants must be seen as a powerful tool in the fight for supremacy between capitalism and communism. It was part of the smokescreen put up by the producers of atomic bombs to hide the threat of atomic war behind the idea of the atom as a bringer and even a guarantee of peace.

by the eye, seeking to move instead into the realm of music and sound. As such, it emphasizes the sensual and the body, which are usually dismissed in linguistic approaches to language as structure and difference. This shift opens up a world that was partially inaccessible to us as long as we approached it through our eyes.[3]

For readers who are familiar with Jelinek's writing, it is surely no surprise that the author dedicated a play to Fukushima. Indeed, Jelinek writes almost obsessively about catastrophes of all "scales,"[4] from a fire in the tunnel of a glacier funicular in Austria to the collapse of a clothing factory in Bangladesh.[5] And although I use "scale" here in the way that we commonly do to differentiate between events on a global versus a local scale, Jelinek's plays challenge the concept of "scale" itself as an analytical tool. Consequently, in the context of Jelinek's plays, which intricately interconnect the micro and macro levels of catastrophes, we must speak of "topology" rather than using the geometrical measurement of scale.[6] *Kein Licht* is part of a group of texts that the author has published on Fukushima. These also include *Epilog?* (2012) and *Kein Licht: Prolog?* (2012–15), as

---

3. In her work on *Kein Licht*, literary scholar Bärbel Lücke states that Jelinek focuses on the smallest particles in order to reveal the complex pattern with which we are confronted when we want to grasp something like Fukushima: "She involves herself with the nuclear fallout, with the elements and the elementary particles, with the beta decay and the gamma radiation, in other words the microworld of the quanta, and in the process she brings to light the deep layers of our 'objective' reality, the layers of 'reality' and its effective forces, that are hidden from our bare senses" ("Sie mischt sich unter den *nuclear fallout*, unter die Elemente wie unter die Elementarteilchen, unter den Beta-Zerfall und die Gammastrahlung, also die Mikrowelt der Quanten, und macht so die Tiefenschichten unserer 'objektiven' Wirklichkeit, die den bloßen Sinnen verborgenen Schichten der 'Wirklichkeit' und ihre Wirkkräfte sichtbar") (Lücke, "Fukushima," 326). Although I agree that Jelinek's text confronts us with things that are too small to perceive with our eyes, I want to push beyond thinking in terms of cognition as connected to the gaze, as well as the image of archeological work on the layers of the ground, instead emphasizing the ear and seismology.

4. Jelinek herself claims, in "Das Parasitärdrama," that her plays are nothing without the catastrophic occurrences she writes about.

5. See Jelinek, *Das Werk*, and Jelinek, *Nach Nora*. These are just two examples of an entire group of works that uses natural/technical disasters as a point of departure. I return to this complex in the conclusion of this book.

6. I rely here on the argument for replacing "scale" with "topology" in Barad, "Troubling Time/s" (63). See also the introduction to this book.

well as a short statement in the Austrian weekly magazine *profil* and a text that reflects on the changed direction of nuclear and climate politics in the United States under the presidency of Donald Trump.[7] All of these, and particularly the last text, prove that for Jelinek, catastrophes like the one in Fukushima never stand by themselves. They are presented as entangled in a larger system of violence and exploitation in a world shaped by capitalism, militarism, imperialism, and nationalism that in turn creates shared but uneven patterns of violence.[8]

Jelinek's ongoing work on disastrous events has inspired scholars to discuss her writing in terms of a "theater of catastrophe."[9] However, Jelinek's plays never use a linear storyline to try to reconstruct the incidents she is writing about. We find neither characters that represent single individuals and their actions nor a plot that follows a logic of cause and effect. Instead, the plays are characterized by breathless speech that weaves together a wide range of fields, spaces, and times, never fully present or absent. Given the specific characteristics of Jelinek's plays, scholars speak of them as *Textflächen* (text surfaces). This term was in fact coined by Jelinek herself, but soon became established in the scholarship as well.[10]

---

7. Jelinek's short statement in *profil* was published in the context of a larger article on the question of how artists approach natural disasters and technological incidents (Jelinek, "Zu Japan"). She wrote the text *Der Einzige, sein Eigentum*, in which she particularly focuses on the United States, for the director Nicolas Stemann's 2017 staging of *Kein Licht* at the Ruhrtriennale in Bochum.

8. The way in which Jelinek presents and perceives catastrophes deeply resonates with Nancy's argument that we now experience catastrophes as equivalent (Nancy, *After Fukushima*).

9. Schößler, "Die Sehnsucht," 86.

10. Jelinek first used the term *Sprachflächen* (language surfaces) to characterize her texts, later introducing "text surfaces." The author regularly uses both terms—whether in her plays, in interviews, or in poetological texts—to describe her writing for the theater (e.g., Tiedemann, "Das Deutsche scheut das Triviale"; Jelinek, "Textflächen"; Jelinek, "Grußwort nach Japan"; Jelinek, "Immer hinauf auf den Steg"). Lehmann (*Postdramatic Theatre*, 18) introduced the term *Sprachfläche* as coined by Jelinek to scholarship. Another important study that further theorizes text and speech surfaces is Vogel and Eder, *Lob der Oberfläche*. Today, "text surface" has become an almost ubiquitous categorization for plays without dialogue (see Felber, *Travelling Gestures*; and Millner, "Prae—Post—Next?"). For an overview of the most important scholarly positions, see Hochholdinger-Reiterer, "Spricht wer?"

Given that Jelinek's text surfaces are polyphonic, they challenge theatrical institutions and their conventional modes of staging, as the question occurs of who should appear and speak on stage. And while this is true for all of Jelinek's plays since the 1980s, *Kein Licht* poses an even greater challenge when it comes to questions of theatrical form. The director Nicolas Stemann, who has staged more world premieres of Jelinek's plays than any other director and is well versed in approaching her text surfaces, characterizes the play as her most abstract text, taking the question of who is speaking to a new extreme.[11]

Kein Licht is divided between two speakers, "A" and "B," and yet they do not carry on a dialogue.[12] The relationship between the indicated speaker and the words that are uttered is hard to grasp, as the voices that speak through A and B cannot be identified with those entities. Indeed, A and B appear to be mere husks that could be filled with anything. Accordingly, they refer to themselves and each other in multiple ways. The spectrum of possibilities includes first and second violin, quantum particles, light, radiation, a search party, but also survivors of an unidentified catastrophe. The identification of body with speech is complicated even further when we consider that the play demands at least three actors, as indicated on the website of Jelinek's publisher, Rowohlt Theaterverlag.[13] Does this mean A and B can in fact be split into smaller entities, like atoms? Or is there a body onstage that does not speak at all? The play does not give us any answer to this question. As is typical for Jelinek's works, there are no stage directions.

A and B are not dramatic characters but rather sensors that receive, record, and make audible the sounds and voices dispersed over time and in space. The words that A and B utter are borrowed from writers and philosophers such as Sophocles, Rilke, Goethe, Schiller, Brecht, Benjamin, Heidegger, and Girard, as well as from

---

11. See Schmidt, "Gedankenstromlogorrhoe."
12. Lücke therefore calls this a "Dia(Poly)Log" (Lücke, "Fukushima"). I do not think this label goes far enough, however, because it still suggests a communicative situation with clearly distinct speakers, whereas Jelinek's play pushes toward the limits of language and radically deprives us of any origin at all for the speech.
13. *No Light (Kein Licht)*.

current media reports. At first glance, what is expressed seems random and arbitrary. However, on a closer look, we understand that the overwhelming soundscape produced by A and B is the very fiber of any meaning that arises. In other words, it is the void, as the indeterminate potential for everything that is and might yet be.

Kein Licht is a provocation to the theater in that it radically deprives us of any visual impression, thus challenging conventional forms of representation. The text incorporates the invisibility of radiation in order to confront us with things that are too small for us to see but that nevertheless have an immense impact on us and can slowly transform not only individual bodies but entire environments. Given that Jelinek links radiation and music, and given the importance of the soundscape that accompanies the spoken words, the adaptations of the play so far have stressed music.[14] Karin Beier, for example, the director of the play's world premiere, has emphasized that her production should be understood as a concert—more concretely, an oratorio or requiem—rather than a conventional play.[15] Stemann went even further, working with the French composer Philippe Manoury to adapt the play for the musical theater.[16] Nonetheless, we can see that even these stagings struggle when it comes to re/presenting things that are invisible to our eyes. Instead of confronting us with the limitations of our gaze and pushing to the limits of sight, they tend to reintroduce visual elements.

---

14. *Kein Licht* has been staged several times, not only in the German-speaking context but also in Japan. And yet it has been less successful than other plays by Jelinek, which may have to do with the fact that it is one of her most complex, puzzling pieces and that it challenges theater and theatrical conventions even more than her other pieces do.

15. Beier, "Dionysos und Apollon zugleich," 76. As Beier claims in the same interview, Jelinek's text on Fukushima was shared with Beier when Beier was already working on another production, her own work *Demokratie in Abendstunden*, that emphasized music and specifically stressed identifying the speakers onstage as musicians in an orchestra, an idea that Jelinek then also took up for her own play (Beier, "Dionysos und Apollon zugleich," 78).

16. This version of the piece was based on *Kein Licht* as well as *Epilog?* and a new essay that Jelinek wrote specifically for this adaptation entitled *Der Einzige, sein Eigentum (Hello Darkness, My Old Friend)*. The opera, announced as a "Thinkspiel," premiered on October 18, 2017, at the Opéra Comique in Paris. For a detailed analysis of this production, see van Daele, "The Absence of Traditional Characters."

In Stemann's production, for example, radiation is represented by a greenish substance onstage, making it seem contained, easily graspable and manageable by human cognition.

In the following pages, I work slowly through the ever-changing topology that unfolds in *Kein Licht*. True to Jelinek's form, I do not immediately present a possible reading of each thread but rather introduce them only to slowly show where and how they are connected and how we might understand them. At the center of my analysis is the interweaving of music and quantum physics,[17] which, although it is at first glance highly confounding, introduces questions of temporality into the play that are key to understanding how Jelinek makes the void, as indeterminate potential, palpable. I examine the importance for Jelinek's theater of what she herself calls "chaos," which, I argue, should be understood as the void and, as such, as the realm from which all meaning arises. I also revisit the intricate relationship between life and death that is so central to Jelinek's theater. Although this chapter focuses on *Kein Licht*, I also offer some more general insights into possible new understandings of Jelinek's theater, presenting new perspectives on central categories and concepts like "who is speaking," representation, and catharsis by reading them through the void.

Undoing Time: Music and Radiation

Even though *Kein Licht* was published as an immediate reaction to Fukushima, the text is deprived of any clear markers that tell us to read the play in such a way. This is already evident from the fact

---

17. Music and quantum physics are indeed not usually discussed together. Alexander's *The Jazz of Physics* is an interesting exception, using music as an analogy to explain complex questions of quantum mechanics and showing that some of the most important physicists, including Einstein, were deeply inspired by musicians from Mozart to Coltrane. At the same time, musicians often compose in dialogue with new findings in physics. A good example is *Into the Labyrinth: A History of Physics from Galileo to Dark Matter*, a composition by the physicist and guitarist Alberto Rojo and the percussionist Michael Gould that premiered at the Keene Theater in Ann Arbor, Michigan, in 2023 and that included parts of Jelinek's *Kein Licht*.

that Fukushima is not mentioned even once. Instead, the play is created out of diverse voices and a cascade of screams and murmurs, establishing an attitude toward the present that forces us to perceive it as a ghostly space in which all im/possible voices of im/possible past, present, and future catastrophes become in/audible or im/material, without ever being truly present or absent.

This haunting sphere emerges from an idiosyncratic superimposition of music and quantum physics.[18] The link between music and quantum physics is key for the play as through it, *Kein Licht* confronts us with the fine line between the immaterial and the material and with temporal diffraction. Moreover, it forces us to perceive theater no longer as primarily a place for seeing but as a place for hearing.[19]

The sonic takes center stage from the very first lines, introducing the semantic field of sound and hearing, which becomes the primary mode of perception in the play: "A: Hey, I can hardly hear your voice, can you do something about this? Can't you get it to sound louder? I don't want to hear myself, you've got to somehow drown me out. Actually, I've been thinking for a while now that I can't hear myself either, even though I've got my ear right at the control panel, where I try to capture them, the sounds."[20] These first few lines start up a complex constellation of hearing and not-hearing as well as of silence and sound. A addresses someone with the complaint that that other person's voice (are A and B parts in an orchestra? voices in a choir? regular speakers?) is not loud enough to drown

---

18. In the existing performative approaches to *Kein Licht*, music and quantum physics have so far been disentangled. We can see this in the different productions of the play, which have a tendency to identify A and B as musicians rather than explore what it might entail when music and quantum physics pass through each other. We have seen that Beier stressed that her world premiere of the play should be understood as a concert, and such understandings of the play are fostered by the publisher's description, where the speakers are simply identified as musicians in an orchestra (*No Light* [*Kein Licht*]).

19. See the introduction and chapter 1, where I discuss this in greater detail.

20. Jelinek, *Kein Licht*. Private translation by Gitta Honegger. "A: He, ich hör deine Stimme kaum, kannst du da nicht was machen? Kannst du sie nicht lauter tönen lassen? Ich möchte mich selbst nicht hören, du mußt mich irgendwie übertönen. Dabei glaube ich schon längere Zeit, daß ich auch mich nicht hören kann, obwohl ich das Ohr direkt am Schaltpult habe, wo ich versuche, sie zu greifen, die Töne."

out A's own voice. At the same time, A's own voice, too, seems to be muted. While the lines suggest two voices speaking simultaneously instead of one after the other (as in a dialogue), we also have to wonder whether anything is audible at all or whether what we have instead are silent murmurs not perceptible to our ears.

When there is sound that we cannot perceive, how do we even know that it's there? How can we sense it? The reference to the control panel is striking, suggesting the need for a technological tool for perceiving sounds and confronting us with the limits of our own senses. Furthermore, A speaks of trying to "grasp" (*greifen*) the sounds (what is translated above as "capture"), in the sense of "touching" them, and in so doing reminds us of the material, bodily quality of sounds, which may, even when they are not audible, still be sensed through vibrations in our bodily tissues.

The first lines set the tone for the entire play, which unsettles our conventional understanding of what is perceptible and therefore considered to be *something*, versus what is imperceptible and consequently considered to be *nothing*. In challenging our conventional modes of perception, the text forces us to attune our senses to the complex interplay of im/materiality, in/visibility, and in/audibility. This happens through a link between music and quantum physics; in particular, between musical sound and radiation. Sound and radiation share the quality that they force us to perceive in/visibility, in/audibility, and im/materiality anew. While the opening lines only hint at the possibility of the entanglement of music and radiation, by stressing physical phenomena like the superimposition of sound waves, such references intensify over the course of the play. Slowly, musical terminology and terms from quantum physics become more and more enmeshed. This is initiated with A and B associating the Geiger counter, used to measure ionizing radiation, with the violin (called *Geige* in German). In this context it is stressed that radiation, when measured, produces sound; but even more importantly, the half note and the half-life now seem to apply to both realms:

> Earlier, my tone had a half-life of about 50 minutes, so then I should hear it, even in half an hour I should still hear it. The tone I played, should still be there. But what about the other tones? Are they also disintegrating

after, no before, no after 50 minutes? Does that mean 50 minutes before they have even been played? Does the sound run backwards? Well now, my tones you can only find as long as my tone-generating reactor is still running, as long as my turbines are still running on their secret paths where nobody can see them and by means of which the inaudible becomes audible and is finally coming, but the creators, the reactors, that is, those who react, because creators don't exist, only reactors to something that can't be seen, as the name says already, whatever, I turned them off already days ago.[21]

This passage links nuclear energy, creation, and creative production, while playfully engaging with the question of what it means to act versus what it means to react. What is most striking about the passage, though, is how rhythm and sound are infused with notions of radioactive decay and the survival of atoms, which introduces questions of time and temporality. In giving music a half-life and in complicating how we think of musical time, multiple temporalities are introduced that seem to be in constant flux and that contradict any notion of time as moving forward. Instead, the text presents these temporalities as easily reversible.

Thus, *Kein Licht* suggests that there are different temporalities inherent in music and quantum physics that inhabit each other. One temporality we find in the play is time linked to capitalism, militarism, nationalism, and imperialism, marked by an understanding of time as unfolding linearly. This temporality is evoked by notions like "being behind," "moving forward," being "late," or talking about what "lies ahead." While *Kein Licht* confronts us with voices connected to the violence that is unleashed by time thought

---

21. Jelinek, *Kein Licht*. Private translation by Gitta Honegger. "Mein Ton vorhin hatte eine Halbwertszeit von etwa 50 Minuten, also müßte ich ihn ja noch hören, sogar in einer halben Stunde müßte ich ihn immer noch hören. Es müßte immer noch anhalten, daß ich meinen Ton gespielt habe. Aber was ist mit den andren Tönen? Zerfallen die auch schon nach, nein, vor, nein, nach 50 Minuten? Heißt das 50 Minuten, bevor sie überhaupt gespielt wurden? Läuft der Schall rückwärts? Also meine Töne kannst du nur finden, solang mein Tonerzeugungs-Reaktor noch läuft, solang meine Turbinen noch laufen auf ihren Schleichwegen, wo sie keiner sieht und mit denen das Unhörbare hörbar wird und endlich kommt, aber die Schöpfer, die Reaktoren, also die Reagierer, denn Schöpfer gibts keine, nur Reagierer auf etwas, das man nicht sieht, Reaktoren, die ja nicht Schöpfer sind, sondern eben auf etwas reagieren, das sagt schon der Name, egal, die habe ich bereits vor Tagen abgeschaltet."

of as progress, the play simultaneously points to an undoing of such time from within. This undoing of time is set in motion through the claim that music is time ("Musik ist Zeit"), which is repeated three times in the play. How are we to understand this claim?

Music is time art, par excellence, and as such considered to have its own temporality: musical time.[22] And yet, the music in *Kein Licht* seems disconnected from its own time and linked instead to the rhythm and lifetime of the atom. The fact that music is deprived of its own time hints at the universal, homogenous time of capitalism, which aligns everything to the rhythm of the atom.[23] And yet, it is not the rhythm of the atom in general that music is attuned to. Instead, music is particularly synchronized to the time of radioactive decay, introducing the recurring motif of music as something that will soon disappear or has already done so. "Music is time and we don't have that anymore," we read in the play.[24] The lines anticipate an end that is yet to come or that has already happened. While it is not surprising to be confronted with such an apocalyptic image in a text inspired by Fukushima, the implications are more complex than simply reminding us that doomsday is near or that we have already arrived there. The music in *Kein Licht* is connected to the end times, suggesting not simply the apocalypse but the end of linear time itself. *Kein Licht* cracks open time as thought of in terms of capitalist progress, moving at an ever-faster pace toward the destruction of the entire planet, and reveals another time that also inhabits these end times.

How, then, does the play undo linear time and the narratives of an end time in order to subsequently end linear time altogether? To answer this, we need to keep in mind that in *Kein Licht*, music is not just ephemeral but also finite. This evokes a radical reworking of how we conceive of who and what can live and die, as Barad

---

22. See Alperson, "Musical Time," for a discussion of music as time art and musical time, as well as a great historical overview of different conceptualizations of time, starting with Kant.
23. Barad, "Troubling Time/s," 60.
24. Jelinek, *Kein Licht*. Private translation by Gitta Honegger. "Musik ist Zeit, und die haben wir nicht mehr"; Here, we can also see the close references to Heidegger. Particularly to his main study *Being and Time*.

claims for the nuclear age. In their essay on the atomic bombing of Hiroshima and Nagasaki, Barad writes that "in the twentieth century, time is given a finite lifetime, a decay time. Moments live and die. Time, like space, is subject to diffraction, splitting, dispersal, entanglement."[25] The diffraction of time entails that we find a multiplicity of times in every moment, which is an ineliminable feature of existing material conditions.

If, as stated in *Kein Licht*, music *is* time, then music, too, has become mortal in the twentieth century and as such is subject to diffraction, splitting, dispersal, and entanglement. With this in mind, the play evokes Walter Benjamin's seminal essay "The Work of Art in the Age of Mechanical Reproduction" in order to try to register the complex entanglements of time and space in music: "This mixture of chaos and senselessness would be linked to all possibilites of limitless *technical and mechanical reproducibility*, any nothing can be randomly repeated and repeatedly brought out, it would remain a nothing, but it could be repeated over and over again with technical devices, the repeatable chaos, and one wouldn't know anymore, if it is still going on or it was another chaos already."[26] By having lines from Benjamin's essay running through the speech of A and B, Jelinek is introducing another text that links art and quantum physics, as the literary scholar Peter Fenves argues. Fenves shows that Benjamin's conceptualization of *aura* in this essay is deeply inspired by quantum physics and specifically by the notion of *Verschränkung* (entanglement), which becomes palpable in Benjamin's very definition of aura: "Uniqueness and permanence are as closely linked [*verschränkt*] in the latter as are transitoriness and

---

25. Barad, "No Small Matter," G106. See also the discussion of the ephemeral of the inanimate in Barad, "No Small Matter," G112–13. Barad follows quantum field theory, which states that particles can live and die as they are "born out of the void, go through transformations, die, return to the void, and are reborn" (G112).

26. Jelinek, *Kein Licht*. My emphasis. Private translation by Gitta Honegger. "Diese Mischung aus Chaos und Sinnlosigkeit wäre verknüpft mit allen Möglichkeiten der grenzenlosen technischen Reproduzierbarkeit, jedes Nichts kann ja beliebig wiederholt und wiederholt hervorgeholt werden, es bliebe ein Nichts, aber es könnte mit technischen Geräten immer wieder wiederholt werden, das wiederholbare Chaos, und man wüßte nicht mehr, ob es noch andauert oder schon ein anderes Chaos wäre."

reproducibility in the former."[27] While the published manuscript only hints at Benjamin's involvement with quantum physics, the importance of this field to his writing becomes much clearer when we also consider an unpublished fragment of Benjamin's (originally intended to be part of the essay) that refers to Arthur Stanley Eddington's *The Nature of the Physical World*.[28] Jelinek's play makes use of this hidden possible meaning of aura, as something that entangles seemingly disparate temporal and spatial positions, when it associatively evokes Benjamin's study through the semantic fields of originality, transitoriness, reproduction, preservation, and endurance, which pass in and out of each other, inspiring a mixing of the seemingly contradictory temporalities of "passing by" and "returning," "elapsing" and "staying," "vanishing" and "lasting."

While Benjamin is interested in the observer of a work of art, Jelinek discusses music in relation to the musician: "Music is the controlled autonomy of its producers, but it is already slipping away from us, undressing us, becoming uncontrollable, even though we have learned and practiced to control it."[29] In *Kein Licht*, the music created can be synchronized to the body of the musician. Music, though, can also separate itself from the musician's body and flee from it. And it is in between control and slippage that the entanglements of time can be reconfigured. We can understand this better if we consider a short essay that Jelinek published about her organ teacher, Leopold Marksteiner: "Back then, at any rate, he offered his student a place where the world was not any slower,

---

27. Benjamin, "The Work of Art in the Age of Mechanical Reproduction," 223. In the German version, we find the term *verschränkt* (entangled) instead of *verbunden* (linked); *verschränkt* better emphasizes the link to quantum physics: "Einmaligkeit und Dauer sind in diesem so eng verschränkt wie Flüchtigkeit und Wiederholbarkeit in jener" (Benjamin, *Das Kunstwerk*, 15).

28. See Fenves, "The Problem of Popularization," and Fenves, "Aura und Irrtum." In both of these insightful articles, Fenves discusses the unpublished fragment, intended for the essay on "The Work of Art in the Age of Mechanical Reproduction," that makes reference to Eddington's *The Nature of the Physical World*.

29. Jelinek, *Kein Licht*. Private translation by Gitta Honegger. "Musik ist kontrollierte Autonomie ihrer Erzeuger, doch schon ist sie dabei, uns zu entgleiten, sich unserer zu entkleiden, sie wird unkontrollierbar, obwohl wir doch gelernt und geübt haben, sie zu kontrollieren."

but where it could be countered by something: an audibility of the flow of time. That which is music. I don't mean the burbling vanishing of time in the outflow of the radio, the record player, and later the CD player, but time that you could hear in its flow and at the same time navigate yourself, time whose run had to be carefully coxed so that you would not lose it."[30]

As we can see here, music, for Jelinek, has the ability to counter and to resist common conventions and categories of the world. According to her, the creation of music not only makes the passage of time perceptible but also means being able to control its flow. She clearly differentiates between playing music and listening to it in its reproduced versions. While the latter makes time flow by and disappear, the former, that is playing music oneself, carries the potential to undo time. Only in the entanglement of the musician's body with the invisible sound do we find a possibility that one could "lose" time: that it could hurry away, pass by its creator, or intersect and overlap with other times. In short, time here appears dispersed and diffracted.

In *Kein Licht*, this relationship is further complicated. Not only does music enter and pass through an abstract body that is disconnected from the natural body in the sense of a "body without organs" (Deleuze) but the play introduces the body *with* its organs when it describes music as something that inscribes itself onto the body and starts to reconfigure its materiality: "The body can mistake our tones for something else and then even incorporate them into the bones, so they say. So then at some point we'll have become our tones! Maybe our bodies have already stored what we produced as tones in the skeleton and we just haven't noticed it. We absorbed

---

30. Jelinek, "Die Zeit flieht." Private translation by Gitta Honegger. "Er hat damals jedenfalls seiner Schülerin einen Ort angeboten, an dem die Welt zwar auch nicht langsamer war, an dem man ihr aber etwas entgegensetzen konnte: eine Hörbarkeit des Zeitablaufs. Das, was Musik ist. Ich meine nicht das gurgelnde Verschwinden von Zeit im Abfluß des Radios, des Plattenspielers, später des CD-players, sondern Zeit, die man, in ihrem Verlauf, hören konnte und gleichzeitig selber steuerte, Zeit, die man, in ihrem Ablauf, sorgfältig gliedern mußte, damit man sie nicht verlor."

it unwittingly."³¹ When *Kein Licht* suggests that music penetrates the body and starts to reconfigure its materiality, ephemerality and duration enter into a complex relation.

Suggesting its long-lasting effects on the body, Jelinek goes so far as to compare music's impact to that of radiation. As Barad writes, it is precisely radiation's ephemerality and materiality that hint at other possible temporalities that allow us to understand that in each moment, multiple times meet and interact: "The temporality of radiation exposure is not immediacy; or rather, it reworks this notion, which must then rework calculations of how to understand what comes before and after, while thinking generationally. Radio-activity inhabits time-beings and resynchronizes and reconfigures temporalities/spacetimematterings. Radioactive decay elongates, disperses, and exponentially frays time's coherence. Time is unstable, continually leaking away from itself."³² What Barad lays out here resonates with what I have described earlier as a haunting that now also comes from the future. A nuclear disaster cannot be captured by simply looking into the losses and devastation connected to the specific moment of the explosion or meltdown. Instead, as Barad emphasizes, radiation reworks time and brings past, present, and future into ever-new constellations. The nuclear radiation of today might, for instance, cause future bodily mutations that turn into cancer cells.³³ Jelinek provocatively links music to such forms of haunting. In *Kein Licht*, sounds do not simply appear and disappear; even though they are silent, they materialize and become written into the very flesh and bones of our bodies. This means that they are not fully lost. Instead, they can and have become a future.

---

31. Jelinek, *Kein Licht*. Private translation by Gitta Honegger. "Der Körper kann unsere Töne mit etwas anderem verwechseln und dann sogar in die Knochen einbauen, so sagt man. Wir werden dann irgendwann unsere Töne geworden sein! Unsere Körper haben das, was wir als Töne erzeugt haben, vielleicht schon in ihr Skelett eingelagert, und wir haben davon nichts gemerkt. Wir haben es aufgenommen, ohne es zu merken." Deleuze first introduces this concept in *The Logic of Sense* and expands it in his co-written book with Félix Guattari, *Anti-Oedipus*.
32. Barad, "Troubling Time/s," 63.
33. Schwab, *Radioactive Ghosts*, ix.

Speaking Silence: On Chaos and Nothingness

Throughout *Kein Licht*, A and B seem to be in a chaotic situation. They talk about following tracks in the hopes of finding something that they describe as invisible and inaudible. They repeatedly mention that it is hard for them to hear each other, and they emphasize that they are breathless. B's very first lines speak of A this way, when A's panting is described as threatening to drown out the very sound that A seeks to catch:

> No wonder that you are so breathless that just your panting drowns out the sound you want to catch. The animal you put to flight! There you're running after your sounds, but those are mine. You're running on the wrong track! How could there ever be an exit? This is a narrow path, nothing leads out of it, the walls are meters high, steep and smooth, and below, the puddles glow in their own, uniquely beautiful light, which we, only we, have thrown on them. We certainly hope that this will also show us in a good light. But light, radiance, warmth cannot be heard. What kind of hiss is this? We are being robbed of energy! The dead radiate, they are not appealing and not responsive. I grant you my sounds so that you don't have to hear your own. That's what you want, isn't it? For someone to intervene at the last moment and tear your sounds away from you. Your sounds don't pull it off the way you want them to? You think that mine are getting through? I only play second fiddle, I accompany you but can't yet see where to, while I move more diligently and quicker. Along. But I am not your driver, and by that I don't mean the hardware, the bus driver, I mean a rather soft-hearted driver, the kind that non-huntable animals have. Whom they take for a shepherd. But that's not what it is. It's what goes into their houses and lights a fire under their ass. That's what I call energy. And the others do too.[34]

---

34. Jelinek, *Kein Licht*. Private translation by Gitta Honegger. "Kein Wunder, wenn du so atemlos bist, daß schon dein Schnaufen den Ton übertönt, den du erjagen willst. Dieses Tier treibst du in die Flucht! Da rennst du hinter deinen Tönen her, aber es sind meine. Du rennst den falschen Weg! Wie sollte ein Ausstieg je möglich sein? Das ist ein Hohlweg, aus dem nichts herausführt, die Wände sind meterhoch, steil und glatt, und unten leuchten die Lachen in ihrem eigenen schönen Licht, das aber wir, wir allein, auf sie geworfen haben. Wir hoffen wohl, daß das ein gutes Licht auch auf uns wirft. Aber Licht, Strahlen, Wärme kann man nicht hören. Was ist das für ein Fauchen? Energie wird uns geraubt! Die Toten strahlen, sie sind nicht ansprechend und nicht ansprechbar. Ich verleihe dir meine Töne, damit du deine nicht hören mußt. Das ist es doch, was du willst. Daß jemand im letzten Moment eingreift und deine Töne von dir wegzerrt. Deine Töne verlaufen nicht so, wie du möchtest? Glaubst du, daß meine es

A and B claim to be searching for something, but their hunt is chaotic and unsuccessful. They mention that they are walking along the wrong paths; they run backward and are clearly disoriented. As readers of the play, we try to follow the conversation, but reading here almost feels like joining the chase, trying to keep pace with A and B in an effort not to lose them. Given that all we hear are fragments of stories and hints at seemingly disparate times and spaces, we know we must follow them closely in the hope that they will eventually fill in the gaps. Thus, we run after and with A and B, without knowing where they are going or what they are trying to find.

In this chase, wordplays make us jump between seemingly disconnected realms. The German term *Treiber* can mean "beater," "electronic driver," "slave driver," or "driving force," while the verb *treiben* can mean "hunt" or "drive," inspiring wordplay that leaps from "hunt" to "hardware drive" to "sheperd." Later on, "values" (*Werte*) become readable as both "radiation levels" and "note values"; water and tears interfere with each other, and music, physics, and physiology intermingle. All of these seemingly free associations with the word *Treiber* (driver), however, stress the sense of something chasing after an unknown goal or target. The audience desperately seeks to grab hold of what is being expressed, and yet whatever is said only adds to the already overwhelming pattern of confusion, rather than helping us to make sense of it.

Faced with this text that relies predominantly on continuously reconfigured relations that create an ever-changing topology, the overall feeling for us as the audience is one of being overwhelmed by excessive markers, hinting at so many times and places that we can no longer pinpoint anything. And yet, this is where the void, from which singular and unpredicted meaning can arise, is made possible. In other words, Jelinek's play turns us into a tracking audience. Tracking in *Kein Licht*, though, does not mean finding and

---

schaffen durchzudringen? Ich spiele doch nur die zweite Geige, ich begleite dich, sehe aber noch nicht, wohin, dafür gehe ich umso fleißiger und schneller. Dahin. Aber ich bin nicht dein Treiber, also ich meine nicht die Hardware, den Bustreiber, ich meine so einen eher weichherzigen Treiber, wie nicht jagbare Tiere ihn haben. Den sie für ihren Hirten halten. Ist er aber nicht. Der geht in die Häuser und macht ihnen Feuer unterm Hintern. Das nenne ich Energie! Und die anderen nennen es auch so."

decoding signs.³⁵ Instead, like A and B, we have to embrace the fact that we too are sensors that can receive and record the diverse sounds that reach us. As such, the play invites us to join A and B in spontaneously assembling the voices that reach us and are part of the violent histories of colonialism, capitalism, imperialism, and militarism that meet in Fukushima.

In addition to Barad's interpretation of nothingness and the void, I also want to draw on Michel Serres, whose discussion of music allows me to link music and the void.³⁶ Although Barad stresses the ear and the sonic when speaking of the void, they do not further theorize the void's relationship to music. Serres shares with Barad a relational thinking that radically reworks categories of time, space, causality, and the human and the nonhuman. By synthesizing the work of these two thinkers, I show that music and chaos consist of indeterminate possibilities in which the opposition of meaning and nonsense, of living and dying, is challenged. In short, I argue that when Jelinek speaks of music and chaos, she is referring to what I call the void.

The fact that all meaning in *Kein Licht* belongs to the void is primarily expressed, in the play, through excerpts from Rainer Maria Rilke's *Duineser Elegien* (*Duino Elegies*). Early on, A raises the question of who would hear them speaking through all this diffuse noise:³⁷ "For who, if I cried out, would ever hear me" ("Wer, wenn ich schriee, hörte mich"), thereby citing from the beginning of Rilke's poem cycle: "For who, if I cried out, would ever hear me among the Angels and archangels' / hierarchies?"³⁸ In scattering various stanzas of Rilke's cycle throughout her play, Jelinek is introducing a work that is concerned with the tension between chaos

---

35. While some of my readers might now immediately think of semiotics, I will show throughout the chapter that this form of track reading is not to be confused with semiotics. See also the succinct demonstration of the difference between a semiotics of things and phenomenology from a posthuman position in theater analysis in Ernst, "Akteur-Netzwerk Theorie," 157.

36. I draw particularly on Serres's works *Genesis*; *Musique*; and *The Five Senses*.

37. When I refer to noise here, I am not speaking of noise as an unwanted signal that needs to be eliminated but of something that includes all possible meaning. See Serres, *The Parasite*; as well as the chapter on "The Beauty of Noise" in Alexander, *The Jazz of Physics*.

38. Rilke, *Duino Elegies*, 331.

and order as well as the struggle to create something meaningful in a world that seems fragmented. For Rilke, the human being is torn between chaos and order, beauty and terror, life and death, human and animal. Jelinek's play moves between similar realms, but instead of framing this as an irreconcilable tension, the play embraces movement, entanglement, and constant reconfigurations that surprise us with their ever-new constellations. In other words, it reveals that fragment and form, if they are not misunderstood as creating a totalizing whole, do not necessarily have to be opposites but that, true to plasticity, fragments can be spontaneously organized.

How exactly can we envision this overwhelming soundscape of *Kein Licht*, then? It is not simply the multitude of voices that are speaking at the same time that creates a chaotic atmosphere. The chaotic feeling is intensified by the ever-changing cascade of shrieks and cries that A and B refer to. As they note, this mix of noises, screams, heavy breathing, and other confusing sounds sometimes overpowers their spoken words. What is more, the sound is already there before the first words are spoken. As such, the first lines spoken by A already refer to noise as a constitutive part of everything that is said: "There's only this roar, I don't know, from an animal factory [*Tierfabrik*]? A power failure at the plant? But if the system broke down, why do they screech like that? Throttled at full strength? Automatically turned off? But that doesn't mean that everything is silent. The powers that cannot disappear, because nothing ever disappears, continue to screech in the monster's stomach like cicadas, long after they have been eaten, in the stomachs of cats."[39] Within this soundscape of screams and shrieks, music takes on a specific role. I have already explained that music enters in connection with questions of temporality. Now, I need to shed light on another thread to which music is connected in this play,

---

39. Jelinek, *Kein Licht*. Private translation by Gitta Honegger. "Da ist nur dieses Gebrüll, ich weiß nicht, von einer Tierfabrik? Ausfall einer Anlage? Wenn die Anlage ausgefallen ist, wieso schreien die dann so? Bei voller Kraft abgewürgt? Automatisch abgeschaltet? Aber das heißt ja nicht, daß alles still ist. Die Kräfte, die nicht verschwinden können, weil nie etwas verschwindet, schreien noch im Magen des Ungeheuers wie Zikaden, noch lang nachdem sie schon gefressen sind, in den Mägen von Katzen."

one that becomes obvious when we pay attention to the fact that Jelinek makes reference to Sophocles's satyr play *Ichneutae*.

Sophocles's play is about the newborn Hermes, whom the chorus of satyrs accuses of having stolen Apollo's cattle. When the satyrs set out to find Hermes and the cattle, they discover something unexpected—the sounds of the lyre, invented by Hermes. The satyrs are simultaneously afraid of and captivated by the beauty of the sound, as it blurs the boundary between life and death.[40] Drawing on Serres, we can read the nods in *Kein Licht* toward Sophocles's *Ichneutae* as introducing music as the possibility of all meaning and, as such, also of future becomings that are neither stable nor predictable. In conversation with Bruno Latour, Serres explains that "Hermes is the one who invented the nine-stringed lyre. What is a musical instrument, if not a table on which one can compose a thousand languages, and as many melodies and chants? Its invention opens the way for an infinite number of inventions."[41] Agreeing with Serres, we can argue that music in Jelinek introduces a reworked approach to knowledge and language that allows us to understand that language is only one possible meaningful medium among others, as well as how it positions the human in entanglement with animals and machines. In short, music is revealed as something that hints at future becomings without limiting them to one specific future. It opens up possibilities that might become realized.

Thus, chaos and nothingness in *Kein Licht* cannot be confused with anything or emptiness; instead, they present a realm of potential. A passage that we find closer to the end of *Kein Licht* helps clarify this. A short comment in italics states that A and B no longer share the text between them nor are they speaking in alternation. Instead, they speak and even shout the remaining text simultaneously: "*From here on, in the long passage until the voices are separated again, both should scream together—or divide up their texts themselves. They can also overlap, so that in some passages*

---

40. See the insightful analysis in Felber, *Travelling Gestures*.
41. Serres and Latour, *Conversations on Science, Culture, and Time*, 117.

nothing can be understood at all."⁴² Noise clearly dominates over linguistic language when Jelinek envisions the text as being shouted by more than one speaker at a time, until the two voices, A and B, briefly separate once more at the end of the play.⁴³

Although it is meant to be performed so that the individual words are not comprehensible, the following paragraph is still worth examining. It expresses what the play performs through the superimposition of different voices and sounds, namely the collapse of meaning bound to linguistics and the rise of all possible meanings within chaos and nothingness:

And all this will be as if it were nothing. Nothing to be done but to throw it all out. Surely we would not have thrown out our own notes? That's also a possibility, but before that we would have had to hear them out, trash them, and discard them! So then there is only the worry about whether they have adapted themselves to us and we to them. Everything is nothing, right? Right, no worries: everything's nothing. And if both of us must let our tones disappear, must we go where our tones already are, to where something can finally be heard? Or if we ourselves turned into tones and are therefore inaudible, because no one hears us, maybe we don't even exist, if we are nothing but our own tones? *Tones that are still in their infancy* and can't walk yet.... And in order for reality to become controllable, there has to be someone there, otherwise there is nothing, because without a system, no matter how illogical it is (and nothing could be more illogical than someone wanting an autograph from us, of all people!), how complicated or strangely discordant within itself and intransigent toward us, we would have to improvise, to create something where no one but us understands how things work, no one else, a *chaos of tones.*⁴⁴

---

42. Jelinek, *Kein Licht*. Emphasis in the original. Private translation by Gitta Honegger. "*Ab hier, die lange Passage, bis die Stimmen wieder aufgeteilt sind, sollten beide gemeinsam schreien—oder sich ihre Texte selber aufteilen. Sie können sich auch überschneiden, so daß man passagenweise nichts mehr versteht.*"

43. It is not new for Jelinek to envision her texts as being performed in such a way that noise is emphasized over information and communication. This becomes obvious in the various suggestions she makes for how her text might become present in the context of a staging, ranging from projecting it as an LED ticker to making it available on each member's smartphone during the performance, as recorded text being played in endless repetition, as background sound, or even completely muted.

44. Jelinek, *Kein Licht*. My emphasis. Private translation by Gitta Honegger. "*Und das alles wird sein, als ob es nichts wäre. Kann man alles nur noch wegschmeißen. Wir*

While we are once again confronted here with an overwhelming textual pattern that moves between existence and nonexistence, life and death, meaning and nonsense, and that complicates the relationship between voice and sound, presence and absence, being audible and being mute, I am particularly interested in how chaos here is framed as potential. This paragraph raises the question of how to handle or preside over reality. While the paragraph first evokes traditional epistemological models, when the voice claims that there must be some entity (God? a system?) that helps us to grasp reality, it subsequently points instead to an alternative thinking that embraces chaos, nonsense, and confusion. Serres makes it clear that chaos is not the opposite of order, nor does one derive from the other. Instead, chaos and order open up a rich sphere that allows us to face the im/possibility of communication and to think instead about a movement *toward* meaning and noise that can occur in a wide range of expressions, spanning syntactic language, music, and rhythm ("tones that are still in their infancy," as quoted before). All of these possible expressions are to be found between two extremes, both of which are meaningless, either because they carry the potential for all information and messages in general but none in particular (white noise) or because they are an unchanging monotone. As such, it is important to keep in mind that noise, when we understand it as Serres does, does not refer to something that is meaningless because of a lack of signification. In Serres, noise refers to excess, to a surplus of possible meanings from which meaning can arise. Thus, noise is

---

werden doch nicht unsere eigenen Töne weggeschmissen haben? Das wäre auch noch eine Möglichkeit, aber davor hätten wir sie doch vernehmen, verwerfen und entsorgen müssen! So ist nur die Sorge da, ob sie sich uns angeglichen haben und wir uns ihnen. Alles nichts, oder? Ja, nur keine Sorge: alles nichts. Und ob wir beide und alle unsere Töne verschwinden müssen, ob wir dorthin müssen, wo unsere Töne schon sind, ob wir weg müssen, wohin, wo man dann endlich etwas hört. Oder ob wir selbst unsere Töne geworden sind und daher unhörbar, denn uns hört keiner, vielleicht gibt es uns gar nicht, wenn wir selbst unsere eigenen Töne sind? *Töne, die immer noch in den Kinderschuhen stecken*, aber noch nicht gehen können.... Und damit Wirklichkeit beherrschbar wird, muß da jemand sein, sonst gibt es nichts, denn ohne ein System, und wäre es noch so unlogisch (und nichts könnte unlogischer sein, als daß jemand ausgerechnet von uns ein Autogramm will!), kompliziert oder merkwürdig uneins in sich und uneinsichtig mit uns, müßten wir improvisieren, etwas schaffen, in dem nur wir uns noch auskennen, niemand sonst, ein *Chaos aus Tönen.*"

the groundless foundation of our world. It is constantly present as the noise of our bodies or the world outside of us. In Serres's account of language and knowledge, he captures this in a few words: "no *logos* without noise."[45] Jelinek's *Kein Licht* is full of such noise. Sounds, shouts, breath, and panting accompany the words that we hear. Noise, which here is a constitutive part of all meaning, makes up the overwhelming majority of the play.[46]

Kein Licht is a call to rework our approach to the world and start training our ears for sensory encounters. It introduces the ear as an alternative embodiment, where being or becoming present is replaced by the indeterminate possibility of what was, could be, and might yet come. Music is key here for replacing linear models of communication with a model in flux, in which noise must not necessarily be perceived as the opposite of meaningful information. Music meets quantum physics, as they are both connected to an alternative mode of meaning-making that stresses movement *toward* meaning.

To better grasp this movement *toward* meaning, we can again turn to Barad's interpretation of nothingness and the void based on quantum field theory. Barad argues that given quantum indeterminacy, the zero state of the void cannot be determinate. If this is the case, the void must include all possible time-beings ("quantum fluctuation" or "virtual particles"). This brings me back to the still drumhead that Barad introduces to exemplify what it means if we conceive of the void not as empty but as filled with virtual particles. As Barad stresses, the still drumhead does not mean simply silence but rather the "*indeterminate murmurings of all possible sounds*" or a "*speaking silence.*"[47] Based on this interpretation of the void, Barad describes the void as a spectral realm that is the condition of im/possibility of non/existence.[48] The void reworks the relationship between life and death. It is full of "*innumerable possibilities/imaginings*

---

45. Serres, *Genesis*, 7.
46. For an analysis of disruption and noise in Jelinek's concept of the "secondary drama," see Kovacs, *Drama als Störung*.
47. Barad, "Troubling Time/s," 77. Emphasis in the original.
48. Barad, "Troubling Time/s," 78.

of what was, could be, might yet have been, all coexisting."[49] Jelinek's *Kein Licht* and her plays in general use grammatical constructions that hint at such possibilities when they wildly mix future perfect, perfect, pluperfect, and the subjunctive mood, as we can see in the following paragraph from *Kein Licht*: "Perhaps time rushed over us? I can't find the word that was supposed to touch us and is now touching the Earth, but touching isn't enough, she wants to kiss, she wants to penetrate, I couldn't say the word for what she wants correctly, not even if I could think of it. I can't tell. And when I say it, nobody can hear me, because time took me right out of my mouth. It took the word out of my mouth, because it wanted to say what I couldn't even have known yet."[50]

In Jelinek's theater, we enter a spectral realm that confronts us with all possible noises and movements that have been, that are, and that might yet be.[51] These texts are not outside of the void, and they don't produce the void by surrounding it. They *are* the void. As soon as we understand the void in Jelinek in this way, we can see that what is often captured as "chaos" is, to use Barad's words, the murmurs of the void. This connects with Jelinek's claim that theater is what decays and consumes the bodies of the actors, of the author, of the audience, as I described it in the introduction of this book. Like particles in the void, theater for Jelinek is the realm where language, bodies, matter, etc., emerge and decay. Linking this to *Kein Licht*, we can now grasp another layer that is introduced through Sophocles's *Ichneutae*, that is, the possibility of non/existence. *Ichneutae* is not just about the invention of the lyre; it discusses music as that which entangles the living and the dead. The satyrs are afraid of music, not

---

49. Barad, "Troubling Time/s," 78. Emphasis in the original.
50. Jelinek, *Kein Licht*. Private translation by Gitta Honegger. "Vielleicht ist die Zeit über uns hinweggeeilt? Ich kann dieses Wort nicht finden, das uns hätte rühren sollen und das jetzt die Erde berührt, doch die Berührung reicht ihr nicht, sie will küssen, sie will eindringen, ich könnte das Wort nicht richtig schreiben, was sie will, nicht einmal, wenn es mir einfiele. Ich kann es nicht sagen. Und wenn ich es ausspreche, hört mich keiner, weil die Zeit mich mir selbst aus dem Mund genommen hat. Sie hat mir das Wort aus dem Mund genommen, weil sie sagen wollte, was ich noch gar nicht gewußt haben konnte."
51. Jelinek, "Fremd bin ich."

simply because of the sound but because they understand that the lyre is an instrument made from sheep gut and turtle shell that nonetheless produces living sounds. As such, they stress music as an eerie phenomenon that combines life and death. In writing the void, Jelinek's theater is—to use Barad's words about the void—"a lively tension that troubles the opposition between living and dying (without collapsing their important material differences)."[52] It is a theater shaped by a "strange liveliness" in which "all speak"[53]—the living and the dead, the animate and the inanimate—as meaning is no longer limited to language but flashes up in the "speaking silence" of the void.

Jelinek herself points to the importance of those murmurs or chaos that never allow humans, in the convention of dramatic theater, to appear on stage, but instead produce all possible beings—inanimate or animate: "Chaos breaks out, no, it didn't break loose, it is that which is here. . . . It is a hot chaos that produces everything, and this should be preserved or always generated anew, it all depends. It gapes open, chaos does, and spits something out, but it never is people. It is speaking and nothing else."[54] Jelinek goes on to specify that such utterances are never whole but snatches that are always different when we return to them and reconfigure them with every single performance of the play, as she does not put them in any particular order.

> My speaking on stage is not a putting in order, not even a putting together; that is, after all, what a good chaos is; it leads that which occurred to me, to what it is, which, every night it is presented, gets to make itself present on stage, the one leads to the other. There, that which has been becomes what it is (at that point the text to this play, but which play do I mean, always another one even though it is the same every

---

52. Barad, "Troubling Time/s," 78.
53. Jelinek, "Textflächen."
54. Jelinek, "Es ist Sprechen und aus." Private translation by Gitta Honegger. "Chaos bricht aus, nein, es bricht nicht aus, es ist das, was da ist. . . . Es ist ein heißes Chaos, aus dem alles kommt, und das sollte bewahrt werden oder immer neu hervorgebracht, je nachdem. Es klafft auf, das Chaos, und spuckt etwas aus, aber Menschen sind es nie. Es ist Sprechen und aus."

night? has long since been written), what was becomes what is.... Each night, in the theater, it throws the past into what is and knocks it over with itself. What a hit!⁵⁵

Again, we see that for Jelinek, theater is a ghostly realm in which past, present, and future intermingle and in which the bodies we see onstage appear as eerily teetering between life and death. While Jelinek stresses that her texts do not put things into an order, her plays are not formless. On the contrary, they reconfigure thinking in terms of form as connected to a totalizing whole into thinking in terms of plasticity.

Transforming Catharsis: Dis/affection and Posttraumatic Subjectivity

Finally, we must take into consideration the importance of dis/affection in *Kein Licht* and ask about its implications for Jelinek's theater of the void. A and B repeatedly talk about laughter and tears. This lends itself to associations with a wide range of emotions, from sadness, depression, and anger to happiness and excitement. At the same time, though, A and B insist that neither laughter nor tears need be connected to any emotion. On the contrary, they claim that both of these are mere physical functions that allow the cleansing of the body: "Emotion? My ass. An irritation, as from a speck of dust in the eye. It makes one cry more than when one's mother died. So then, how about laughter, the reverse process?"⁵⁶ The play

---

55. Jelinek, "Es ist Sprechen und aus." Private translation by Gitta Honegger. "Mein Sprechen auf der Bühne ist kein Ordnen, nicht einmal ein Her-Stellen, ein gutes Chaos ist eben beides, es führt das, was war, was mir eingefallen ist, meinetwegen, zu dem, was ist, was jeden Abend, an dem das aufgeführt wird, sich eben aufführt, auf der Bühne, dort wird das eine dem andren zugeführt. Da wird das, was war (der Text zu diesem Stück ist bis dahin, aber welches Stück meine ich dann, immer ein anderes, obwohl es jeden Abend dasselbe ist?, ja längst geschrieben), das, was war, wird also zu dem, was ist.... Es stürzt die Vergangenheit jeden Abend auf der Theaterbühne in das, was ist, hinein und schmeißt es mit sich selbst um. Eine Wucht!"

56. Jelinek, *Kein Licht*. Private translation by Gitta Honegger. "Rührung? Von wegen. Eine Reizung ist es wie die vom Staubkorn im Auge. Da heult man mehr, als

introduces a complex arrangement of affect and disaffection that at the same time complicates the relation between mind and body.

Emotion and the lack of emotion remain important throughout the play, which challenges the place of catharsis in the theater. Since Aristotle's *Poetics*, catharsis has been essential for defining the function of tragedy and more generally of theater and drama. Aristotle claims that tragedy evokes feelings of *eleos* (pity) and *phobos* (terror), but his *Poetics* does not go into greater detail about how those affects might arise. As a result, catharsis has been translated and interpreted in multiple ways over the centuries, generally revealing more about the given interpreter's specific understanding of theater than about Aristotle's text itself.

In the German context, Lessing's interpretation of Aristotle's concept of catharsis and his translation of *eleos* and *phobos* as *Mitleid* (pity) and *Furcht* (fear) introduced the idea of theater as a pedagogical and moral institution. While older interpretations understood *phobos* in terms of *terror* or *horror*, Lessing considered it essential to have recourse to a less violent emotion. He was convinced that only then would the audience be able to identify with the characters onstage, and that identification, he believed, was essential in order for them to feel empathy and ultimately to transform their passions into moral skills.

Lessing's bourgeois-humanitarian concept of the theater is clearly evoked in *Kein Licht* when A asks about *Rührung* (emotion), but immediately challenged in the very next line when *Rührung* is replaced by *Reizung* (irritation). In this play, tears and laughter are neither emotional reactions on the part of the play's characters nor the sign of an emotional roller coaster on the audience's part. As the text's two speakers, A and B, make clear, tears and laughter are simply physical reactions to a physical irritation. Jelinek adopts lines from Girard's short essay "Ein gefährliches Gleichgewicht" (A dangerous equilibrium), in which he introduces an interpretation of catharsis as detached from morals and emotion. Girard links catharsis instead to mere physicality not just by discussing it in the realm of

---

wenn einem die Mutter gestorben ist. Und wie ist das dann mit dem Lachen, dem umgekehrten Vorgang?"

aesthetics but also by including its medical and religious implications. Girard claims that crying and laughing are both connected to the same mechanism of purging and elimination. Like other recent scholars, he rejects any moral implications, stressing that Aristotle thinks of *eleos* and *phobos* as strong bodily reactions and approaches catharsis through the realm of the medical and the ritual.[57]

Given that Jelinek playfully weaves in quotations from Girard's text that stress this alternative reading of catharsis, it might seem that the play is adhering to Girard's understanding of catharsis as an alternative to Lessing's take. And Jelinek does indeed depart from Lessing's vision of the theater as a place for moderate feelings that allow for identification and empathy, a place that is linked to morality. Her play presents neither psychologically motivated characters nor a plot that would allow its audience to identify and feel with the characters onstage. And yet, the play also challenges Girard's ritual and medicine-based definition in that it problematizes purging as an eliminatory practice: "The resetting of an emotion can't have been set in motion, no, they would have told us. Rebooting? Eye, tear, get a move on, what are you waiting for, foreign body or emotion, whatever, tears are running! We have this need for cleansing processes which really are also elimination processes, aren't they. *We want something to be gone that is here.*"[58]

Unlike Girard, Jelinek is wary about theater that promises cleansing. We can understand this better when we consider a conversa-

---

57. This reading was first presented by Jacob Bernays in 1857 in his *Grundzüge der verlorenen Abhandlung des Aristoteles* (Outlines of Aristotle's lost work). Theo Girshausen convincingly shows in his succinct overview of the historical interpretations of catharsis that this understanding of catharsis is shared by most scholars today. Moreover, it was essential to the attempts to rethink theater beyond drama in the second half of the twentieth century and has influenced the approaches of the theater makers who think of theater in close connection with its ritual origins (for example Richard Schechner, Living Theater, Orgien-Mysterien-Theater). See Girshausen, "Katharsis," 168–69.

58. Jelinek, *Kein Licht*. My emphasis. Private translation by Gitta Honegger. "Das Resetten eines Gefühls kann nicht in Gang gesetzt worden sein, nein, das hätte man uns mitgeteilt. Neu booten? Auge, Träne, raus damit, wirds bald, Fremdkörper oder Gefühl, ganz egal, die Tränen fließen! Wir haben dieses Bedürfnis nach den Reinigungsvorgängen, die ja eigentlich auch Eliminationsvorgänge sind, nicht wahr. *Wir wollen, daß etwas weg ist, was da ist.*"

tion that Jelinek had with the dramaturg Rita Thiele, where the author spoke more directly about catharsis, shedding light on her rejection of both of its dominant types—the one shaped by Lessing and that discussed by Girard: "I don't want . . . this abreaction, nor any catharsis either so that people can be freed from fear and terror. That would only be the forever perpetuated drama of the family in which the children remain powerless, the drama from which the 'I' wants to work its way out, whereas I show the powers that keep this 'I' underage, and my own rage, with which I write, is the rage of a minor, a voiceless one,[59] and yet one who speaks continuously, even without a mouth."[60]

Jelinek problematizes the violence inherent in catharsis, with its promise of the cleansing purge. When she speaks of the continuation of the "drama of the family," we find another connection to Girard that makes visible the problem of exclusion that Jelinek finds in Girard's thinking about culture. This time, it has to do with his notion of "mimetic desire," which he first coined in *Deceit, Desire, and the Novel*. Very much in the tradition of Hegel's master-slave dialectics, Girard shows in his analysis of familial dramas in novels by Cervantes, Dostoevsky, Flaubert, Proust, and Stendhal that the subject desires what the other desires and introduces the triangle of subject, model, and object. He argues that in the novels, the protagonists ("subjects") unconsciously identify and desire what an exemplary other (the "model") desires, which subsequently leads to rivalry and the attempt to violently exclude or destroy the exemplary other.[61] In

---

59. The German makes a pun here that cannot be translated into English. Jelinek is playing with the concept of legal immaturity, which is expressed in German as lacking a mouth (to speak with) (*unmündig*), and the actual mouth as an organ of speech.

60. Thiele, "Glücklich ist, wer vergisst?" Private translation by Gitta Honegger. "Ich will . . . diese Abreaktion nicht, auch nicht eine Katharsis, damit die Menschen von Furcht und Schrecken befreit werden können. Das wäre ja nur das ewig perpetuierte Drama der Familie, in der die Kinder immer machtlos bleiben, aus dem sich das Ich herausarbeiten möchte, aber ich zeige die Mächte, die dieses Ich unmündig halten, und meine eigene Wut, mit der ich schreibe, ist die Wut einer Unmündigen, die aber ununterbrochen spricht, auch ohne Mund."

61. See the detailed analysis of Girard in Lawtoo, *Violence and the Mimetic Unconscious*.

Violence and the Sacred, Girard expands on this theory, arguing that this desire shapes the entire social body. It is a theory of society as trapped in the logic of violence. The only solution to violence here is to mimetically repeat the violent acts in such a way as to channel and discharge them against an innocent victim, a scapegoat. Jelinek is suspicious of this kind of cathartic effect.

So then, what kind of catharsis, if any, do we find in Jelinek's theater, given that neither empathy through identification nor cleansing by purging seems to be a fitting model? Analyzing the relationships among fury, speech, and catharsis in Jelinek, the literary scholar Christa Gürtler argues that the texts affect the audience not through the audience's possible identification with the characters onstage but through polyphony and the lack of signification. For Gürtler, this opens up a space that allows the audience to actively apply meaning to the words and thereby inspires it to reflect and to "think further."[62] I agree with Gürtler when she focuses on the specific form, on polyphony, and on the demand that the audience do the work of thinking and working through the subjects raised in the play. And yet, Gürtler does not further explain *how* the specific form inspires this kind of work and what the work might look like.

To understand this better, we must pay attention to the fact that in Jelinek's theater, catharsis no longer relies on affects, which is a radically reworked understanding of the concept. What shapes her theater instead, I argue, is the potential to become disaffected. This surely is a surprising claim. Jelinek's theater has become notorious for confronting audiences with negative feelings like anger, disgust, and despair, feelings that not only drive her literary production but are also highlighted and analyzed in plays like *Wut* (Anger). And yet, the overlooked potential for becoming disaffected is similarly important,[63] carrying as it does a social and political dimension. I see disaffection as a helpful tool for casting light on new modalities of power and new determinations of the subject of power in our

---

62. Gürtler, "Elfriede Jelineks *Wut*," 86.

63. Here, I also include radical theatrical experiments such as the theater of Bertolt Brecht, which promotes "coolness" and thus positions itself in opposition to a theater shaped by catharsis. The negation of emotion still relies on emotion and does not necessarily introduce disaffection.

present. I draw on Malabou's talk "From Sorrow to Indifference," which shows that disaffection is connected to the complex pattern of destructive plasticity.[64] Not only does disaffection open up a space of potential and chance, but it is also a political problem because it produces subjects who lose their power, which also means their power to resist.

In *Kein Licht*, disaffection is introduced through the indifferent tone that accompanies the repeated mentions of laughter and crying. These two manifestations, laughter and crying, allow for associations with the two fundamental passions of joy and sorrow as described by Spinoza in his third book of *Ethics*, which is dedicated to emotions.[65] For Spinoza, affect and power are interrelated. According to him, joy is any passion that increases one's power of action, while sadness is any power that diminishes it. Malabou, meanwhile, suggests a shift in this analysis toward the radical absence of passion, an absence that, as neurobiological research suggests, characterizes our contemporary subjectivity.[66] The disaffected subject, Malabou argues, is deprived of the ability to wonder; it is without passion. It is a subject indifferent to its own indifference;[67] destroyed by accident, yet still existing. Being aware of the emergence of this new subjectivity, Malabou contends that power no longer instrumentalizes sadness, but indifference. As indifferent subjects, our power is not diminished but absent. The new, indifferent subject is bereft of any passion; it doesn't care and is therefore incapable of any form of resistance or political action. In turning to this possibility, Malabou emphasizes that

---

64. For a thorough discussion of destructive plasticity, see chapter 1.
65. Spinoza, *Ethics*, part 3, 107.
66. Malabou, "From Sorrow to Indifference." Malabou draws on the work of the neurobiologist Antonio Damasio (*Feeling and Knowing*), who states that the loss of wonder is the emotional and libidinal disease of our time (Malabou and Johnston, *Self and Emotional Life*, 11). In line with other neurobiologists, Damasio sheds light on the radical changes brought forth by severe brain lesions, including trauma, which can cause the subject to act without emotion, or "in cold blood." If this is true, Malabou argues, then we are confronted here with a new subjectivity that radically differs from the auto-affected subject, touched by wonder, as thought of in continental philosophy.
67. This, of course, makes possible a connection with Heiner Müller and the subjectivity revealed in his *The Task*, as analyzed in chapter 2.

destructive plasticity does not necessarily lead to liberation but complicates it by taking into consideration that disaffection can lead to apolitical subjects.

Jelinek's *Kein Licht* confronts us with this new subjectivity. A and B comment on and speak about death and devastation in a cold voice. Even when they are talking about the screams of dying animals that are being wiped out in a catastrophic event, they are calm and detached from what they are saying. With this lack of passion, the play allows us to experience a posttraumatic subjectivity that is shaped by the loss of the capacity for wonder.[68] Jelinek, like Malabou, understands that the most important question today is how to resist this tendency to become disaffected and thus passive and absent as a political agent. In Jelinek, we can see a search for how the subject can break away from his or her fate and how s/he can escape when trapped in a body and mind that are characterized by coolness. In short, her theater is aware of the negative side of destructive plasticity, while at the same time it seeks to make use of it as a possible way to break free from determination and enclosure.

While confronting us with a cool, indifferent tone, Jelinek's theater is simultaneously fueled by negative affect, which resists the lack of concern that prevents the subject from making sense or giving meaning to catastrophes but also from becoming a potential aggressor. Like the author-persona[69] that is an essential voice in Jelinek's plays, expressing the constant struggle, fight, and work that are attached to the attempt of maintaining negative feelings, we are reminded to feel angry, to feel outraged, and to make these feelings the basis for a practice of meaning-making that allows resistance.

Confronting us with theatrical texts that appear at first impossible to grasp and are at the very least hard to pin down, Jelinek invites us to experiment with new ways of interpreting and making sense in times when we seem to have lost our capacity to give meaning to the ongoing violent events that are happening at an ever-faster

---

68. Here, as already mentioned in the introduction, we see a line that connects Jelinek's theater to Samuel Beckett, whose plays also investigate this kind of subjectivity.

69. For a detailed analysis of the author-persona's voice in Jelinek's work, see Clar, "*Ich bleibe, aber weg.*"

pace. Thus, the shift from *Rührung* (emotion) to *Reizung* (irritation) that is expressed in *Kein Licht* seems essential. Jelinek's theater is aware of the dangers of disaffection, and thus continues to irritate us. In so doing, it forces us to do the necessary work that it demands to stay affected in our present. In other words, it invites us to practice making meaning when everything around us seems utterly meaningless.

4

Darkness, Movement, and Metamorphosis

Radical Possibility in Christoph Schlingensief

> The expansion of the dark phase, that's actually what I'm interested in right now.
> —Christoph Schlingensief, *Mea Culpa*

Of all the theater makers discussed in this book, Christoph Schlingensief is the most difficult to position within the category of theater. This has to do with the fact that he worked in almost all media. Not only does his oeuvre encompass film, theater, opera, performance art, installations, and media art but it also brings all of them together, interrogating one medium through another and thus allowing their discrepancies and discontinuities to emerge.[1] My

---

Epigraph: "Die Ausweitung der Dunkelphase, das ist eigentlich das, woran ich gerade interessiert bin."

1. This has been thoroughly discussed in scholarship, where Schlingensief is usually characterized as an artist who continually explored concepts that relied on

decision to discuss Schlingensief as a theater artist stems from the fact that most of his works were commissioned by key German-language theater institutions and, as such, contributed to expanding the concept of theater from the early 1990s, when Schlingensief first worked in the theater, until his death in 2010. Schlingensief can be seen as a director who probed and continually challenged the boundaries of established theatrical institutions. He did this by bringing other art forms, such as opera, installation art, and film, into these institutions. At the same time, he not only broke down the fourth wall that separates stage and audience, he broke down the walls of these institutions entirely, opening the theater up to the public sphere, where many of his performances took place. In my analysis, and understanding this complexity in Schlingensief, I do not reduce his work to theater per se but take seriously the fact that his theatrical works include all other media. This is clearly marked when I pay close attention to the cinematic principles that are at the core of his version of the theater of the void and which he predominantly explored after his first encounter with opera and, in particular, with Richard Wagner's *Parsifal*, which he staged in Bayreuth in the years 2004 through 2007.[2]

Schlingensief's engagement with the void is probably best captured in the short film of a hare decomposing[3] that ends his production of *Parsifal*. The film shows us the decomposition process of organic material, which normally takes weeks, using time-lapse

---

the combination of different media and genres, such as the *Gesamtkunstwerk* (total work of art). See early, seminal publications such as Forrest and Scheer, *Christoph Schlingensief*; and Janke and Kovacs, *Der Gesamtkünstler*.

2. Schlingensief's production premiered in 2004 at the Bayreuth Festival Theatre. The German and international media were scandalized at this production by the enfant terrible Schlingensief and, beginning months before the premiere, they framed the relationship between the director and the Wagner family as an antagonistic one, a perception that Schlingensief fueled. Long after the premiere, the production continued to cause outrage, resulting in its cancellation in 2007, a year sooner than usually announced.

3. The video is from Alexander Kluge's film archive and was produced in the basement of the Humboldt University, Berlin, filmed with a 35mm Arriflex camera with a time-lapse motor. The decaying process was captured over the course of several weeks. For a detailed description of the production process, see Alexander Kluge, "The Complete Version of a Baroque Invention by Christoph Schlingensief," 243.

photography. Typically for Schlingensief, the black-and-white film is grainy and full of larger and smaller disturbances, including overexposures, so that it is hard for the audience to distinguish between the defective material and the depiction of maggots that slowly begin to consume the decaying tissue of the animal. The entire sequence is highly ambivalent and unsettling, as it blurs the boundaries between life and death. This process finds its peak in the moment at which the actual decomposition becomes visible and the body of the hare twitches, giving the viewer the impression at first that the hare is alive and about to jump up. This short film opened up a new reading for the last lines of Wagner's opera, "Redemption to the Redeemer," as it is contrary to the usual interpretation of the end of *Parsifal* in terms of salvation and transformation into a superior life.[4] The short hare video became a recurring element in Schlingensief's theater, finding its way into almost all of his works after 2004.[5] There is no simple answer to the question of what it is that makes this small sequence so significant. And yet it clearly stands out from the sheer, overwhelming amount of visual and filmic material that Schlingensief included in his theatrical works. And while we cannot easily pin down what makes this video so special, we can name some aspects of the film that are also fundamental to Schlingensief's theater more generally: the work with disruptions, ruptures, and superimposition; light and dark; the hare as an ancient and ambivalent symbol for fertility and death; the tension-filled relationship between tradition and the new; metamorphosis and transformation; and the wound as a productive force.[6]

---

4. The short video was the most discussed and criticized moment of the director's already controversial production of *Parsifal*. See, for example, Spahn, "Das Bayreuther Hühnermassaker"; and Eichler, "A Hullabaloo for an Opening at Bayreuth."

5. The video was shown in the context of Schlingensief's "Animatographische Editionen" (Animatographic editions, 2006–2007), a series that includes *House of Obsession (Iceland Edition)*, *The African Twintowers (Africa Edition)*, *Odin's Parsipark (German Edition)*, and *Area 7*, at the Burgtheater in Vienna. Moreover, it became an integral part of Schlingensief's final theatrical works that engaged with his lung cancer, such as *Eine Kirche der Angst vor dem Fremden in mir* (*Church of Fear vs. the Alien in Me*, 2008) and *Mea Culpa* (2009).

6. See the insightful analysis in Meister, "Zirkulationen des Schmerzes," particularly 105–8. The importance of the wound allows a link to Müller, where the wound is similarly central, as I discussed in chapter 1.

The hare provides the impetus for my analysis of the void in Schlingensief. Starting from the video, I show that Schlingensief found in Wagner a form of plasticity at work that inspired him to investigate in greater detail some of the cinematographic principles with which he had been working since his early films, which subsequently led to the creation of the "Animatograph" as an ever-revolving and growing stage. While his insistence on using a rotating stage for his production of *Parsifal* was a matter of intuition at first, it later became a central element of his work. As a structure in permanent rotation, it allowed him to reinvent conventional film without the filmic cut. Instead, the rotating stage itself was able to introduce failure, movement, and chance, which involved everyone participating in the work in a process of transformation.

To better explain the function of the rotating stage, I first position the hare film in the broader context of Schlingensief's ongoing work on theater as expanded cinema and on the link between film and failure. This is necessary in order to make evident the importance of cinematic principles to his theatrical work. Schlingensief, who started as a director of low-budget, highly experimental movies, repeatedly emphasized that he had never stopped making film. He considered his theatrical works to be an expansion of his filmic oeuvre. And while the fact that the director himself characterizes his works in that way does not necessarily mean that we will find the principle realized in the actual pieces, Schlingensief's theater is indeed, as I will show, clearly based on cinematic principles. After establishing the importance of film for his theater, I discuss how his works first and foremost explore the difference between single frames of a movie that can occur horizontally (in the dark phase)[7] or vertically (in the superimposition of images). This then brings me to the materiality of film, particularly the life of its own that the material itself develops during the creative process.[8] Both the

---

7. Schlingensief here is not only inspired by his mentor Werner Nekes but also clearly draws from Alexander Kluge and his investigation of the dark phase. For an in-depth analysis of the dark in Kluge, see Langston, *Dark Matter*.

8. Schlingensief was introduced to the possibilities that occur in the difference between two single images of a movie by his mentor Nekes (1944–2017), the experimental filmmaker, who defined this difference as the smallest cinematographic

difference between single frames and the experiments with the material are attempts to remove the performance from the director's control and to allow unexpected creative processes to happen. Consequently, the works fluctuate between intention/determination and contingency, between creation and destruction. It is precisely in this fluctuation that the void becomes visible as the indeterminate source of all that is and might yet be and that it enters Schlingensief's theater as a radical potential for singular and unexpected becomings. After developing both these crucial principles, I return to the hare and discuss how Schlingensief breaks away from salvation and redemption to introduce a form of healing into his theater that is true to plasticity. I close by reflecting on how Schlingensief's theater of the void reinvents and transforms the notion of *Gesamtkunstwerk* (total work of art) that is inextricably linked with Wagner.

Accidents Happen: Theater and Film

To gain some initial insight into the importance of film and failure for Schlingensief's theater, we can focus on one particular moment in the director's career: in 2005, with the production of *The African Twintowers*, Schlingensief announced his return to film, a medium he had officially abandoned in 1997 with *Die 120 Tage von Bottrop (The 120 Days of Bottrop)*.[9] But the situation was in fact somewhat more complicated. For one thing, Schlingensief had never really stopped making films; he had just brought film into the theater, both through his dominant use of filmic material, which was usually projected on several screens simultaneously, and through his

---

unit (Nekes, "Whatever Happens between the Pictures"). I will return to this point later in this chapter.

9. The movie was meant as a farewell to New German Cinema and to moviemaking in general. Its subtitle, *Der letzte Neue Deutsche Film (The Last New German Movie)*, underscored the farewell through its allusion to New German Cinema, the specific school of filmmaking that had dominated German cinema from the 1960s to the early 1980s, with directors like Rainer Werner Fassbinder, Werner Herzog, Alexander Kluge, and Hans-Jürgen Syberberg. For a detailed discussion of Schlingensief and his relationship to New German Cinema, see Langston, "Junger und Neuer Deutscher Film."

experiments in treating theater as live film. But in addition, *The African Twintowers* cannot be classified as a normal feature-length film, since it was never completed—at least not in any conventional way—but instead documented its own failure.[10]

The African Twintowers was the result of an accident instigated by the director himself. At the very beginning of the shooting, Schlingensief announced that the script had been stolen from him and was thus lost forever.[11] Then, in addition to the script being missing, he himself became more and more unreliable, often disappearing for hours and leaving the crew without a director. With no outline or clear direction, Schlingensief's team was left bored and confused, and when it came time for shoots was forced to improvise and react spontaneously.[12] And yet, this was exactly the situation Schlingensief had wanted to set up, convinced as he was that it was only under such circumstances that something unexpected could happen. Deprived of any guidelines, the team then created a movie for which no one could claim authorship, as *The African Twintowers* started drawing from film history. On shooting days, the crew reenacted films such as Luchino Visconti's *The Damned*, Russ Meyer's *Faster, Pussycat! Kill! Kill!*, Wim Wenders's *The State of Things*, and Fritz Lang's *The Nibelungs*. Working in this chaotic, disorganized way, Schlingensief collected more than 180 hours of extensive film footage, which was never edited. Thus, *The African Twintowers* exceeds any possibility of conventional on-screen presentation. The film was never shown in a movie theater. But the overwhelming amount of material that had been collected was presented in various constellations, including being displayed on parallel screens in theaters and museums.[13]

---

10. This is captured in the documentary *The African Twin Towers* (2009) and in the short movie *Say Goodbye to the Story (ATT 1/11)* (2011), both directed by Schlingensief.

11. Of course, the fact that the script was never shared with the crew and the cast already indicates that Schlingensief had never had any intention of following a script.

12. See the 2009 documentary produced by Schlingensief, *The African Twin Towers*, that documents the failure of the movie production and captures the frustration and irritation felt by the entire team.

13. The theater presentations included one at Hebbel am Ufer (HAU), Berlin, in 2008, and showings as part of Schlingensief's "Animatographic Editions," e.g., at

The African Twintowers was part of Schlingensief's "Animatographic Editions," a long-term project that grew out of the director's work in Bayreuth and the introduction of a rotating stage into his work.[14] The Animatograph was film, performance, action art, live concert, and installation; at the same time, it did not fit seamlessly into any of these categories. At the core of the Animatograph was a rotating stage that included additional structures that actors and the public could enter, walk through, and play on at the same time. The specific spatial arrangement varied depending on where the Animatograph was set up. Thus, some versions managed with only one revolving stage construction, while others significantly expanded this minimal installation and integrated a multitude of other stages and installations.[15] The Animatograph was composed mainly of materials found on-site. In addition, it gathered objects from the environment and functioned as both projector and projection surface.

Schlingensief described the Animatograph as a "cinema of the future" ("Schlingensief-Installation in der Burg").[16] What that future meant to him, however, was also necessarily a reinvestigation of historical principles and techniques from the prehistory of film.[17] That is where he believed he would find practices that could allow failures to happen and might help him to make the void possible in the

---

Area 7, Burgtheater Wien, in 2006. The museum presentations included a showing on parallel screens at the exhibition *18 Bilder pro Sekunde* (18 images per second), Haus der Kunst, Munich, in 2007, and at Neue Galerie, Graz, in 2008.

14. For a detailed discussion of this series, see Berka, *Schlingensiefs Animatograph*; and Hegenbart, "Animatographische Editionen."

15. This was the case for the German edition, *Odins Parsipark*, which took place at the former Neuhardenberg military airport in Brandenburg, Germany, in 2005 and at *Area 7* at the Burgtheater in Vienna in 2006.

16. Schlingensief emphasized the importance of film to the conception of the Animatograph in several places. In *Kaprow City*, he referred to the Animatograph as a "film reel" (Schlingensief, "*Kaprow City*, Program Notes").

17. Werner Nekes (with whom Schlingensief studied, as mentioned above) had the world's largest collection of optical objects and believed that the future of film could only arise from deep engagement with these historical objects. It was Nekes who introduced Schlingensief to these objects, and Schlingensief kept returning to him in order to discuss his theatrical settings, particularly his Animatograph. See Kovacs, "Zwischen Bildern"; see also Langston, "Junger und Neuer Deutscher Film," who emphasizes Alexander Kluge's importance in making Schlingensief fully understand and appreciate these objects.

usually highly controlled realm of theater. Early film proves to be an exceptional medium for failure. As the film scholar Mary Ann Doane argues, early machines for the production of the illusion of movement confronted their users with failure, because these devices relied on the fact that viewers could not trust their own senses. In other words, these mechanical devices were linked to defects that meant that the "body is no longer a transparent entity taken for granted but is subject to temporality and error."[18]

Schlingensief's very choice of the word Animatograph referred to the early history of film, emphasizing how essential the return to early mechanical devices was for the production of optical illusions in the context of his theater.[19] Once we understand this, the entire setting and layout of each "Animatographic Edition" becomes revealed as a reworked and revised version of those devices, machines, and inventions.[20] For example, Schlingensief constructed a structure for *Kaprow City* (2007) that resembled Thomas Edison's Black Maria (1893), the first recording and projection studio developed in the United States. In so doing, he emphasized the work in progress, inviting the audience into a setting where film was no longer limited to the final product that is cut before it is shown to an audience.

In addition to the Black Maria reconstruction, Schlingensief experimented with machines and techniques linked to experimentations with moving pictures from before the invention of film, such as the peep box. The setting of his controversial piece *Bitte liebt Österreich* (*Please Love Austria*, 2000) can be interpreted as an enlarged version of a peep show, because the fenced-in containers in the public

---

18. Doane, *The Emergence of Cinematic Time*, 81.
19. Schlingensief took the name "Animatograph" from Robert W. Paul's camera and projection apparatus of the same name, which Paul patented in 1896 and initially advertised as a "Theatrograph." With this invention, Paul wanted to renew stage design by replacing the traditional painted stage backdrops with projected images. The connection with Paul has been thoroughly discussed in the scholarship on Schlingensief. See, e.g., Hegenbart, "Psychic Interiors"; and Schaub, "Sich in den Weltzusammenhang hineindrehen."
20. While there are numerous articles and major works that address Schlingensief's references to Paul's Animatograph in detail, studies devoted to other such references are scarce. Exceptions include Kovacs, "Zwischen Bildern"; Hegenbart, "Psychic Interiors," 93; and Langston, "Junger und Neuer Deutscher Film."

space that were at the center of the work consisted of peepholes that promised passersby glimpses into the interior of the container. Work involving various versions of a peep box, in which Schlingensief positioned a variety of larger and smaller wooden boxes with holes and slits, remained central to the "Animatographic Editions." These constructions were intended to arouse the audience's curiosity, suggesting that through the constructions the audience could look into foreign worlds. In addition, Schlingensief adopted the zoetrope and the panorama, which had similar functions.

Schlingensief was also interested in early movement studies at the intersection of photography and the moving image, incorporating Étienne-Jules Marey and his invention of the photographic rifle (1881–82) as well as Eadweard Muybridge's famous motion studies (1872–79) into his "Animatographic Editions." He even dedicated the short film *Diana II: Muybridge-Film*,[21] which became part of *Kaprow City*, to Muybridge. In this reference to Muybridge, who is considered the father of the moving image,[22] Schlingensief points us toward a very specific aspect of the prehistory of early cinema, allowing us to better understand where he locates the potential of becoming that I call in this book the void. Muybridge studies are interested in the relationship between stillness and movement, and between individual images.[23] Like Muybridge, Schlingensief was attentive to the relationship between two images, particularly in their contradictions, dis/continuities, and ruptures. This becomes evident in his ongoing work on the expansion of the darkness between single frames and his work with superimposition.

---

21. At the beginning and end of this film, Schlingensief demonstrates the movement that Muybridge breaks down into individual images in his studies to subsequently have individual images fade away in the middle section of the film, superimposing movement and individual images, and allowing the movement to merge into a series of individual images. In his TV series *Die Piloten* (*The Pilots*, 2007), which is also part of the "Animatographic Editions," Schlingensief again references Muybridge. *Die Piloten* was promoted by Schlingensief as being a talk show in the dark phase that takes place between images.

22. Haas, *Muybridge*.

23. The film scholar Tom Gunning points out that Muybridge's fascinating power comes from the fact that with his series of images, he made things visible in their contradictions (Gunning, "Never Seen This Picture Before," 272).

Darkness and Superimposition

Schlingensief began making movies out of a deep fascination with the relationships between image and image and between image and sound. In Schlingensief's work, these relationships are never harmonious, because what he wanted to explore was the possibilities that arise from their discrepancies and ruptures. Here, two cinematic principles are central: the dark phase and superimposition. Both of these principles allowed Schlingensief to emphasize the moment that does not force an image with a predefined meaning on us but that instead inspires work and a form of meaning production that evolves from the interaction between the viewer and the cinematic material and the possibilities carried by that cinematic material.[24] He considered the dark between images not as an empty space but the realm of all possibility. By conceiving the dark in this way, it became crucial to his works as a place where the unexpected can appear and a creative process can take place that is not highly controlled. These two principles of the dark phase and superimposition, which were already an important part of his early feature films, were ones that he continued to experiment with in the context of his theatrical work, whether through the intensive use of film, usually projected onto several screens simultaneously as well as onto the bodies of the actors, or through the translation of these principles into the spatial arrangement of his theatrical works.

Both the expansion of the dark phase and the superimposition of images evolve from the difference between single frames, which Werner Nekes, the experimental filmmaker and Schlingensief's mentor, defined as the smallest element of cinematographic language and termed *kine*. Schlingensief shared his mentor's conviction that the exploration of the *kine* allowed insights into the creation of movement and that these insights could in turn expand the possibilities of film, film production, and film projection. In Schlingensief's case, this also included the realm of theater.

---

24. Here, again, Schlingensief is close to Kluge and how he understands the dark phase in film. See, for example, Kluge's conversation with Oskar Negt (Kluge, "What Does Nothingness Mean?").

In the cinematographic investigation of the smallest difference between single frames, Schlingensief saw a way to explore the relationship between stability and fluctuation, a relationship that he considered essential to everything that has been, is, and might yet be. He was inspired by neuroscience and the workings of our brain. As a child, Schlingensief had gone with his father to attend a lecture by a neuroscientist, from which he remembered one crucial insight: "to remember is to forget." Schlingensief was captivated by the plasticity of the brain. In particular, he was absorbed by the fact that the brain continuously re-forms itself, as some synapses stabilize but others decay, and by the type of flickering in-between this process creates, in which images can occur that are completely disconnected from reality and our actual experience.[25] Film, for Schlingensief, was a means to explore the plastic workings of the brain and the diffraction of time and space that results from those workings. Above all, he was interested in a subjectivity in which destruction and transformation are inseparable and in which error and failure not only destroy but, at the same time, also bear great potential for a re-formation and transformation of the subject. The dark phase between images, for Schlingensief, creates the realm that allows us to better understand that destruction and transformation, and life and death, teeter on a fine line and never fully settle.

There is barely a work that Schlingensief made in which he did not clearly refer to and make use of the darkness between single frames. This meant, first and foremost, experiments into the expansion of the darkness, where the single frames per minute are so reduced that movement is no longer a smooth process. Only then, according to Schlingensief, can we understand that movement and stillness, light and dark, destruction and transformation, life and death are not contradictions but rather coconstitute each other and are inseparably entangled. Schlingensief criticizes the emphasis on light in film, himself choosing to emphasize the importance of darkness instead: "Film is the blank space, the dark space. I always separate the image I see from the darkness in which it moves. Without darkness, there is no movement."[26]

---

25. Kluge, "Parsifal verlernen," 54:08–55:01.
26. Dax, "Ich glaube an die Peinlichkeit."

Darkness, Movement, and Metamorphosis   149

Schlingensief's concern with making visible the darkness that is constitutive for film, or even moving it to the center of attention, enters into his work predominantly through his provocative references to the director Jean-Luc Godard, who defined twenty-four frames per second as cinematic truth. Schlingensief overwrites this principle with his own truth of the radical reduction of frames, as it is only then that the dark gets enough room:

> According to Godard, a film consists of 24 frames per second. He says: "24 truths in a second." But there Godard is mistaken: that is at least 6 frames too many, because one starts to see a fluid movement beginning at 18 frames, even almost at 12 frames per second. So please remember: as of 12 frames it is almost fluid, as of 16 frames it is quite fluid, as of 18 frames it is fluid. But at 25, it's already so superfluous that there's no dark phase at all, and that phase is crucial. 18 frames per second is right.[27]

This commitment to the reduction in the number of frames per second finds its way into a large number of Schlingensief's works. The importance he places on the dark phase is probably best captured by his own short appearance in one of his last productions, *Mea Culpa* (2009), in which he projects and comments on individual scenes from past works that range from his 1985 film *Menu total* to his staging of Wagner's *Flying Dutchman* (2007). From the latter, he shows recordings from the rehearsal, in which the orchestra is positioned in the middle of the Amazon rainforest. We can hear his past instructions from the rehearsals, which he partially repeats and partially changes during his commentaries in *Mea Culpa* in order to finally reassure us that the reduction in the number of frames is at the core of his theater: "The expansion of the dark phase, that's

---

27. Schlingensief, "*Kaprow City*, Program Notes." Schlingensief wasn't consistent when talking about the number of frames per second in Godard. As we can see in this quote, he speaks about twenty-four and twenty-five frames per second. I decided not to correct this. "Laut Godard besteht ein Film aus 24 Bildern pro Sekunde. Er sagt: '24 Wahrheiten in der Sekunde.' Aber da irrt sich Godard, das sind mindestens 6 Bilder zu viel, weil der Mensch ab achtzehn Bildern, ja fast schon ab zwölf Bilder pro Sekunde anfängt, eine flüssige Bewegung zu sehen. Also bitte merken: Ab zwölf Bilder fast flüssig, ab sechzehn Bilder ziemlich flüssig, ab achtzehn Bilder flüssig. Aber bei 25 ist es schon so überflüssig, dass es gar nicht mehr zur Dunkelphase kommt, und die ist entscheidend. Achtzehn Bilder pro Sekunde sind richtig."

actually what I'm interested in right now. The dark section is getting longer and longer. It's getting darker and darker. It also stays dark longer than it used to. And Godard says 25 frames per second is the truth, right? Complete nonsense. There are people who can already see everything flowing perfectly starting at 13 frames per second. Me too, by the way. I only need 6 frames."[28]

Not only is the dark area between single frames essential for experiments with the relationship between movement and standstill, but it is also important for Schlingensief because of the way in which it changes how we perceive single images. The darkness is never nothing because we can perceive fluctuations and flickerings that remind us that it is a realm of potential and the groundless ground from which everything that we get to see in Schlingensief's theater forms. With an emphasis on the dark, on flickering, and on the production of decelerated movement, the images that are presented to us seem uncanny, monstrous, and eerie: they confront us with both movement and stillness, with both continuity and rupture, and with the possibility of images coming to life that might, however, also disappear immediately into darkness.

Closely connected to the dark phase is the superimposition of single images, which fascinated Schlingensief since his early childhood. This, too, had to do with a certain childhood experience. Schlingensief's father, a passionate maker of home movies, once forgot to change the film during a summer family trip to the beach, thus creating a double exposure. When the family watched the movie later at home, they could see the young Christoph lying next to his mother on the beach as well as shots of the beach and random people walking. Due to the superimposition of the frames, though, it seemed like the people were walking over and through the bodies of the boy and his mother. Schlingensief incorporated

---

28. Schlingensief, *Mea Culpa*. "Die Ausweitung der Dunkelphase, das ist eigentlich das, woran ich gerade interessiert bin. Das Dunkle wird immer länger. Es wird immer dunkler. Es bleibt auch länger dunkel als früher. Und Godard sagt 25 Bilder pro Sekunde wären die Wahrheit, ja? Völliger Quatsch. Es gibt Leute, die können ab 13 Bilder pro Sekunde schon hervorragend alles im Fluss sehen. Ich auch übrigens. Ich brauch' nur sechs Bilder."

this short home movie into many of his works, particularly the later ones in which he confronted the possibility of his early death.

Working with double and multiple exposures remained important for Schlingensief throughout his entire career. It entered his work as a means to create fragmented and hybrid images that established connections with diverse times and spaces. At first, this was limited to the films that he shot for the theater. Later, however, he also used the technique of superimposition in relation to the stage. In addition to using screens, he projected images onto the bodies of the actors, the audience, and elements of the stage in order to create complex temporal and spatial arrangements. This intensified the incongruities between the present and absent body, between existence and nonexistence, and emphasized the vast topology that unfolds in Schlingensief's works.

The "Animatographic Editions" are what best allow us to understand these forms of superimposition and multiple exposure that occupied Schlingensief until his death. In leaving the conventional theater space that separates the stage from the audience and creating instead his own spatial setting of diverse rotating platforms and projections which the audience could explore freely and at its own pace, he made it possible for different times and seemingly distant places to intermingle in a process of constant transformation. *The African Twintowers*, for example, included video projections from the earlier versions in Iceland and Germany while at the same time superimposing them with new images created in Namibia, where the structure was erected. Anyone who entered the continuously rotating platform in Namibia became part of a vast topography that linked Icelandic sagas, German history, and African myths. This came to a peak in Schlingensief's *Area 7: Matthäusexpedition* (*Area 7—St. Matthew's Expedition*), the biggest and final version of the Animatograph, realized at the Burgtheater in Vienna in 2006.

Area 7 occupied the entire space of the theater, thus dissolving the boundaries between stage, audience, foyer, and hallways. It consisted of numerous (revolving) stages that included not just live action but also textiles that were used as projection screens for videos Schlingensief had produced in Iceland, Namibia, and Germany in earlier versions of the work, as well as footage from his past

152   Chapter 4

Figure 1. *Area 7*. Christoph Schlingensief. Burgtheater
Vienna, 2006. © Georg Soulek

Darkness, Movement, and Metamorphosis 153

Figure 2. *Area 7*. Christoph Schlingensief. Burgtheater Vienna, 2006. © Georg Soulek

Figure 3. *Area 7*. Christoph Schlingensief. Burgtheater Vienna, 2006. © Georg Soulek

works. *Area 7* deeply challenged conventional modes of perception and cognitive patterns. As the art critic Sabine Vogel described it in her review of the piece, "too many images and words collide in his highly willful approach to meaning and logic."[29] This was a result of the installation being in continuous motion. Schlingensief forced the audience and the performers into the vast space of possibilities that arranged such seemingly unrelated and distanced fields as action art, physics, music, politics, religion, and environment alongside each other. In *Area 7*, German history met Icelandic and African mythology, animals met gods and historical figures, canonical texts met the avant-garde, Michael Jackson met Joseph Beuys, and living organisms met broken technological equipment. Namibia and the music of Bach were suddenly in proximity. Icelandic myths no longer seemed distant from the atrocities of World War II. In short, our usual thinking in terms of scale and within Newtonian categories of time and space collapsed, or rather exploded into constellations in which past, present, and future were constantly rearranged, and the local and the global seemed inseparable. In this installation, nothing existed that was not already entangled with multiple others. At the same time, differentiations between life and death, subject and object, human and nonhuman, here and there, nature and culture became blurred. Even more so, everyone and everything in this performance was paradoxically woven through each other: life and death, subject and object, human and nonhuman, here and there, culture and nature. This is due to the fact that, true to plasticity, the fragmentation that we experience in Schlingensief is not the opposite of synthesis. On the contrary, the Animatograph, with its continuous movement, not only cuts but also momentarily synthesizes these fragments and as such allows its audience to experience the ongoing practice of forming and transforming.[30]

---

29. Vogel, "Christoph Schlingensief."
30. For a detailed discussion of synthesis, see chapter 1, where I explain that synthesis must not be confused with a totalizing whole.

The Independent Life of the Material and Continued Movement

Along with the dark phase and superimposition, the materiality of film is key to Schlingensief's theater. He was primarily concerned with the fact that the material has a life of its own, which can create an artwork without any intention of the director. Here, too, Schlingensief repeatedly shared an anecdote to explain what he meant when he referred to the life and creative potential of the filmic material itself. In his first feature film, *Tunguska—Die Kisten sind da* (*Tunguska—The Crates Are Here*, 1984), he simulated the burning of the film itself. When the film premiered at the Hof International Film Festival, however, the film reel actually did start to burn, thus responding to Schlingensief's cinematographic trick with a surprising creation beyond the director's intention. For Schlingensief, the experience of sitting in the audience and helplessly observing how the film was melting made him understand that destruction and the unanticipated accident do not necessarily have to mean annihilation. Instead, we can perceive them as the radical possibility for new and different becomings.[31] From this moment on, Schlingensief obsessively worked on creating situations in which he lost control of the material so that an unforeseen event could happen. This remained true throughout his career.

Film is surely an exemplary medium for error and failure. As noted above, its coming into being cannot be separated from erroneous vision. How, though, did error and the independent life of the material make it into Schlingensief's theatrical works? How did he transpose this singular quality of film into theater? Here, his exploration of Wagner becomes important, in particular his introduction of a rotating stage into his production of *Parsifal*. As Alain Badiou argues in his thought-provoking *Five Lessons on Wagner*, the opera presents a complex approach to destruction and creation, life and

---

31. For Schlingensief's repeated sharing and discussion of this anecdote, see, for example, Kluge, "In erster Linie bin ich Filmemacher," 113; Schlingensief, *Kaprow City*; and Schlaich, *Interviewfilm*. This anecdote also came up in several interviews and became a part of numerous stagings by Schlingensief.

death, endurance and change that is fundamentally shaped by musical plasticity and metamorphosis. Badiou challenges established readings of Wagner that position him on the side of a teleological thinking that leads to resurrection and points out that the musical plasticity in Wagner contradicts the content of the opera and, in so doing, allows unpredictable transformations to take place that intrude into the teleological narrative structure and characters.[32] Schlingensief paid close attention to this specific quality of *Parsifal*, which he stressed in his own production of it in Bayreuth.[33] Being attentive to possibility and potential in Wagner, he once again turned to film as he began to understand that that was where he found the potential that he also needed to introduce into theater. In short, Schlingensief's engagement with *Parsifal* ultimately turned into a more conscious work with filmic principles in his theater, which became visible in his turn to the Animatograph as a "living film reel" that emphasized ongoing movement and metamorphosis.[34]

With the use of a rotating stage in *Parsifal*, which Schlingensief later called the "Ur-Animatograph," he introduced a structure that allowed the unanticipated to happen—a structure that was radically disconnected from the director's control or from his own appearance or presence onstage.[35] The form of failure that is introduced

---

32. Badiou, *Five Lessons on Wagner*, 89. Badiou claims for Wagner's operas: "What will enable a subject to be different by the end of a monologue . . . is structured much more crucially by the *transformative* role played by the themes than by their mere indicative role. . . . The essence of the Wagnerian theme lies in its potential to be transformed. It is this transformation that really conveys the subjective metamorphosis, thereby making the decision appear immanently, not in terms of 'I was such and such a way before, but now I am different' but rather in terms of a change from one state to the other in the discourse itself" (*Five Lessons on Wagner*, 89. Emphasis in the Original).

33. See Franziska Schößler's analysis of Schlingensief's *Mea Culpa*. Schößler ("Intermedialität und das 'Fremde in mir'") argues that Badiou's interpretation of Wagner, along with Žižek and Dolar's *Opera's Second Death*, can almost be considered a manual for how to understand Schlingensief's theater and his take on Wagner. I agree with her on this reading.

34. Schlingensief, "*Kaprow City*, Program Notes."

35. Here my reading clearly differs from established interpretations that see this autonomy from the artist as only having been realized in his final work, the Opera Village Africa in Burkina Faso (see Knapp, "Radikale Autonomie und Eigenleben im Film *Tunguska: Die Kisten sind da*," 105–7).

by the Animatograph stands in stark contrast to the unanticipated accident in Schlingensief's early works from the 1990s to the early 2000s, which relied on the presence of the director himself to disrupt the rehearsed protocol and force the actors to improvise—meaning, in other words, that it was still bound to the director's intentions. Comparing the Animatograph to Schlingensief's early works, it becomes obvious that it was only with the spatial setting of the rotating stage that he was fully able to realize the potential of the cinematographic principles he had been experimenting with from his first movie onward. In short, the Animatograph allowed Schlingensief to introduce a form of movement that he had been missing in his earlier works.[36]

The revolving stage corresponds to the approach of translating cinematographic modes of seeing into space and experimenting with them. On the one hand, the movement of the Animatograph is circular and does not progress but instead with each turn absorbs something that then becomes part of the rotating movement, and thus it expands or grows. On the other hand, however, it brings the viewers into motion and as such opens up new perspectives at every moment. This allows them to leave behind their entrenched patterns of perception and to explore a theatrical piece with all their senses. Confronted with a structure in ongoing motion, we are deprived of the image as something that we can frame and observe from a distance. But we also cannot limit the success of the Animatograph to the simple fact that the actors and audience are able to step onto it and freely move around it. There is something else at work that fulfills what Schlingensief was seeking to accomplish with his art, something that he captures when he compares the Animatograph to a living organism.

Terms like "organic" and "living" already gained importance in the context of Schlingensief's preparation for the staging of *Parsifal*.

---

36. Over the course of his career, Schlingensief became increasingly critical of his early films. For example, in a 1998 interview, he spoke of his films in terms of "snail movies" ("Schnecken-Filme") to stress that even though "they appear full of strength and motion, in reality you don't advance a centimeter." "Es wirkt wie Kraft, wie Bewegung, aber in Wirklichkeit kommt man keinen Zentimeter weiter" (Schlingensief, "Wir sind zwar nicht gut, aber wir sind da," 27).

But it was only with the Animatograph that they began to clearly dominate his works; they then remained important through his very last project, the Opera Village Africa in Burkina Faso, about which Schlingensief stated that "at its best, art is an organism that connects with life."[37] Organic metaphors are nothing unusual in the context of art. Indeed, they dominate the avant-garde and neo-avant-garde discourses of the twentieth century, the discursive contexts in which the scholarship has regularly positioned Schlingensief.[38] In Schlingensief, though, the organic is more than a mere metaphor used to mystify art in an attempt to make it become alive. Instead, Schlingensief's theater makes use of the vitality of matter and includes matter's own creativity in its artistic process.

In its attempt to highlight plasticity, the Animatograph went beyond everything else that Schlingensief had experimented with in his earlier works. It introduced movement into his theater, actually creating a void through the constant fluctuation, shaped by gaps and leaps from which the unexpected can arise without the director being personally involved in its creation. Human actors and matter both share the fact that they are created out of nothing, that they are formed through an error, an explosion, and, in their most radical form, through destruction. As such, matter in Schlingensief is not introduced as lifeless and formless, awaiting to be formed by the artist. Instead, Schlingensief's creative process must be understood as a dialogue and a form of relational cocreation and cosculpturing among the production team, the audience, and the inherent creative potential of the matter itself. In Schlingensief, plasticity is present in both its positive and its negative versions. Schlingensief's theater is clearly shaped by strong moments of disruption and by

---

37. Schlingensief, "Die Kunst ist." "Die Kunst ist im besten Fall ein Organismus, der sich mit dem Leben verbindet."

38. For the positioning of Schlingensief in the avant-garde, see Knapp, Lindholm, and Pogoda, *Christoph Schlingensief und die Avantgarde*; and Deutsch-Schreiner and Pewny, "Avant-garde! Marmelade! Avant-garde! Marmelade!" When it comes to the metaphor of art as an organism, Frederick Kiesler is a particularly interesting figure for comparison. He, too, wanted to renew theater with the help of innovative spatial settings that allowed the free movement of actors and audience. See Kovacs, "Flowing Space."

violent blasts. This is evident in the intense use of violence that is characteristic of his works and that enters them through the recurrent motif of the explosion (be it through an atomic bomb, as in his early movie *United Trash*, or through his repeated urge to cause high culture to explode), scenes of intense outrage, blood, weapons, and the destruction of large parts of the stage. And yet it is precisely these violent acts that allow the process of forming, re-forming, and transforming to take place. This brings us back, once again, to the video of the hare.

Movement, Metamorphosis, and the Wound as the Limit of the Image

The short movie of the decomposing hare that ends Schlingensief's *Parsifal* production and that becomes a central, recurrent sequence in all his subsequent works is only one example of the importance of the hare as a symbol, motif, and living organism within Schlingensief's theater. The hare appears in his works in such varied forms as, for example, a corpse for whom he plays songs from Wagner's operas, a living animal trapped in a cage, a stuffed animal to whom he explains the performance, and, in its preserved form, a religious relic. While the references that Schlingensief evokes range from art history (e.g., Dürer's *Feldhase*) to East Asian tales, the hare is most dominant in his works linked to the German performance artist Joseph Beuys, in particular to Beuys's seminal 1965 work *Wie man dem toten Hasen die Bilder erklärt* (*How to Explain Pictures to a Dead Hare*).

For Beuys, the hare was a symbol of incarnation and of humans' capacity for the active work of transformation that can bring about radical change or revolution: "[The hare] has a strong affinity to women, to birth and to menstruation, and generally to the chemical transformation of blood. That's what the hare demonstrates to us all when he hollows out his form: the movement of incarnation. The hare incarnates himself into the earth, which is what we human beings can only radically achieve with our thinking: he rubs, pushes, and digs himself into Materia (earth); finally penetrates (hare) its laws, and through this work his thinking is sharpened, then transformed, and becomes revolutionary."[39] Beuys relies here on the rich associations that the hare evokes because of its deep historical, symbolic meanings that span diverse cultures and religions. For him, this makes the hare an intriguing counterfigure to reason, a model for alternative forms of knowledge production and for the formation of the subject based on spirituality.[40] At the center of Beuys's interest in the hare is its function as a symbol for the human ability, as well as the ability of all other living organisms, to change, to transform, and to become radically other. In short, for Beuys, the incarnation symbolized by the hare is a model for how we as individuals, as a society, and on a planetary level can change.

Incarnation for Beuys is closely connected to movement, which he defines as the core trans/formative practice. Linking it back to Christianity, he speaks of resurrection through movement because it allows for the channeling of organic energy: "The principle of resurrection, transforming the old structure, which dies or stagnates, into a vibrant, life-enhancing, and soul- and spirit-promoting form. This is the expanded concept of art."[41] Thus, as we can see, the hare for Beuys is interconnected with spirituality, self-transcendence, and resurrection. While Schlingensief breaks with such an understanding and seeks to find a mode of transformation without redemption,[42] he is still deeply invested in metamorphosis and transformation as an underlying principle of life, as highlighted in Beuys's work, and almost notoriously returns to Beuys's practices that emphasize that the artistic work is a form of sculpting: that it is, in particular, a social sculpture (*Soziale Plastik*).

When the hare enters Schlingensief's theater as a symbol of rebirth and transformation, it is because Schlingensief, like Beuys, sees change and transformation as connected to the practice of movement. Movement is the underlying principle of his work from the

---

39. Beuys in Tisdall, *Joseph Beuys*, 101.
40. This is reflected in the strong connection between his performative works and shamanism.
41. Beuys in Rosenthal, "Joseph Beuys," 25.
42. In this context, note Schlingensief's comment about the Opera Village Africa, as quoted on the website of the project (Schlingensief, "We Will Not Redeem.")

beginning, but becomes best visible with the Animatograph and all his subsequent works.[43] The importance of transformation becomes evident in diverse contexts in Schlingensief's oeuvre, and he often thematizes it using the term "metamorphosis" or, as in the title and text of one of his last, unfinished works, "metanoia." Although metanoia emphasizes connotations of Christianity and thus of spirituality more generally, in Schlingensief, death ultimately does not lead to a superior form of life.

When we try to better understand the mode of transformation that underlies Schlingensief's theater, the injury, suffering, and wounds that I introduced in the context of his short hare film will become important once again. Here, too, Schlingensief is closely aligned with Beuys in that they are both convinced that transformation can only happen if we are willing to reveal our wound; this is another instance in which we can see the links to Wagner's *Parsifal*. The sick, suffering, and dying subject is the focus of Schlingensief's attention. Illness shapes Schlingensief's theater from his earliest works on, but it becomes more explicit in the projects that he carried out that are closer to *Parsifal*, for example Schlingensief's *Kunst und Gemüse, A. Hipler* (*Art and Vegetables, A. Hipler*, 2004), which includes the subtitle "Theater ALS Krankheit" ("Theater AS Illness"). The German subtitle, with the word *ALS* ("as") in capital letters, already names the most important part of the work: in this piece, Angela Jansen, a woman with ALS (amyotrophic lateral sclerosis), is positioned in the middle of the audience in her hospital bed, from which, with the help of a machine, she functions as director for the evening.

The question of the sick person's position in relation to society gains even more importance after Schlingensief's own cancer diagnosis. From that point on, his working through the question of who

---

43. Movement, for example, was already at the center of some of Schlingensief's *Aktionen* in the public sphere, such as *Chance 2000*. In this piece of performance art, he founded a party that officially ran for the German parliament in the 1998 German elections. The entire project was characterized by diverse forms of movement, including protest walks through Berlin, a shopping trip to the KaDeWe department store, and a concerted outing to Lake Wolfgang in Austria in an attempt to flood the house of Germany's then chancellor Helmut Kohl.

the sick person is and how that person can have a future and autonomy in the world becomes even more pronounced. We can see this in his "fluxus oratorio" *Eine Kirche der Angst vor dem Fremden in mir* (*Church of Fear vs. the Alien Within*, 2008). Quoting Heiner Müller, Schlingensief claims: "The essential thing is the transformation. Dying. And the fear of this last transformation is universal; it can be relied upon, it can be built upon. And this is also the fear held by the priest and the fear held by the congregation. And the special thing is not the presence of the living priest or of the living worshipper, but the absence of the potentially dying person."[44] Right next to that, Schlingensief adopts a credo from Beuys that builds the center of the performance: "He who shows his wound will be healed; he who hides it will not be healed."[45] What is emphasized here is the centrality of the wound, without which no healing process can be initiated, as well as plasticity as the underlying principle of all life. The wound is subsequently also tackled through the question of how best to represent it in the theatrical context. Schlingensief exposes the limits of a theater that is trapped in conventional forms of representation when reduced to the gaze and the eye. The wound cannot be made visible; it escapes any such presentation. Schlingensief reveals this by repeatedly returning to an image, namely the X-ray of his missing lung, which he embeds in a Christian ritual and places in a monstrance. While the monstrance is a receptacle for displaying sacred relics and as such meant to present a visible object to our gaze (the Latin *monstrare*="to show, to point out"), Schlingensief uses it to uncover the *limits* of any visual representation of the wound. In the X-ray, the wound is the dark spot: the black hole or void. When Schlingensief shifts our focus to the black hole, he shows that, paradoxically, the end of the image allows a theatrical piece to develop

---

44. Schlingensief, *Eine Kirche der Angst vor dem Fremden in mir*. "Das wesentliche ist die Verwandlung. Das Sterben. Und die Angst vor dieser letzten Verwandlung ist allgemein, auf die kann man sich verlassen, auf die kann man bauen. Und das ist auch die Angst des Priesters und die Angst der Gemeinde. Und das Besondere ist eben nicht die Anwesenheit des lebenden Priesters oder des lebenden Gottesdienstbesuchers, sondern die Abwesenheit des potenziell Sterbenden."

45. Schlingensief, *Eine Kirche der Angst vor dem Fremden in mir*. "Wer seine Wunde zeigt, wird geheilt, wer sie verbirgt, wird nicht geheilt."

that is overflowing with all kinds of possible images, although these images never fully stabilize but instead fluctuate on the edge between existence and nonexistence.

Even though Schlingensief is explicitly working through his personal experience of undergoing surgery and treatment for lung cancer, his individual experience is always also entangled with broader questions of individual/social/planetary change, freedom, and autonomy. The theater scholar Jasmin Degeling points this out when she reminds us of the specific context of the Beuys quotation on which Schlingensief relies. For Beuys, the wound is clearly the wound of a society, as his comment on his work *Zeige deine Wunde* (*Show Your Wound*, 1976) makes clear. Beuys writes, "Show your wound, because you have to reveal the disease that you want to heal. The space ... speaks of society's disease. Then, of course, the traumatic character is addressed. A wound that you show can be healed."[46] While the importance of the revelation of the wound at first suggests a psychoanalytical reading, in Schlingensief there is doubt expressed about whether the subject is actually able to reveal this wound. The possibility that Schlingensief proposes instead is that the subject and, more broadly, society might suffer from an event that cannot be assimilated into or appropriated by the subject. Thus, Schlingensief's exploration of the wound is closer to Malabou's cerebral subject than to psychoanalysis.[47] Showing the wound here is not the revelation of the repressed. Instead, it confronts us with wounds that we cannot make sense of and to which we are hermeneutically blind. Images of life-threatening cancer cells and of Schlingensief's wound are accompanied by an overwhelming number of highly unsettling, monstrous images and voices that force us to experience individual, societal, and planetary wounds at an ever-faster pace. And yet, although it is trapped in an enclosed system shaped by violence and injury, the wound nevertheless carries the potential for change and freedom, as Schlingensief

---

46. Beuys, in Degeling, "Heilung durch Kunst?," 188. "Zeige deine Wunde, weil man die Krankheit offenbaren muss, die man heilen will. Der Raum ... spricht von der Krankheit der Gesellschaft. Dann ist natürlich der traumatische Charakter angesprochen. Eine Wunde, die man zeigt, kann geheilt werden."

47. Malabou, *The New Wounded*, 203.

links it to the destructive form of plasticity and reveals that explosions can open up spaces for alternative becomings, for transformation, metamorphosis, revolution, and freedom.

Practicing Possible Endings: The Death of Art and Its Regeneration

The wound, the status of the one who suffers, and questions of individual transformation and radical changes of entire societies relate Schlingensief and Wagner (through Beuys).[48] Wagner was occupied with concepts like rebirth and regeneration from the early 1840s until his death in 1883.[49] Like Schlingensief, he linked these questions directly to the arts. We can see this not only in his operas but also in his theoretical reflections on the total work of art that builds on ancient Greek tragedy. While Wagner praised ancient Greek tragedy for its combination of different arts, we must keep in mind that at its center is the healing function of theater, which is captured in the principle of catharsis.[50]

Schlingensief, too, considered the healing function of ancient Greek tragedy to be important, but he believed it to have been lost in his time. His theatrical works must be seen as an attempt to reconnect to theater's potential for healing. This becomes obvious in his work with ritual and figurations from ancient Greek tragedy, his adherence to catharsis, and his repeated claim that his theater administers poison in small doses, which is essential for healing.[51]

---

48. Beuys's "social sculpture" has been thoroughly discussed in the research as a reinvention of Wagner's *Gesamtkunstwerk*. See, e.g., von Graevenitz, "Erlösungskunst oder Befreiungspolitik."
49. For a detailed discussion of Wagner's regenerational writings and the importance of notions like rebirth, see Molnar, "Inception of Wagner's Doctrine."
50. Molnar, "Inception of Wagner's Doctrine," 85.
51. See, for example, Schlingensief's statement that, "In the past, opera in Greek theaters was associated with the healing process. In Epidaurus, actual prescriptions were issued, doctors prescribed visits to the theater or opera. In those days, art and culture were also there to help people, something that we overstuffed European culture warriors have of course completely forgotten. We don't go to the opera to be cured, but a) we sit around there stupidly and think, where am I going to eat later, and b) we can't

Subsequently, we can see that even though Schlingensief was critical of Wagner, he did not simply reject Wagner's idea of the total work of art. Instead, he wanted to cause it to be exploded so that it could be reinvented and formed anew: "Because I always had the feeling that we also have to blow up this high culture. Not destroy it, I don't mean that, but simply let people in who don't really have anything to do with it and who will give it vitality again. I still can't quite get away from a term like the total work of art."[52]

What is it about Wagner's idea that continues to attract Schlingensief? I argue that it lies in Schlingensief's awareness of the total work of art as a theatrical means of making visible the precarious ontology that he experiences in our present, an ontology that radically challenges the line between life and death. This brings us back to the importance of the symbol of the hare. As Alexander Kluge points out, the hare was one of the most important links between Schlingensief and Wagner, whose "Good Friday Spell" in the third act of the opera was inspired by the hare. Wagner, like Schlingensief and Beuys, saw the hare as a fertility symbol and at the same time as a carrier of the "theatricality of Golgotha."[53] In short, the

---

be cured anyway." (Schlingensief, *Ich weiß, Ich war's*, 165). "Früher war es so, dass die Oper in den griechischen Theatern verbunden war mit der Genesung der Menschen. Da wurden in Epidaurus richtig Rezepte ausgestellt, da gab's Ärzte, die ihnen Theaterbesuche oder Opernbesuche verschrieben haben. Damals war Kunst und Kultur eben auch zur Heilung da, was wir vollgefressenen, europäischen Kulturkämpfer natürlich völlig verlernt haben. Wir gehen nicht in die Oper, um geheilt zu werden, sondern a) sitzen wir da blöd rum und denken, wo gehe ich denn nachher essen, und b) sind wir sowieso nicht heilbar." We also need to keep in mind that in his later works, where he predominantly focuses on his own cancer, Schlingensief introduces intriguing perspectives that involve reading Wagner through contemporary, neoliberal discourses around wellness and self-care, for example in Schlingensief's *Mea Culpa*, where he translates *Parsifal* into the setting of an Ayurvedic clinic. See Degeling, "Heilung durch Kunst?"

52. Schlingensief, *Ich weiß, Ich war's*, 166. "Denn ich hatte ja auch immer das Gefühl, man muss sie auch sprengen, diese Hochkultur. Nicht zerstören, das meine ich nicht, sondern man muss einfach Leute reinlassen, die damit eigentlich nichts zu tun haben und die da mal wieder Kraft reingeben. Ich kann auch immer noch nicht ganz Abstand nehmen von so einem Begriff wie Gesamtkunstwerk."

53. Kluge also points out that Wagner read an article by Alfred-Erwin Jahn that appeared in volume 14 of *Zeitschrift für deutsche Vorzeitforschung* (Journal of German prehistoric studies) in 1809 and that made Wagner think of the symbol of the hare in the context of compassion: "The suffering of the cross and the mirth of 'na-

hare symbolizes the thin knife-edge between life and death that both Schlingensief and Wagner considered essential for change and thus for the possibility of a future.

But why, then, in spite of all the resonances between Wagner and Schlingensief, has the final scene with the decomposing hare been perceived as an attack on and blunt contradiction of Wagner's praise of redemption? This final scene in Schlingensief clearly differs from common interpretations of Wagner that see him as an artist who synchronizes all elements in such a way that a totalizing whole can emerge, and as an artist who elevates art to a religion that forms a cohesive, violent, enclosed community in the ritual of performance.[54] Schlingensief's last scene clashes with the dominant understandings of *Parsifal* as an opera that promotes the mystification of art and that associates art with redemption, eternity, and the deferral of time.[55] Instead, Schlingensief insists on another possible reading of Wagner, arguing that *Parsifal* is not about redemption but about the acceptance of disappearance. "'Redemption to the Redeemer' signals the hard-won agreement with one's own disappearance. It means farewell to the world and farewell to art and farewell to oneself."[56] As he describes it again elsewhere, "The end is conceived as decay dancing on the music, giving birth to new life."[57] Schlingensief subsequently adopts this reading for Wagner's total work of art in general when he questions the endurance and monumentality of Bayreuth and instead stresses its ephemerality. "I think that Wagner's most beautiful idea was to build a dedicated opera house

---

ture's vernal laughter': the contrast seemed to him an opposite expression of the 'taxing burden of compassion.'" (Kluge, "The Complete Version of a Baroque Invention by Christoph Schlingensief," 243).

54. Annuß, "Christoph Schlingensiefs autobiografische Inszenierungen," 292. For a critique of such interpretations of Wagner, see Badiou, *Five Lessons on Wagner*.

55. See Lore Knapp, who positions Wagner in the broader context of the avant-garde and its attempt to create art that becomes life (Knapp, "Radikale Autonomie," 102–5).

56. Kaiser, "Es waren 100.000 Robben." "'Erlösung dem Erlöser' signalisiert das schwer erkämpfte Einverständnis mit dem eigenen Verschwinden. Das heißt Abschied von der Welt und Abschied von der Kunst und Abschied von sich selbst."

57. Schlingensief in Michalzik, "Der Todestag." "Das Ende ist gedacht als auf der Musik tanzende Verwesung, die neues Leben gebiert."

for each opera, to do a single performance, and then to burn down the house along with the score. That is fantastic because it means accepting decay and celebrating one's own end. I want to have that freedom."[58] The acceptance of decay and acknowledgment of one's own finitude, which are important for Schlingensief, hint at a form of regeneration as described by Malabou.[59]

In Schlingensief, healing and rebirth are not transcendental or metaphysical, even though he hints at both as he works through the questions of how to accept disappearance and how to think of an ending. The transformation of the hare in Schlingensief does not lead to the process of sublation, resurrection, and transformation into a superior life. Instead, the hare symbolizes the very banal process of suffering and dying and the radical possibilities that that process opens: death is framed not as the end but as an opening to exploring the possibilities of an ending.[60] We can understand this better if we include one more work in our discussion, Schlingensief's *Sterben Lernen: Herr Andersen stirbt in 60 Minuten* (Learning to die: Mr. Andersen dies in 60 minutes, 2009). This work promotes the idea that "immortality can kill" and links it not only to the individual's acceptance of their own death but also to the mortality of art. This is stressed in the performance when the slogan "Sterben lernen der Kunst" ("art learning to die") becomes important. How can we read this strange phrase? Schlingensief repeatedly emphasized that Wagner's music was deadly. He even went so far as to predict that the result of his staging of *Parsifal* might be his own death.[61] After his lung cancer diagnosis, he stuck to that

---

58. Schlingensief in Laudenbach, "Weehee, Weehee." "Die schönste Idee von Wagner finde ich, für eine Oper ein eigenes Opernhaus zu bauen, eine einzige Aufführung zu machen und danach das Haus samt der Partitur zu verbrennen. Das ist toll, weil es bedeutet, Verwesung zu akzeptieren und das eigene Ende zu feiern. Diese Freiheit will ich haben."
59. Malabou, "Again: The Wounds of the Spirit." For a detailed discussion see chapter 1.
60. See Badiou, *Five Lessons on Wagner*. See also the notes by Carl Hegemann, the dramaturg for Schlingensief's *Parsifal* production. Hegemann, "Werkstatt Bayreuth," 268.
61. "I am convinced I'll get cancer after *Parsifal*, like Heiner Müller." Schlingensief in Laudenbach, "Weehee, Weehee." "I'm very moved when I hear that *Parsifal*

claim even more fiercely.[62] As the literary scholar Lore Knapp argues, Schlingensief drew the conclusion that when eternal art is deadly, then art has to become mortal.[63] Only then will it no longer lead to death but be able to become a source of healing.

Schlingensief critically challenged dominant twentieth-century approaches that wanted to bring art closer to life through a mystification of art as eternal. We can see this in his numerous returns to the artistic practices of the early avant-garde, which he took up in his works only to go beyond them. I want to suggest that the mortality that Schlingensief wants to make productive is not the result of yet another form of the mystification of the vitality of art,[64] as Knapp claims, but rather the acknowledgment of plasticity and transformation as the underlying principle of art and life. In art and in life, destruction and construction, determination and contingency, explosion and possibility are inseparably interwoven with each other.

Therefore, beginning with *Parsifal* and spanning his work from the "Animatographische Editionen" to his works on cancer, Schlingensief's theater can be read as a rehearsal, as ongoing practice for how to die and how to come to an end.[65] In his production of *Parsifal*, this exploration is still closely connected to the figure of Parsifal himself. This changes, however, in Schlingensief's later works, which are deeply shaped by his own experience with illness and death. In these works, he shifts his focus and makes the figure of the director himself the point for this inquiry. All of Schlingensief's later works, with the exception of the long-term Opera Village Africa project in Burkina Faso,[66] work through different possible deaths and endings. *Eine Kirche der Angst vor dem Fremden in mir* stages the future

---

was Wagner's departure from the world. Deep inside I have imagined that it's my departing piece." Schlingensief in Michalzik, "Schlingensief in Angst und Schrecken," quoted in Malzacher, "Citizen of the Other Place," 198.

62. Schlingensief, *So schön wie hier kanns im Himmel gar nicht sein*, 171.
63. Knapp, "Radikale Autonomie," 103.
64. Knapp, "Radikale Autonomie," 103.
65. See also Hegemann, "Sterben lernen?," where Hegemann characterizes Schlingensief's theater as a "practice in dying" (333).
66. This long-term project was meant to secure Schlingensief's legacy. In his final works, he included the idea for the Opera Village Africa in his reflections on possible endings and critically challenged his own need to create a lasting legacy.

dead director's own memorial service, in which Christian ritual and the traditions of avant-garde art (particularly those of the Fluxus group and its happenings) are intertwined in order to investigate practices of endings; *Mea Culpa* adopts Wagner's *Parsifal* as a way to think through death as metamorphosis; and *Sterben lernen: Herr Andersen stirbt in 60 Minuten* transfers the illness to the fictional character of Mr. Andersen in order to repeatedly rehearse the last minutes of a person's life.

In Schlingensief, death, destruction, and explosion are essential in order for the subject to experience freedom, because these processes guarantee that one will be able to break away from a given script and form anew. Only through such an explosion is something like healing possible. In Schlingensief's work, however, healing does not mean transforming into a superior life, nor can we understand it from a deconstructive angle, as a healing that produces cuts and traces. The Animatograph, as a spatial structure that eliminates the filmic cut and replaces it with constant movement and transformation, makes this clear. Badiou argues that the finale of Wagner's *Parsifal* represents the "transmutation of sovereignty into gentleness," meaning that it replaces "moribund, narcissistic, deathly Christianity with a new, reaffirmed Christianity around the idea of a central, innocent self-denial."[67] Badiou suggests that, understanding the finale in such a way, Amfortas's cure is "actually a kind of death" that allows a metamorphosis from power into gentleness;[68] I argue that Schlingensief's hare film must be read in a similar way and that, more generally, Schlingensief's theater explores this potential for change and metamorphosis introduced by Wagner's music. Yet Schlingensief then goes beyond Wagner: for Schlingensief, change and transformation are no longer bound to Christianity and self-denial but connected instead to forms of ease, pleasure, and joy for the plastic subject.

---

67. Badiou, *Five Lessons on Wagner*, 112.
68. Badiou, *Five Lessons on Wagner*, 112.

5

D-Dramatik or "Darwin-Type Theater"

Unpredictability and Singularity in René Pollesch

> I really can't explain it using Newton anymore,
> this thing between us.
> —René Pollesch, *Probleme Probleme Probleme*

At the beginning of René Pollesch's *Probleme Probleme Probleme*[1] (Problems problems problems, 2019), Marie Rosa Tietjen enters the

---

An earlier version of this chapter was published in *Seminar: A Journal of Germanic Studies* 58, no. 3 (2022): https://doi.org/10.3138/seminar.58.3.4. Reprinted with permission from University of Toronto Press, © *Seminar: A Journal of Germanic Studies*. That earlier version, however, did not consider Pollesch's interest in Darwin nor discuss Pollesch's theater through the void.

Epigraph: "Ich kann mir das mit Newton wirklich nicht mehr erklären, das hier zwischen uns."

1. The word *Probleme* here, in its ambiguity, evokes scientific problems or "troubles," the scientific method, the troubles science is involved in, and the troubling potential of the sciences.

stage, seemingly exhausted. She is in conversation with Sophie Rois and Angelika Richter, two other performers who enter with her.[2] Even though she is walking onto the stage, however, she does not address or take notice of the audience but simply keeps speaking to Rois and Richter in a colloquial manner, more like a backstage conversation than an opening sentence onstage. Consequently, the audience is forced to pay close attention in an effort to pick up even parts of the conversation. Sitting in the theater for this entrance, it does not feel as though someone is *performing* for us. Nor does it feel like someone is performing *for us*.

This disconcerting relationship between the stage and the audience speaks to the main characteristics of Pollesch's theater. Pollesch investigates how Brecht's radical demand for a "theater without an audience," as Brecht formulates it in the context of his *Lehrstücke* (learning plays),[3] can be implemented in our present. He criticizes a theater that wants to *present* something *to* the audience and that assumes a continuous relationship between stage and auditorium. Instead of unquestioningly accepting such a relationship and assuming that the director and actors will be able to communicate their intentions to the audience without interruptions, and that those intentions are guaranteed to be understood by the audience, Pollesch asks, "What if this audience didn't exist?"[4] Here Pollesch radicalizes Brecht's critique of bourgeois illusory theater in which he shows not only that the drama creates a false illusion on stage but that the spectators themselves and their relationship to the stage

---

2. Pollesch never uses characters in his plays, but always the actual names of the performers.

3. The English translation was suggested by Brecht himself. It differs from the German, which stresses the role of the educator when speaking of *Lehre* (education) rather than the role of learning (*lernen*). And yet the English better captures Brecht's attempt to create a theater for learning through participation.

4. Pollesch, *Der Schnittchenkauf*, 10. "Was wäre, wenn dieser Zuschauer nicht existiert?" Pollesch can be read with Jacques Rancière and his reflections on pedagogy as formulated in *The Ignorant Schoolmaster*, as well as with his claims in *The Emancipated Spectator*. Pollesch and Schlingensief share their deep concern with the position of the audience and the fact that they both challenge the usually unquestioned relationship between stage and audience. For a detailed analysis of this aspect in Schlingensief, see Kovacs, "Götterdämmerung im Ruhrgebiet."

are similarly an illusion. Pollesch repeatedly talks about the tearing down of the imaginary fourth wall between stage and auditorium that Brecht called for, making the point that it is no more than an empty phrase and that nothing changes in the relationship between spectator and stage as long as we leave the position of the spectator unquestioned. Pollesch therefore ironically and provocatively counters this demand with the opposite alternative, namely the materialization of the fourth wall, since it is only when the spectators are no longer shown anything and when the actors are no longer playing *for* a spectator that theater can be radically renewed.[5]

The uncertainty about the audience leads to another question: If the actors are not playing *for us*, who is the audience? Given that, even though we as spectators fulfill all the conventional codes of the theater—we have bought a ticket, we sit down in our seats at the right time, and we become quiet when the start of the performance is signaled—the actors are no longer perceiving, addressing, or accepting us as an audience and we are forced to think more carefully about our own position in the context of the theater. Not only do we get the feeling that it requires work from our side for us to gain a meaningful part in the performance (even if that means nothing more than being accepted in the role of the spectator) but the situation also allows a sense of ghostliness to arise—a sense that does not affect the audience in the theatrical works by the other playwrights and directors described in this book. Because they are used to theatrical conventions, the audience cannot but feel like intruders from the past or future when they are confronted with a piece that addresses someone but obviously not the present audience. And because of this feeling of being displaced and having fallen out of time, the audience is forced to engage more sincerely with both positions (of the audience and of the stage) and to engage with temporalities that push beyond time, as linear floating.

In this chapter, I discuss how Pollesch's interest in the sciences, particularly quantum physics and Darwin's theory of evolution, informs his theater of the void and his rethinking of the relationship between theater and the audience as well as the relation between

---

5. Pollesch, *Der Schnittchenkauf*, 18–19.

theater and the world. His engagement with the sciences allows him to introduce the void as a realm of possibilities without necessarily relying on the kind of catastrophic event that still so crucially fuels Müller, Jelinek, and Schlingensief. For Pollesch, catastrophes are too intermingled with our thinking in terms of the "dramatic" and "tragic," a kind of thinking that shapes our approach to the world and is primarily constructed by way of Hollywood blockbusters, along with the mass media and their daily headlines. Pollesch is critical about the affective regime that is linked to this kind of capitalist sensationalism; he makes it clear that emotions have become a mere surplus value in our neoliberal societies.[6] Being sensitive to the role of emotions in our present, though, does not mean that Pollesch simply abandons tragedy. Instead, he believes that we need a farewell to tragedy, because only such a farewell will reveal that the tragic is actually lost in our present. "Tragedy—this term should be rendered useless for the audience. The audience should realize, based on your tragic stories, that this is exactly what is missing."[7] Pollesch's theater confronts us with the intense emotions produced in our societies—predominantly with the desire to love or be loved—only to confront us with their superficiality. The big emotions present on stage are always accompanied by a kind of indifference on the part of the actors portraying them, because Pollesch is convinced that in our highly affected capitalist societies, only indifference can promise freedom.[8] This indifference is accompanied by the radical questioning of prevalent understandings of the notions of Self and Other, as well as of the human as such. Once again, science becomes an important tool with which to question the category of humankind.

---

6. Here Pollesch is close to Müller and his critique of the indulgence of apocalyptic thinking in the 1980s. But what we find more strongly reflected in Pollesch is a neoliberal society shaped by the post-1989 loss of an alternative economic and political system. For a detailed analysis, see the chapter on Pollesch in Sieg, *Choreographing the Global*.

7. Pollesch, *Der Schnittchenkauf*, 13. "Tragödie—dieser Begriff müsste für das Auditorium unbrauchbar gemacht werden. Die Zuschauer müssten merken, anhand eurer tragischen Geschichten, dass genau das fehlt."

8. Pollesch, *Der Schnittchenkauf*, 14.

Pollesch adopts Brecht's belief that theater must engage with the newest findings in the sciences if it wishes to have a future. This becomes clear in Pollesch's poetological text *Der Schnittchenkauf* (Buying canapés, 2011–12), which paraphrases Brecht's unfinished theoretical piece *Der Messingkauf* (*The Messingkauf Dialogues*, also sometimes translated more literally as *Buying Brass*), written during the late 1930s and early 1940s, in which Brecht lays out the importance of the sciences to his theater. Pollesch specifically makes reference to Brecht's differentiation between two types of theater, *K-Dramatik* and *P-Dramatik*, and he wants to overcome the former through the latter. While the *K* in *K-Dramatik* refers to the *Karussell* ("merry-go-round" or "carousel") and describes a kind of theater that relies on the audience's empathetic involvement, the *P-Dramatik* is based on the principles of the planetarium, meaning that it is a scientific theater that inspires critical observation.[9] Pollesch adopts this differentiation but replaces Brecht's terms with *R-Dramatik* (representational-type theater) and *D-Dramatik* (Darwin-type theater). While the first references the same type of bourgeois theater that Brecht had in mind when he described *K-Dramatik*, the latter highlights Darwin and thus specifies what kind of science Pollesch has in mind for reenvisioning theater. In this shift to Darwin, Pollesch replaces Brecht's focus on critical observation, as the essence of everything that is and might yet be, with mutability. In other words, Pollesch shifts his focus to the void that is the ontological point of departure in Darwin's *On the Origin of Species*.

With his *D-Dramatik*, Darwin-type theater, Pollesch reinvents Brecht's theater of the scientific age, which stressed a critical observation from a distance, as a theater of the void in which being is conceived as without essence and substance, shaped instead by indeterminacy and mutability. Yet, while observation and thus the focus on the eye are replaced by the experience of the void as the indeterminate source of all that is and might yet be, scientific observation nevertheless still plays a role. Observation now is part of an entangled, intra-active phenomenon in which things are not a predetermined given but only *become determinate* through the exclusion of

---

9. Brecht, "K-Typus und P-Typus," 387–89.

others in the moment of observation. What becomes determinate, though, does not depend on the observer but happens intra-actively between the audience, performers, stage, and director.

In the first part of this chapter, I draw attention to the way in which Pollesch starts to integrate the sciences into his theater, beginning with the work of the feminist biologist and philosopher of science Donna Haraway. For Pollesch's theater, Haraway's notion of diffraction as an alternative critical practice to reflection is central, as it offers a new way of thinking about difference that is not trapped in the production of the same elsewhere.[10] Scholars have so far mostly thought of Pollesch's references to Haraway as mere intertextual markers. I will show, however, that these references indicate a critical engagement with drama and representational theater that relies, for Pollesch, on identification and empathy and that promotes the human as its center. After discussing Haraway's importance for Pollesch's theater, I will shed light on how Darwin enters the discussion and explain why he becomes a central reference point for Pollesch's theater. In the second part of this chapter, I will focus on Pollesch's turn to quantum physics and link it to his attempts to challenge theater as an intentional institution that follows predefined rules which reproduce norms. Following Karen Barad, we can recognize how quantum physics allows for a queering of such norms, as it basically reveals nature as queer, monstrous, and unruly. Barad's interpretation of the double-slit experiment becomes important in that it is closely linked to the notion of diffraction in Haraway. Yet, in making diffraction the basis of a new ontology and epistemology (*ontoepistemology*), Barad expands it even further.[11] I take this as my starting point for discussing Pollesch's concrete interventions into Brecht and for showing what a Darwin-type theater that starts from nothing means for Pollesch. Ultimately, I ask whether and how Pollesch's theater claims to be a realistic kind of theater, maintaining a relationship with the world, but not the relationship of a mirror.

---

10. Haraway, *Modest_Witness*.
11. Barad combines ontology and epistemology in their writings to emphasize that they cannot be separated but are deeply entangled.

What Is the Human? Rethinking Theater through Biology

Pollesch has repeatedly challenged the reduction of theater to the historical form of drama and its mode of representation as linked to the eye, as this would cement a particular notion of the human and would define theater as an anthropocentric space. For Pollesch, drama is too involved in exploring the universal essence and truth of human nature, which reduces the human to soul and spirit; what he wants to do in his theater instead is to take the material reality of all living beings into account. So, while conventional representational theater is involved in the re/production of norms that center on the white, heterosexual, able-bodied, middle-to-upper-class male, Pollesch seeks to find a new theatrical practice that goes beyond a metaphysics of the human. In framing the performers' bodies as living organisms rather than embodied minds, he breaks with the idea of universal truths, drawing heavily on Haraway's reconceptualization of the human in relationship to other species.[12]

Beginning in 2005, when Pollesch began engaging with Haraway's works, her writings served as the starting point for a number of his plays, from *Cappuccetto Rosso* (2005) to *Passing* (2020). This engagement is sometimes evident in the title of his plays, such as his 2019 play *(Life on earth can be sweet) Donna*, while at other times it is more obscure. However, Haraway's writings have also influenced Pollesch's theatrical practice more generally. He regularly finds settings that translate her arguments into comedic genres and into explicit conversations about relationships between humans and nonhumans. His plays often include artificial animals and technical stage devices that no longer function as props but instead become performers on their own. Moreover, in the last few years of his life, an interest in science fiction was clearly observable in Pollesch's plays, inspired by Haraway's practice of *sf* as first introduced in her *Staying with the Trouble*. In Haraway's own generative language, *sf* can stand for a number of things, including string figures, science

---

12. See Haraway, *Modest_Witness*; Haraway, *Staying with the Trouble*; and Haraway, *When Species Meet*.

fiction, science facts, and speculative fabulation. Despite this wide range of possible meanings, however, *sf* always remains connected to the playful practice of multispecies world-making. It follows relationships and weaves multiple species together, dissolving and transforming existing knots of the pattern while also creating new ones.

Even though Pollesch's interest in science fiction came rather late, other practices that Haraway subsumes under *sf* shaped Pollesch's theater from his early successful performances at the Volksbühne in Berlin, particularly her thinking about difference, thought, and alterity in terms of diffraction. Haraway uses diffraction as a metaphor to challenge a thinking in terms of reflection and to emphasize a more complex relationship between Self and Other, one that is attentive to patterns of interference. Diffraction is an important concept for Haraway's critique of representationalism, which Pollesch applies to his critique of representational theater. The German studies scholar Jack Davis has convincingly shown that Haraway functioned as an important inspiration for Pollesch's *Cappuccetto Rosso* (2005).[13] To confront the mechanisms of representational theater, Pollesch makes the bodies of the actors readable here not as human beings but as an "assemblage of nonhuman forces."[14] This becomes evident when one of the actresses, Caroline Peters, claims that her body is being eaten up by a fungus. Therefore, she concludes, what we see can no longer be conceptualized as "the human"; instead, what we are seeing is a eukaryotic organism. While Davis does not deal with the notion of diffraction in his analysis, I consider this notion to be crucial to a better understanding of Pollesch's theater. In his earlier works, it introduces the critical potential that can be gained from thinking about the body as an assemblage of human and nonhuman forces rather than treating the corporeal as an enclosed entity; in his later works, it allows him to connect theatrical practice with quantum physics.

As Haraway suggests, diffraction replaces thinking of the other either as sameness or as radical other with thinking in terms of a

---

13. This is the first of Pollesch's plays to explicitly connect his critique of representational theater with an ecological and posthuman discourse.
14. Davis, "Who's Afraid of Kommissar Rex?," 33.

threading and going through one another.[15] She relies on optical metaphors in order to set diffraction apart from reflexivity, a mode that has, she argues, dominated Western philosophy and science. Thinking of difference in terms of diffraction changes our critical practice: "Reflexivity has been much recommended as a critical practice, but my suspicion is that reflexivity, like reflection, only displaces the same elsewhere, setting up worries about copy and original and the search for the authentic and really real."[16] Because diffraction opens critical consciousness to diverse metaphors of difference while dismantling any notion of original, it is a compelling concept with which to think about Pollesch. His theater contains practices like fragmentation, sampling, and collage, meaning that the plays create a complex patchwork of quotes from pop culture, Hollywood movies, and theory. These practices have been linked to postmodernism and read as nonpolitical art that has lost its connection to the world,[17] but when it is read through Haraway, Pollesch's sampling, in particular, can be understood as something other than mere postmodern play. Sampling is connected to a critical mode that can be considered diffraction.

Pollesch challenges drama and representational theater as forms promoting a critical practice of reflection that violently excludes everyone and everything that is not part of the Western conceptualization of the human. In Pollesch's theater, this particularly entails a focus on gender norms. More concretely, he attacks the conceptualization of theater as a moral institution as defined by Friedrich Schiller.[18] Pollesch criticizes this kind of theater as being defined by mimesis, understood as imitation, and often conceived as a mirror of the world; in Haraway's words, it contributes to the "production of the same elsewhere."[19] Pollesch's theater does not

---

15. Diffraction as conceived by Haraway allows a link to Foucault's trans-subjectivation and the thinking about difference and change in Malabou's philosophy of plasticity. See chapter 1.
16. Haraway, *Modest_Witness*, 16.
17. See above all the critique of Pollesch in Stegemann, *Lob des Realismus*, 184–88.
18. Schiller, "Die Schaubühne als moralische Anstalt betrachtet."
19. Haraway, *Modest_Witness*, 16.

reflect onstage on discourses from other spheres, nor is it disconnected from the world. Instead, it investigates its own entanglements in the production of differences by making heterogeneous histories visible and allowing us to examine diverse histories of and interactions between theater, gender, technology, and capitalism. Moreover, while theater as a moral institution is concerned with the social life of human beings, Pollesch, in keeping with Haraway, theorizes a theater in which the human and the nonhuman are entangled. This shift becomes explicit when he provocatively rewrites Schiller's 1784 speech "Theater Considered as a Moral Institution":[20] "What is wanted is the theater as a moral institution or as a conservationist recollection or as a medium of humane values in society. But what that totally neglects or, if you will, intentionally neglects is to question the human and to problematize whether the human being or reality can still be processed with the categories of humanity at all. How about the morality of beetles or of monkeys for a change?"[21]

Pollesch urges us to critically question any framework based on the category of humanity and the human more generally. This does not imply an antihuman perspective. Instead, as I have already noted, it is connected to his critique of thinking of the human in terms of a universal essence and truth, a kind of thinking that he seeks to undermine. His theater replaces the exploration of *the* human with an attention to individual beings and their relationships to their environment, social contexts, etc. In other words, Pollesch

---

20. Schiller's original speech was inspired by the question "What can a theater of good standing actually achieve?" The speech concludes, "Each takes joy in others' delights, which then, magnified in beauty and strength, are reflected back to him from a hundred eyes, and now his bosom has room for a *single* sentiment, and this is: to be truly *human*." (Schiller, "Theater Considered as a Moral Institution.") Emphasis in the original. Schiller's understanding of what good theater can do has shaped the theatrical landscape in the German-speaking countries ever since.

21. Pollesch and Raddatz, "Die Probleme der Anderen," 25. "Gewollt wird das Theater als moralische Anstalt oder als konservierende Rückbesinnung oder als Medium der humanen Werte in der Gesellschaft. Dabei wird aber total verpasst oder, wenn man so will, gewollt verpasst, das Menschliche in Frage zu stellen und zu problematisieren, ob der Mensch oder die Realität mit den Kategorien der Humanität überhaupt noch zu bearbeiten ist. Wie wäre es zur Abwechslung mal mit der Moral der Käfer oder der der Affen?"

rejects an understanding of the human as predefined or as having any particular essence or substance, instead viewing the human as an indeterminate being in constant transformation. Similarly, his theater is opposed to the idea that the world is composed of preexisting, independent entities. Instead, he highlights the world as constituted through relationships and in the meeting of matter and meaning. In short, Pollesch views the world as becoming, as a worldmaking or "worlding," instead of the world as being.

Thus, it is not surprising that Charles Darwin becomes central to Pollesch's theater, as reflected in his poetological text *Der Schnittchenkauf*. Drawing on new research on Darwin that appeared around the biologist's two hundredth birthday in 2009, Pollesch, clearly influenced by the historian Philipp Sarasin's new approach to the biologist, views Darwin not simply as a promoter of the survival of the fittest but as a thinker of mutability.[22] By reading him alongside Foucault, Sarasin presents Darwin as a key philosopher who radically challenged any stable distinction between nature and culture and any thinking about being in terms of essence and substance. In so doing, Sarasin reveals the historicity that Darwin finds in nature since, according to Darwin, biological evolution cannot be separated from culture because it takes place in the tension between determination and contingency, conscious work and accident.[23]

For Pollesch, this new interpretation of Darwin is crucial, as it undermines thinking about the human and other species in terms of determined beings. We can see this when Pollesch makes explicit references to Darwin as someone who allows us to understand that evolution is random and that similarities are linked to a shared

---

22. See Sarasin, *Darwin und Foucault*. Pollesch may have attended Sarasin's 2007 talk "Foucault liest Darwin: Bemerkungen zu einer stillen Referenz" (Foucault reads Darwin: Notes on an implied reference) at Berlin's Center for Literary and Cultural Research, or at least read about it in the newspaper *taz*, since Pollesch explicitly refers to the example of the cat that was central in this talk and in the report in the *taz* ("Die Katze ohne Plan").

23. Sarasin's argument very much aligns with Malabou's reading of the void in Darwin (see the introduction of this book).

D-Dramatik *or "Darwin-Type Theater"* 181

living experience rather than to any predetermined characteristics: "There is nothing here to talk about and nothing to communicate but body, body, body. And when we say soul here, we only say soul because of the body, that [soul] is the body, that there in front of us! There is nothing in there that responds as hope to the scratching of the skin. The scratching is outside. Yes, I know, you would like to conclude from the scratching on your body that there is an inside, and tell yourself a drama that you think is your life, yes, I know. But there is no drama."[24] Again, we see here that Pollesch opposes drama as an art form that promotes an understanding of a universal essence and truth of human nature that reduces the human to soul and spirit. Instead, he turns to the body and to material existence in order to then introduce into his theater Darwin's emphasis on a being's mutability and plasticity, rather than stability. In understanding Darwin this way, Pollesch makes him the basis of his theater, which seeks to emphasize that existence is something that starts from the void and allows the quasi-infinite possibility of structural change constituted by the absence of predetermination.

Once more, this allows Pollesch to set his theater apart from conventional drama. As Pollesch makes clear in *Der Schnittchenkauf*, Darwin's theory means that we must radically rethink what makes a conversation between different entities possible, given that all modes of conversation that have so far been established still rely on the mistaken assumption of a shared human essence. In other words, Darwin allows Pollesch to question a theater based on dialogue. What Pollesch claims instead is that theater first and foremost needs to admit that we do not know how to actually communicate and connect to each other, as language obviously fails: "The

---

24. Pollesch, *Der Schnittchenkauf*, 11. "Es gibt hier nichts zu bereden und nichts mitzuteilen als Körper, Körper, Körper. Und wenn wir hier Seele sagen, sagen wir nur Seele wegen dem Körper, die ist der Körper, das da vor uns! Es gibt nichts da drinnen, was auf das Kratzen an der Haut als Hoffnung aufspringt. Das Kratzen ist draußen. Ja, ich weiß, du würdest gerne vom Kratzen an deinem Körper auf ein Inneres schließen, und dir ein Drama erzählen, das du für dein Leben hältst, ja, ich weiß. Aber es gibt kein Drama."

similarity of our bodies does not form the basis for a successful conversation. Indeed, it could be that when someone tells a story, one body to the other, that only one hand understands it, and the other cannot follow the story."[25]

Not yet fully able to grasp what a theater based on Darwin might look like, Pollesch starts by saying what "Darwin-type theater" is not. First of all, for Pollesch, theater has to stop relying on any form of relation or communication based on empathy. In this, he clearly connects with Brecht, seeing emotions and empathy as having been appropriated by capitalism and now being nothing but a form of surplus value, as I have already noted. Similarly, Pollesch criticizes the need for theater to tell a story, as formulated in Aristotle's *Poetics*, as a means of touching our emotions. Instead, he calls for a theater in which we remain indifferent but at the same time open to actual and meaningful relationships: "On the contrary, the person on the stage should be able to sit atop the ruins of a tragic story, indifferently checking to see whether their stocking seam has gone crooked."[26] For Pollesch, theater needs to rethink its entire situation, since the new way of thinking about existence applies not only to the stage but also to the audience. Pollesch makes it clear that theater must acknowledge that if *the* human does not exist, we also have to bid farewell to *the* audience. Instead—and this is the starting point for Pollesch's theater—we have to acknowledge the bodies that are assembled in a specific room on a specific day for a singular event, and to take their relationship seriously. This is Pollesch's point of departure when he reinvents theater as Darwin-type theater.

---

25. Pollesch, *Der Schnittchenkauf*, 11. "Die Ähnlichkeit unserer Körper bildet keine Grundlage für eine gelungene Konversation. Es könnte nämlich sein, dass, wenn jemand eine Geschichte erzählt, ein Körper dem anderen, dass es nur die eine Hand versteht, und die andere kann der Geschichte nicht folgen."

26. Pollesch, *Der Schnittchenkauf*, 14. "Der Mensch auf der Bühne sollte ganz im Gegenteil auf den Trümmern einer tragischen Geschichte sitzen können, und er sieht unbeteiligt darauf, ob sich seine Strumpfnaht verzogen hat."

Queerness and Groundlessness: Pollesch's Theater through Quantum Physics

While references to biology are almost ubiquitous in Pollesch, his works contain only one reference to quantum physics. Nonetheless, this reference is no less important for only appearing once. It introduces another way for Pollesch to promote a theater that is attentive to the queer, obscene, and monstrous nature of all existence (and when I use the word "nature" here, we need to keep in mind that in the context of Darwin, it is as much culture as nature). To better understand the importance of quantum physics for Pollesch, we must turn once again to *Probleme Probleme Probleme* and take a closer look at what is suggested there.

The opening scene of the performance introduces a sequence of actions that are hard to make sense of: the three actresses repeatedly enter and exit through two similar-looking rectangular openings in a wooden wall that is covered with curtains.[27] These portals are the only openings connecting the front of the stage with the back, which remains invisible to the audience for the first part of the performance. The actresses neither address nor pay attention to the audience, and they repeat the same conversation whenever they come through one of the portals. The evening seems to be stuck in an endless loop.

The dynamics of the scene shift when two more performers, Sachiko Hara and Bettina Stucky, join the original three, Tietjen, Rois, and Richter. Now the group starts going through both portals at the same time while repeating the conversation (two of them through one portal, three through the other). They are dressed in black and white so that the interplay of their bodies creates a new black-and-white pattern whenever they step through the portals. For the audience, it is hard to make sense of this opening scene. In any attempt to follow the conversation, though, one topic stands out—Tietjen's complaints about a double performance (*Doppelvorstellung*) that she has to be in. Not only does it leave us wondering

---

27. The stage design is by Barbara Steiner.

what Tietjen means by a double performance, it also suggests that the evening might already be underway or, even worse, that it is already over. Rois ultimately offers an alternative interpretive frame for the claim of a double performance that leaves the realm of theater and instead connects the evening to quantum physics or, more concretely, to the double-slit experiment:

> M: You know what, I'm really exhausted. These double performances really totally wear me out. And I can't remember whether I've already said that today.
> S: What?
> M: Well, this here.
> A: Tell me, am I cross-eyed, or are there two stages here?
> M: Well, you heard it. It was a double show.
> . . .
> S: We played the double show at the same time? Listen! We're not in a theater here, we're in a . . .
> H: She was right! We were not in a theater, we were in the most important experiment of modern physics. The double-slit experiment. Of course, nobody knew how we got into it.
> S: Yes. It was strange. We were in the middle of an experiment. Something I didn't really want to have anything to do with in the theater. But it was the double-slit experiment, after all. A hundred years ago a little experiment with light introduced us to the idea that logic cannot be applied everywhere: and we were in the middle of it. We didn't know when it had started. Maybe it had been going on forever.[28]

---

28. Pollesch, *Probleme, Probleme, Probleme*. Transcript from the performance.
"M: Wisst ihr, ich bin ganz schön fertig. Diese Doppelvorstellungen machen mich ganz schön fertig. Und ich kann mich nicht erinnern, ob ich das nicht heute schon mal gesagt habe.
S: Was denn?
M: Na, das hier.
A: Sagt mal, schiel ich oder sind das zwei Bühnen?
M: Du hast es doch gehört. Es war eine Doppelvorstellung.
. . .
S: Wir haben die Doppelvorstellung gleichzeitig gespielt? Hört mal! Wir sind hier nicht im Theater, wir sind in einem . . .

In referring to the double-slit experiment, Pollesch introduces one of the most important experiments in modern physics into his play. This experiment consists of light that is sent through two parallel slits in a screen in order to then hit a second screen on the other side of the wall, on which a black-and-white pattern of interference (diffraction) becomes visible. The experiment was first conducted by Thomas Young in the early 1800s and showed that light behaves like waves; before the experiment, light had been understood as a particle. With the advent of quantum physics, the experiment became essential to proving that not only does light behave like a particle, meaning that it bounces off a surface, but it *also* behaves like a wave, meaning that it breaks up and creates patterns of interference when it encounters an obstacle. In short, the double-slit experiment revealed the essential paradox of quantum physics: namely that things can exist in more than one state at a time.

The double-slit experiment is key to understanding not just *Probleme Probleme Probleme* but also Pollesch's theater in general. His theater creates the unassignable place par excellence, as it deprives us of any certainty and instead confronts us with bodies and identities in constant mutation, always appearing to be more than one thing at a time. In other words, the reference to the double-slit experiment in *Probleme Probleme Probleme* goes beyond the obvious and consciously naïve adaptation of the stage setting and costumes, shaping the very core of Pollesch's theater.

While the use of the wooden wall with its two portals translates the double-slit experiment to the stage, adopting its setting and the movement of the light particles for the choreography of the initial scene, the rest of the production translates the paradoxical quantum phenomenon of existing in more than one state at a time into diverse

---

H: Sie hatte recht! Wir waren nicht in einem Theater, sondern im wichtigsten Experiment der modernen Physik. Dem Doppelspaltexperiment. Natürlich wusste keiner, wie wir da hineingeraten waren.
S: Ja. Es war merkwürdig. Wir waren mitten in einem Experiment. Etwas, womit ich im Theater eigentlich nichts zu tun haben wollte. Aber es war immerhin das Doppelspaltexperiment. Ein simples Experiment mit Licht eröffnete uns vor 100 Jahren, dass Logik nicht überall anzuwenden ist: und wir waren mittendrin. Wir wussten nicht, wann es angefangen hatte. Vielleicht lief es schon ewig."

Figure 4. *Probleme Probleme Probleme*. René Pollesch. Deutsches SchauSpielHaus Hamburg, 2019. Actresses from left to right: Angelika Richter, Marie Rosa Tietjen, Bettina Stucky, Sophie Rois, and Sachiko Hara. © Thomas Aurin

paradoxical constellations: the visible front of the stage is framed as the backstage of the invisible back part of the stage by the way in which the actresses speak about it, but at the same time, the front of the stage is the stage that we, the audience, see and is thus the main stage; in addition, the two portals onstage sometimes demarcate two separate stages on the left and the right, and sometimes function as connectors between front and back. The clear separations that exist in a conventional play between spaces like the stage and the backstage become blurred in *Probleme Probleme Probleme*. The entrance is also the exit; mediated videos are also unmediated scenes. Furthermore, the performers claim to be performing two plays simultaneously, Heinrich von Kleist's *Das Käthchen von Heilbronn* and William Shakespeare's *A Midsummer Night's Dream*, and they seem to be in both a rehearsal and a performance. During the whole play, the performers switch between lines from *Das Käthchen von Heilbronn* and *A Midsummer Night's Dream* while commenting on their

Figure 5. *Probleme Probleme Probleme*. René Pollesch. Deutsches SchauSpielHaus Hamburg, 2019. Actresses from left to right: Angelika Richter, Bettina Stucky, Sophie Rois, and Sachiko Hara. © Thomas Aurin

own situation of being trapped in this "double performance." Simultaneously, the performers treat the show as a finalized piece that is being presented to the audience while also continuously interrupting each other, as is typical for a rehearsal.

During the show, there is one line, uttered in the middle of a discussion about a possible romantic relationship, that clearly signals a shift from classical to quantum physics and therefore illustrates the critical practice behind the paradoxical situation explained above: "I really can't explain it using Newton anymore, this thing between us."[29] More than just a funny translation of physics into the social, this line is a key to Pollesch's overall diffractive theatrical practice—conceived not through optics, as in Haraway, but through physics. Concretely, this practice emphasizes a shift from

---

29. Pollesch, *Probleme, Probleme, Probleme*. "Ich kann mir das mit Newton wirklich nicht mehr erklären, das hier zwischen uns."

stable categories and determinations (Newtonian physics) to fluctuation, queerness, and indeterminacy (quantum physics).

Barad's claim that quantum physics brought about a new ontoepistemology that is anchored not in essence and substance but rather in indeterminacy relies on the double-slit experiment, which allowed quantum physics to develop as a field. As Barad explains, in classical Newtonian physics the double-slit experiment is the "ultimate ontological sorting machine" that draws stable boundaries between waves and particles.[30] What it shows based on quantum physics, however, as Barad argues, is actually the contingency and mutability of identity. This interpretation of the double-slit experiment helps Barad to identify diffraction as a queer phenomenon, or as something that no longer sorts and separates things but instead foregrounds the fact that it is one movement of differentiating-entangling (cutting together-apart[31]). Here we can see an important link to Pollesch's theater. Viewing conventional theater as a similar "sorting machine," Pollesch wants to move beyond such a logic and create a theater that finally breaks with the ongoing reproduction of norms: "I do not believe that theater should be a place where it is mainly 'healthy' people who have their say. What society calls 'healthy.' What that means in the theater is that we then mostly see attempts to represent and further cement what society presents as 'healthy.' Heterosexuality, productivity, and so on."[32]

Pollesch gives a concrete example of how strongly theater is trapped in the production of norms when he claims that the simple stage direction "A man enters" is already enough to reveal the normalizing function of traditional theater. He highlights that in the German theatrical landscape, this sentence will broadly be interpreted as "A white, heterosexual man enters." According to Pollesch, if some other body was expected to appear, it would have to be

---

30. Barad, "Diffracting Diffraction," 173.
31. See footnote 21 in the introduction of this book.
32. Pollesch, "Ich würde gern in der U-Bahn schreien," 320. "Ich glaube, Theater darf kein Ort sein, in dem vor allem 'Gesunde' zu Wort kommen. Was man so gesellschaftlich 'gesund' nennt. Im Theater kommen dann meistens nur Versuche heraus, das zu repräsentieren und weiter zu zementieren, was die Gesellschaft als 'gesund' ausgibt. Heterosexualität, Leistungsfähigkeit und so weiter."

explicitly marked.³³ Pollesch wants to counteract this by making possible a theatrical void in which the unexpected and the singular can appear. Turning again to Barad, we can ask what the double-slit experiment might offer to Pollesch's theater in this context. To find an answer, we need to pay attention to the notion of diffraction as an alternative mode to reflection and as what allows Barad to link quantum physics to Haraway's critique of Western critical thought. In Barad, diffraction is developed as a concept that challenges any metaphysics of the subject and that instead introduces a performative approach to science studies and knowledge production more generally, which ultimately undermines the reproduction of norms: "*Performative* approaches call into question representationalism's claim that there are representations, on the one hand, and ontologically separate entities awaiting representation, on the other, and focus inquiry on the practices or performances of representing, as well as the productive effects of those practices and the conditions for their efficacy."³⁴ This performative approach has two important implications for how difference can be understood. First, it troubles representationalism—the mirror—which frames identity and difference as concepts with absolute boundaries. Instead of thinking of the other as a "non-I" that stabilizes and maintains the "self," in the sense of a reflection or mirror, diffraction allows the appearance of—and here Barad references Haraway and her use of a wording used by the filmmaker and theorist Trinh Minh-ha—"inappropriate/d others," who cannot be fixed by difference.³⁵ In short, diffraction asks us to be attentive to the practices that constitute difference.

When entities lack clear boundaries that set them apart, notions of determination also change. Here Barad relies on Niels Bohr, who proved, based on quantum physics, that "there aren't little things wandering aimlessly in the void that possess the complete set of properties that Newtonian physics assumes . . . ; rather, there is something fundamental about the nature of measurement interactions such that, given a particular measuring apparatus, certain

---

33. Pollesch and Raddatz, "Die Probleme der Anderen," 25.
34. Barad, *Meeting the Universe Halfway*, 49.
35. Barad, "Diffracting Diffraction," 172.

properties *become determinate*, while others are specifically excluded. Which properties become determinate is not governed by the desires or will of the experimenter but rather by the specificity of the experimental apparatus."[36] Drawing from Bohr, Barad stresses a performative approach, which rejects any assumption that there are preexisting, individual entities that later encounter each other, instead emphasizing the becoming of entities in their relationality. Thus, Barad's interpretation of the double-slit experiment presents an understanding of being as anchored not in essence and substance but in indeterminacy and mutability. Through quantum physics, Barad conceptualizes an ontology of the void that is similar to Darwin's. But Barad goes one step further, also taking into account the position of the observer in an experimental setting, which, they argue, must be radically reconsidered.

Barad argues that recognizing the importance of the observer for the status of the observed does not simply mean that the observer intervenes in an experiment, since intervention still assumes a preexisting, individual entity. Instead, the observer and the observed coconstitute each other in the moment of observation. As such, Barad speaks not about the observer and the observed but about the apparatus, which is not merely an instrument of observation. On the contrary, apparatuses are "*specific material configurations, or rather, dynamic (re)configurations of the world through which bodies are intraactively materialized.*"[37] Consequently, for Barad, *phenomenon* and *apparatus* are terms that can be linked to entangled world-making.

How exactly does this coconstitution unfold? Drawing from Bohr, Barad shows that apparatuses operate based on exclusion. Following Bohr's "complementarity principle," they describe the way in which phenomena can act in more than one state at a time. However, only one of the states can be observed at any given moment. As such, it is impossible for all quantities to become determinate. On the contrary, the determinate quantities are complementary to the indeterminate ones and vice versa.[38] Instead of accounting for the impossibility of

---

36. Barad, *Meeting the Universe Halfway*, 19. Emphasis in the original.
37. Barad, *Meeting the Universe Halfway*, 169–70. Emphasis in the original.
38. Barad, *Meeting the Universe Halfway*, 20.

determining all quantities by applying metaphysical assumptions,[39] though, Barad argues with Bohr, that we must consider the actual experimental conditions that allow one to measure and create meaning. This, again, shows that difference is no longer understood as an absolute boundary between object and subject, here and there, now and then, this and that, but rather as the effect of exclusions produced through the specific constellation of the apparatus. It is a cutting together-apart that produces not absolute separations but rather entanglements that are constantly reconfigured.[40]

Through Bohr's complementarity principle, Barad sheds light on the political dimension of their performative approach to scientific practices. They argue that their theory can also be expanded to social constructs such as gender, sexuality, class, race, and ethnicity. These are neither determinate nor properties of individual persons but are entangled in discursive-material becoming. Quoting Judith Butler and their analysis of the differential practices that produce the more or less "human," be it inhuman or nonhuman, Barad summarizes: "Any proposal for a new political collective must take account of not merely the practices that produce distinctions between the human and the nonhuman but *the practices through which their differential constitution is produced.*"[41] Hence, the "through"—the encounter, meeting, and going through of in/determinate entities—and the relationships come into focus.

What Barad shows here is that the double-slit experiment, which in Newtonian physics is the ultimate sorting machine, in quantum physics is revealed as a mode of queer critique. And Pollesch, likewise, suggests that such a reinterpretation is also possible for theater. Theater doesn't have to be the institution that secures norms

---

39. Barad prefers Niels Bohr's complementarity principle over Werner Heisenberg's uncertainty principle, which would lead to that kind of metaphysical assumption. Heisenberg's principle suggests that in the moments of observation, electrons are disturbed and thus cannot fully be observed and described. But, as Barad argues, while Heisenberg develops an epistemological principle that engages with the question of what we can know, Bohr's principle yields rather to questions of "what can be said to simultaneously exist" (Barad, *Meeting the Universe Halfway*, 115–18).
40. Barad, "Diffracting Diffraction," 174.
41. Barad, *Meeting the Universe Halfway*, 59. Emphasis in the original.

but can instead become a queer space, inhabited by all kinds of monstrous entities. Barad's focus on the position of the observer in an experimental setting has important implications for Pollesch. It allows him to rework the position of the director and the audience, having them share the position of the coconstitutive observer/observed in an experiment who only come into being in the moment of their intra-action.

This is a radical step, similar to Schlingensief, as even the most experimental forms of political theater had never before managed to break with the intention of the director, which then had to be communicated to an audience.[42] Pollesch clearly sees this as the most shocking deficiency of political theater: "Behind it is this seriousness of the left, of the leftist heterosexual man who conducts from the barricades. And the audience wants that instructor. The one who preaches down from the pulpit the interpretation of *Intrigue and Love* or *Nathan the Wise*. This hierarchy is the worst thing of all."[43] Connecting the position of the omnipotent director to the audience's desire to be activated from above, which are both hallmarks of twentieth-century political theater, Pollesch finds this constellation insufficient for two reasons. First, "*the* audience" does not exist and, as such, any vision of it being activated will not really change the rules and norms of conventional theater but only contribute to the standards already established, cementing the position of the director as the center and intentional grounding rather than dismantling it. Second, Pollesch understands a claim for activation as being no more than a mere *intervention* into the stage action. To use Barad's words here, this type of theater is still trapped in a thinking of preexisting, individual entities. Pollesch is concerned that such an intervention does not go far enough. His theater is therefore deeply shaped by an awareness of creating an apparatus

---

42. For a discussion of how Schlingensief breaks with the intention of the director see chapter 4.

43. Pollesch, "Der Ort, an dem Wirklichkeit anders vorkommt," 317. "Dahinter steckt dieser Ernst der Linken, des linken heterosexuellen Mannes, der von der Barrikade aus dirigiert. Und das Publikum will den Unterweiser. Der von der Kanzel herab die Lesart von *Kabale und Liebe* oder *Nathan der Weise* predigt. Diese Hierarchie ist ja das Schlimmste überhaupt."

in which the audience and the stage *coconstitute* each other. In other words, Pollesch seeks to create a space that is without qualities, without privilege, without legacies, and without tradition. In his vision of theater, entities that are similarly undetermined can meet and experience, from the shared experience of the void, how things become determinate, appear, and disappear, and within this process make the unpredicted and singular possible.

A Theater That Starts from Nothing

How exactly does Pollesch's theater make such a space possible? How does this concretely shape his theatrical practice? First and foremost, it happens in the process of creating a piece. Following Brecht's conception of his *Lehrstücke* as a theater without an audience and without a rehearsal, Pollesch imagines a theater where the production process does not simply focus on creating a polished final product that is then shared with the audience. On the contrary, he stresses the coproduction and cocreation of all elements of a performance by emphasizing theater as work and as a practice. This ultimately means that even when the plays are performed in front of an audience, the making of the piece remains visible. For example, the actors reflect on and refer to the rehearsal process. Additionally, they are often accompanied by the prompter, who otherwise usually remains invisible in the theater, in order to emphasize that the words being spoken by the actors are not authentic to them but that it requires labor and practice to make them audible on the stage.

Pollesch is aware of the importance of the shared process. Like Schlingensief, who deprives the actors of a finalized script, Pollesch never presents the actors with an already existing, finalized text. Instead, he shares an observation or a problem that is of interest to him with the other members of the production team. He approaches the questions or topics by finding a theoretical text that helps him think them through. The working process then starts with a joint reading. This reading is accompanied by applying the abstract terms and concepts of the theoretical text to the everyday experiences of the team members as well as by translating them into mass cultural phenomena, accomplished in part by the team watching Hollywood movies together. Then, based on the conversations with the team, the first element that takes shape for the piece is the stage design. "The first author of our performances is the stage designer,"[44] Pollesch writes. This emphasizes not only that the unassigned place does not preexist but that it needs to be created. Moreover, it underscores that theater is more than the spoken words. Only later in the rehearsal process does Pollesch start to write a text that he shares with the actors, and that he then continually rewrites based on the actors' relationship to the text. If the team involved in the production does not share Pollesch's interest in a question or a problem, they find a new problem that is relevant to all of them and with which they want to engage. Hence, the text does not exist separately from the space, the people, the movement, and the objects that are part of the working process.

Understanding this production process better, we can see why the play can never result in a conventional theatrical dialogue. None of the individual actors can claim ownership of specific sentences. Instead, they share the sentences and develop a curiosity about the differing outcomes, depending on who says what. This process is also the basis for Pollesch's insistence that the texts cannot be restaged. This restriction is not grounded in any claims of ownership or originality but is connected to the understanding that a play is dependent on its specific situation. Repeating a play in a different theater, with different performers involved in its making, would drastically change the outcome.

When the plays are ultimately performed in front of an audience, we can see that what Pollesch's theater wants to create is a place that is not yet predefined. As such, all the markers that usually guide and prepare the audience for a performance are eliminated. This means, for example, that most of the time, the title Pollesch chooses for individual pieces is unrelated to what actually unfolds on stage. Similarly, Pollesch avoids providing any synopsis of the play, instead sharing

---

44. Pollesch, *Schnittchenkauf*, 5. "Der erste Autor unserer Abende ist der Bühnenbildner."

only a short sequence from the performance on the theater's website or in program booklets. In short, when we enter a Pollesch play, we usually do not know what to expect. For example, in his piece *Carol Reed* (2017),[45] the title refers to the British director Carol Reed, who set his famous 1949 Cold War spy movie *The Third Man* in Vienna. Yet there is not a single reference to Reed in the entire play.

Moreover, the majority of Pollesch's works begin with the actors noticing that the set has disappeared or that they are in the wrong set. For example, in *Carol Reed*, the actor Martin Wuttke enters the stage only to realize that something is missing: "Mon Dieu, where is the set?"[46] *Carol Reed* subsequently turns to Alfred Hitchcock and his theory of the MacGuffin in order to work through the question of how an action can be inspired and how it can unfold without reproducing norms and a form of storytelling that are based on the production of empathy. Hitchcock uses the term "MacGuffin" to describe an object that sets the story in motion but remains meaningless to the audience.[47] Pollesch adopts the MacGuffin for his own theater as a way to create an alternative to a drama that has a coherent storyline and psychologically motivated characters. And yet, in the context of his theater, Pollesch clearly transforms the function of Hitchcock's MacGuffin. In Hitchcock's movies, the MacGuffin disappears as soon as it has set the plot in motion.[48] In Pollesch's play, by contrast, the MacGuffin—even though meaningless in the sense that it does not function as a signifier that represents something else—does not disappear but rather gains importance as the play goes on. What is stressed here is that we are confronted with a Darwin-type theater that starts from nothing and where nothing we see or hear is meaningful in a way that awaits our interpretation. On the contrary, we are faced with a performance in which nothing

---

45. *Carol Reed* premiered in 2017 at the Akademietheater, one of the Vienna Burgtheater's three venues. My quotations from the play are based on a recording of the dress rehearsal on April 28, 2017.
46. Pollesch, *Carol Reed*. "Mon Dieu, wo ist denn das Bühnenbild?"
47. Truffaut, *Hitchcock*, 138.
48. As François Truffaut summarizes it in his conversation with Hitchcock: "As the action moves forward, the MacGuffin will pretty much be forgotten" (Truffaut, *Hitchcock*, 138).

seems to make sense. But it is precisely in this lack that the void, as the indeterminate source of all that is and might yet be, becomes palpable in Pollesch's theater.

Toward a New Realism: World-Making

Pollesch's theater has often been criticized for its lack of any connection to the world or the real.[49] Such a reading is the result of framing his practices in terms of a postmodernism or a postdramatic theater that seemingly turns away from representational theater and drama, which are related to the world by imitation and representation. While the latter present an enclosed fictional cosmos, a world in its totality—whether through the stage functioning as the mirror of an outside world or as a world of its own[50] —it is hard to grasp how Pollesch's theater might maintain a relationship to the world and to the real. Here, the void becomes important because it allows us to better define the relationship between Pollesch's theater and the world.

Pollesch's theater, which is more interested in the *effects* of difference than it is constituted by difference itself, no longer suggests totality as the model for the real but instead proposes that the real is iteratively constituted in the mutual encounters between different elements. Consequently, we need to pay attention to how representation is reworked in Pollesch. Barad stresses that representationalism, with its understanding of a world composed of individuals, promotes a tripartite logic of knowledge, the known, and the knower, with the knower mediating between the signifier and the signified.[51] What underlies this logic is the assumption of an ontological gap between independently existing entities. In the context of theater, this would translate into the questions of how one can accurately represent the world, and how one can accurately represent the individual within a given character. But such questions no

---

49. Most recently, Bernd Stegemann argued for a new realism on the stage in order to combat the postmodern practices that he found in Pollesch (Stegemann, *Lob des Realismus*, 184–98).

50. Lehmann, *Postdramatic Theatre*, 22.

51. Barad, *Meeting the Universe Halfway*, 46.

longer apply to Pollesch. On the contrary, his theater closes the gap that representational theater, in following that logic, creates.

When theater adheres to a representational logic, with knowledge clearly positioned on the side of the production team, it takes on the function of the mediator. Its main concern is to make things intelligible for the audience and thus to bridge the gap between stage and audience. Pollesch's intervention, however, does away with any such setup. His theater is no longer a mediator because there is no independently existing world, individual, and so forth. Instead, his theater is part of the iterative constitution of phenomena, part of world-making. This has an impact not only on the relationship between stage and audience but also on the structure of the production team itself. In such a theater, the audience intersects with the production team in the moment of performance. When knowledge is dispersed and intra-actively produced, the director can no longer be positioned as the one who comments on and observes preexisting problems from a distance.

This finally brings me to the question of what importance the visual aspect and the gaze have in Pollesch's theater. While I have stressed, in discussing Müller, Jelinek, and Schlingensief, that they challenge conventional forms of representation by breaking with the importance of the image and the gaze in theater, Pollesch's theater seems to continue to rely on the gaze, given that the terms I have used to speak about his theater have not pushed beyond the sphere of observation. And yet, in Pollesch, seeing is radically different from and no longer connected to the theatrical gaze. He works with sets that complicate our understanding of our eyes as reliable tools with which to perceive the world. The sets are shaped in such a way that most of the time, large parts of the stage are hidden and can only be made visible with the help of video cameras and projections, which give the audience an intimate view of enclosed spaces. While such practices have predominantly been discussed as a critique of technology and mass media, I argue that they introduce a specific mode of seeing that allows a link to quantum physics. Using the example of a scanning tunneling microscope (STM), Barad explains that quantum physics drastically changes how we think about seeing, because the particles are so small that an optical microscope does not allow one to see them at all. The STM is used instead to "see" a particle when it scans the surface: it is a practice that is no longer bound to optics and the eye but involves multiple parts coming together. "Seeing," then, does not simply mean just looking through a lens and seeing; it is sensory and must be practiced. It includes understanding all of the elements of the process of arriving at an image. Barad stresses again that it is not about the observer as the one who intervenes. If we no longer think in terms of preexisting entities, we also have to give up on thinking of an entity that is positioned outside. Instead, what we have is the becoming determinate of entities in their mutual exchange.[52] This is the kind of seeing that Pollesch's stages demand from their audience and from everyone involved in the performance: that is, a form of seeing that lets go of an optical understanding of sight. The audience has to become attentive to the circumstances of the production process and realize that it is not outside but, in fact, within the observed phenomena and thus part of the production of cuts, boundaries, and exclusions.

In such a theater, realism must be understood in a new way. Here, too, Barad offers a compelling alternative that I suggest applying to Pollesch's theater. Barad emphasizes that a conceptualization of realism that continues to be based on representationalism's metaphysical assumptions of the existence of individual entities with separately determinate properties disregards the fact that "realness does not necessarily imply 'thingness.'"[53] Hence, they promote a realism of phenomena, understood as "neither individual entities nor mental impressions, but entangled material agencies," which they summarize as follows: "The agential realist understanding that I propose is a non-representationalist form of realism that is based on an ontology that does not take for granted the existence of 'words' and 'things' and an epistemology that does not subscribe to a notion of truth based on their correct correspondence."[54]

Barad's *agential realism* allows me to link Pollesch's theater to realism without connecting it to the specific realism, committed to

---

52. Barad, *Meeting the Universe Halfway*, 51–55.
53. Barad, *Meeting the Universe Halfway*, 56.
54. Barad, *Meeting the Universe Halfway*, 56.

representational theater, that dominated the stage at the turn of the twentieth century. Moreover, it also differs from the postmodern "paradoxical realism" that Stegemann identifies in Pollesch's works.[55] In other words, in Pollesch we don't find a realism that promotes the idea of predefined, stable identities, nor one that is merely a contingent game. Agential realism makes it possible to engage with the world in terms of objectivity, responsibility, and ethics while at the same time refuting the simplistic conclusion that giving up on the individual necessarily means neglecting responsibility.[56] On the contrary, Barad's agential realism expands on responsibility by showing that agency is not something that someone can *have* but is instead "about changing possibilities of change entailed in reconfiguring material-discursive apparatuses of bodily production, including the boundary articulations and exclusions that are marked by those practices in the enactment of a causal structure. Particular possibilities for (intra-)acting exist at every moment, and these changing possibilities entail an ethical obligation to intra-act responsibly in the world's becoming, to contest and rework what matters and what is excluded from mattering."[57] In short, Barad defines agential realism as being "not about representations of an independent reality but about the real consequences, interventions, creative possibilities, and responsibilities of intra-acting within and as part of the world."[58] In connecting this understanding of world-making to Pollesch's theater, I emphasize the critical potential of his plays. His theater positions the audience and performers, both human and nonhuman, as part of the world-making, rather than positioning them outside, as observers of a preexisting reality. Instead of reflecting or mirroring discrete worlds, individuals, or objects that he finds outside the theater, Pollesch's plays allow the production team and audience alike to meet the world, to pass through each other, and to gain new understandings of the nature of knowing and being. In so doing, it also

---

55. Stegemann, *Lob des Realismus*, 188, 197.
56. Barad, *Meeting the Universe Halfway*, 172.
57. Barad, *Meeting the Universe Halfway*, 178.
58. Barad, *Meeting the Universe Halfway*, 37.

forces us to realize that we are entangled in the production of exclusions and differences.

Ultimately, we can see that Pollesch continues Brecht's project of finding a theater for the scientific age. However, he does so under new conditions and based on recent scientific findings. While Brecht was still working under the conditions of modernity, Pollesch is dealing with our age of technoscience, in which the distinctions between science and technology, nature and society, subject and object, as well as natural and artificial, become blurred.[59] While Brecht's dialectical materialist approach remains focused on the human, Pollesch repeatedly argues for shifting our attention from the human to the ongoing intra-activity between human and nonhuman.[60] Furthermore, while Brecht's theater is connected to "pedagogy" and the strong binary between active and passive audiences, Pollesch reworks Brecht's pedagogical theater through stronger notions of indeterminacy and interdependency. While Brecht considers theater relevant if it opens up the possibility of *becoming other*, for Pollesch, theater is relevant as a place that starts from nothing and, for that very reason, carries great futurity for becoming in the form of a *becoming other-with*.

---

59. Haraway, *Modest_Witness*, 3–4.

60. In his "Short Organon for the Theatre," Brecht focuses on humans in their social and historical relationships. Not only that, but he explicitly uses the category of the animal as that from which the human is to be set apart: "If the actors do not wish to be apes or parrots, they must acquire the knowledge of the time on how people live together by fighting in the class struggle themselves." (Brecht, "Short Organon for the Theatre," 289) In Pollesch, this expectation for the actors and for theater in general has been transformed. Pollesch would surely argue that actors would do better to become parrots or monkeys than to remain fixated on their humanness. Thus, Pollesch provocatively inscribes the animal into Brecht's dialectical theater: "Humans cannot be the measure of all things! ... Most dogs have a longer pedigree than I do, says Haraway" (Pollesch, "Dialektisches Theater Now!," 303). ("Der Mensch kann doch nicht das Maß aller Dinge sein! ... Die meisten Hunde haben einen längeren Stammbaum als ich, sagt Haraway.")

Conclusion

Theater after the End of the World

> Would it were otherwise.
> —Heiner Müller, "Philoctetes"

When I began writing this book, its focus on the nuclear bomb and the fear of nuclear extinction appeared to anchor the new theatrical form firmly in the bygone Cold War era. Unfortunately, in recent years it has become abundantly clear that the threat of nuclear destruction is not something of the past but rather something that directly defines our present existence. And it is not only the war in Ukraine that has brought such fears back—whether because of the Russian occupation of and possible attacks on nuclear plants in Ukraine or the possible use of nuclear weapons by the Russian army—but recently, scholars have also raised awareness of the potential rise in the foreseeable future of a third atomic superpower

---

Epigraph: "Wärs anders."

in addition to the United States and Russia, as China rapidly expands its nuclear arsenal. Linking military strategy to physics, experts read this new situation in terms of the three-body problem, warning that a move from two nuclear powers to three is not simply a growth by one. Instead, it is a change that would complicate everything to such a degree that it might lead to a thermonuclear war, meaning that the amount of destruction is neither predictable nor thinkable from today's perspective.[1] In other words, we are once again confronted with the mega-concept of a nuclear sublime while already living with the consequences of the nuclear mundane.

Similarly, the effects of global warming have become more visible as catastrophes connected to the changing climate succeed each other at an ever-faster pace. At the same time, broad parts of society and of the political leadership are still treating the threat of the end of a livable world as a mere fictional scenario, so that here too we find ourselves living between a climate sublime and a climate mundane. In short, the tension between the nuclear/climate sublime and the nuclear/climate mundane, discussed in chapter 1, has only deepened.

In this closing chapter, I turn to our present and make explicit that the theater of the void, which began with Heiner Müller, anticipates and thus is able to respond to our present experience of the world. Once again, I turn to Müller's experimental and explosive textual ruptures. I return, in particular, to "The Wound Woyzeck" and a point that Müller makes concerning the relationship between catastrophe, violence, and the future.

In a discussion organized in connection with his Büchner Prize award speech, "The Wound Woyzeck," Müller states that what he is experiencing is the end of a world: "My basic experience is that a world has come to an end, a world that certainly also has comforts. Such that, for many things, we are sorry that they are gone. But that world is over. And the new is, first of all, very diffuse and also, perhaps, very frightening. But the main experience is the end, a world has ended, and the new one has its horrors, its stupidities, its bigotries, and its funny sides and all that, but it is a new

---

1. Broad, "The Terror of Threes."

world."[2] With this observation, Müller is responding to a criticism that futurity in his works is not optimistic and beautiful but dire, presenting a "world of corpses" (*Leichenwelt*). Müller's insistence on experiencing the world as living at the end of a world touches contemporary readers in an almost uncanny way, because it anticipates the contemporary experience of living "after the end of the world," as expressed, for example, by Timothy Morton.[3] In linking Müller with Morton, I seek to emphasize that when Müller speaks of the end of a world, he is not presenting yet another apocalyptic narrative regarding the future. Instead, he is pushing against this kind of end-time story, which for him has nothing but a paralyzing effect, when he emphasizes that there is no need to wait for an end to come because the world has already ended. Like Morton, Müller describes his experience as living *after* the end of a world in order to emphasize that the way in which we conventionally think of "the world," with humans at its center and with clearly distinct entities interacting with and acting on each other, has ended.[4] Consequently, our times demand a new understanding of the world. So far, I have related this predominantly to the violence unleashed in the technoscientific age due to nuclear weaponry. Now, I turn to Morton, who links this new understanding to global warming instead and claims that the new world we are living in is shaped by hyperobjects.

Morton uses the term "hyperobjects" to refer to things "that are massively distributed in time and space relative to humans."[5] These hyperobjects are "viscous" and remain attached to the beings they

---

2. Müller, "Ich bin ein Neger," 409–10. "Was ich als Grunderfahrung habe, ist, daß eine Welt zu Ende gegangen ist, eine Welt, die sicher auch Annehmlichkeiten hat. Wo man auch bei vielem bedauert, daß es zu Ende ist. Aber die ist zu Ende. Und das Neue ist zunächst einmal sehr diffus und auch sehr erschreckend vielleicht. Aber die Haupterfahrung ist das Ende, eine Welt ist zu Ende, und die neue hat ihre Schrecken, ihre Dummheiten, ihre Borniertheiten und ihre komischen Seiten und was alles, aber es ist eine neue Welt."
3. Morton, *Hyperobjects*. We find a similar observation in Tsing, *The Mushroom at the End of the World*, which stresses that we live on a ruined planet but that we can still find life within these ruins.
4. Morton, *Hyperobjects*, 7.
5. Morton, *Hyperobjects*, 1.

engage with; they are nonlocal; and they involve numerous temporalities.⁶ Moreover, they are "invisible to humans for stretches of time" and they "exhibit their effects *interobjectively*," meaning that they can be "detected in a space that consists of interrelationships between aesthetic properties of objects."⁷ However, where Morton uses the term "interobjectively," I suggest instead thinking in terms of *intra-objectively* exhibited effects. This emphasizes that it is not two preexisting objects that are interacting but instead, following Barad's notion of intra-action,⁸ two objects that continuously co-constitute each other.

The last two characteristics that Morton names—invisibility and the mode of detection that these hyperobjects demand (how they exhibit their effects)—are the most important ones for my considerations here. Invisibility relates to the question of what can be perceived and thus is commonly considered *something*, versus what cannot be perceived and thus is commonly considered *nothing*. Such a differentiation, as I have argued, becomes complicated in the theater of the void. Detection, on the other hand, names the mode of perception that becomes dominant in the theater of the void and that I have described as a form of seismology. The close link between a new mode of perception forced on us by hyperobjects and the changed mode of perception in the theater of the void shows the resonances between this new theatrical form and the challenges with which we are confronted in these times of global warming or, more broadly speaking, what I have been calling our technoscientific age.

I approach these resonances by linking Morton's claims with the writer Amitav Ghosh's considerations about literary form and global warming.⁹ Ghosh, inspired by Morton, introduces the uncanny and recognition as central modes for how to relate to a world shaped by hyperobjects. Taking him up on the notion of recognition, I argue that a changed understanding of anagnorisis in the theater of the void is what makes this theater so timely. In so doing, I challenge claims

---

6. Morton, *Hyperobjects*, 1.
7. Morton, *Hyperobjects*, 1. Emphasis in the original.
8. Barad, *Meeting the Universe Halfway*, 33.
9. Ghosh, *The Great Derangement*.

that theater has not yet developed a convincing grammar for how to respond to our present.[10] Then, finally, I once again turn to Morton, who ends his *Hyperobjects* with a short reflection on *Antigone*. In the process, I return to the beginning of this book, where *Antigone* allowed me to emphasize the perpetual movement between life and death, continuity and discontinuity, determination and contingency in the theater of the void. In this chapter, I expand my reading of *Antigone* to the question of how to understand and think of the human in our present. Ultimately, I point out that this theater, concerned as it is with the groundlessness of being and with ways of understanding this groundlessness as a chance for new beginnings after the world has ended, has a future and can be identified in a variety of contemporary theater makers. This stands in stark contrast to the experience of many critics and theatergoers that conventionally characaterized postmodern and postdramatic practices and aesthetics lack relevance or a future.

Uncanny Encounters, or: Anagnorisis in the End Times

Ghosh asks why literature has so far had nothing to say about climate change. While the distinction that he maintains between literature and the "popular genre" of science fiction is surely questionable, Ghosh is nonetheless making an important observation when he links this failure to the very form and conventions of the novel that "came to shape the narrative imagination in precisely that period when the accumulation of carbon in the atmosphere was rewriting the destiny of the earth."[11] In other words, Ghosh is bringing to light the fact that global warming cannot effectively become a subject of literature as long as we hold onto the form that was shaped by the very subjectivity that came into being at the time when human forces and natural forces became entangled in such a way that human and geological time can no longer be separated.[12]

---

10. Malzacher, *Gesellschaftsspiele*; Raddatz, *Das Drama des Anthropozäns*.
11. Ghosh, *The Great Derangement*, 7.
12. This is how the Anthropocene is usually conceived. The entanglement of human and nature is a result of the large amounts of carbon dioxide released into

What is required now is new forms and modes of narrative imagination in our present, shaped as it is by hyperobjects.

We find similar claims in the context of theater about the failure of adequate representation of global warming or the Anthropocene. The most important voices on this topic for German-language theater so far have been Florian Malzacher and Frank M. Raddatz, who have engaged with this question in depth. Malzacher and Raddatz agree that in order to succeed in such a representation, theater would have to offer a new understanding of the human as being intricately entangled with nonhumans. They remain skeptical, though, about how theater might actually decenter the human, given that this art form so clearly evolves around human agency. Moreover, they argue that, precisely for that reason, the theater lacks any ability to represent hyperobjects. As Malzacher writes, "The somewhat old-fashioned, analogue, anthropocentric medium of theater has a harder time than, for example, the visual arts in dealing with developments that want to banish the human from the center of thinking and feeling. The perspective of theater is not one *from* the future, but directed *toward* the future. The theater cannot represent or depict a world in which humanity has dissolved into nature, technology, or data."[13] Raddatz argues, similarly, that "there is currently no convincing theatrical grammar that is able to contain the planetary parameters that have been set in motion—such as global warming, the sustained loss of biodiversity, the melting polar ice caps—in a dramatic context and to present them as a consequence of the actions of certain groups of characters or to represent them in individual psychic segments of the human condition."[14] But such claims

---

the atmosphere due to industrialization. For a critical analysis of the Anthropocene see, e.g., Wark, *Molecular Red*.

13. Malzacher, *Gesellschaftsspiele*, 45. "Das etwas altmodische, analoge, anthropozentrische Medium des Theaters tut sich schwerer als beispielsweise die bildende Kunst, mit Entwicklungen umzugehen, die den Menschen aus dem Zentrum des Denkens und Fühlens verbannen wollen. Die Perspektive des Theaters ist keine *aus* der Zukunft, sondern *auf* die Zukunft gerichtete. Eine Welt, in der sich die Menschheit in Natur, Technologie oder Daten aufgelöst hat, kann das Theater nicht repräsentieren, nicht darstellen."

14. Raddatz, *Das Drama des Anthropozäns*, 8. "Doch existiert momentan noch keine überzeugende theatrale Grammatik, die in Bewegung geratenen planetarischen

about the failure of theater are a result of the continued misidentification of theater with the historical formation of drama. As soon as we let go of this identification of theater with drama, we can see that theater offers an interesting means for wrestling with a world that is not only out of joint but also out of scale, a world that so often seems to confront us with the unthinkable or ungraspable.

To show the potential inherent in the theater of the void, I return to Ghosh, who, although he is primarily tackling the failure of contemporary literature, offers a path for how to reinvent theatrical forms in the close attention he pays to perception and cognition. Like Morton, Ghosh thinks of global warming in terms of the uncanny. This becomes evident right away, at the very beginning of his book, when he asks: "Who can forget those moments when something that seems inanimate turns out to be vitally, even *dangerously* alive?"[15] The danger, in this case, seems to be key, as the examples with which he answers this question all include something inanimate that not only turns out to be alive but turns against us, be it the geometrical pattern of a rug that turns out to be a dog's tail on which we have stepped, causing the dog to attack us, or a vine that reveals itself as a poisonous snake. In short, what Ghosh introduces here is the idea of recognizing a presence of which we are already aware while simultaneously realizing that this presence possesses a similar awareness of us, even though it is not human.[16] For Ghosh, such an awareness is key for how we relate to the world in times of climate change.

Recognition, or, to use the Greek term, *anagnorisis*, is an essential category of theater. Along with peripeteia and pathos, anagnorisis is one of the central elements of the tragic plot mentioned by Aristotle in his *Poetics*. It refers to the "extraordinary emotional effect of recognition"; it is "a change from ignorance to knowledge"[17] and thus

---

Parameter—wie die Erderwärmung, den anhaltenden Verlust von Biodiversität, die schmelzenden Polkappen—in dramatische Kontexte zurückzubinden und als Folge von Handlungen bestimmter Figurengruppen darzustellen beziehungsweise in einzelnen psychischen Segmenten der Conditio humana festzumachen."

15. Ghosh, *The Great Derangement*, 1.
16. Ghosh, *The Great Derangement*, 29.
17. Aristotle, *Poetics*, 18.

"a motif related to *cognition*."[18] While recognition, according to Aristotle, is strongest when it involves humans—because that is when it evokes the eleos (pity) and phobos (fear) that are essential to catharsis—he also emphasizes that it is not limited to human relationships. On the contrary, it can also include inanimate objects.

Anagnorisis is central to Müller's theater. Yet, in Müller's theater, anagnorisis no longer entails a linear path from ignorance to knowledge. It is not connected to a moment at which two distinct heroes or entities meet, nor does it reveal some formerly hidden logic. Moreover, it is no longer simply a motif of human cognition. Rather, it is a shared practice of detection, of sensing past, present, or future voices and sounds. In Müller's theater, anagnorisis refers to the im/possibility of (not) knowing (oneself) and demands from us the ongoing work of making and unmaking sense in a continuously intra-actively reconfigured and vast topology.

Based on this understanding of anagnorisis, let us once again examine recognition in Müller's narrative interruption to *Der Auftrag*, this time by focusing on the uncanniness of the encounters that characterize the short narrative. Everything in "Der Mann im Fahrstuhl" feels uncanny. The text complicates the relationship between animate and inanimate, since the categories of what is alive and what is not no longer seem easily applicable. At the same time, the text presents situations and things that are familiar to us only to then deprive them of their familiarity and reveal them as dreadful. We can link this back to Müller's experience of living after the end of a world. The "I" that finds itself on a remote country street in Peru is experiencing what it means to live *after* the end of the world as we know it and when no alternative understanding of it has yet been found.

While Morton and Ghosh relate the uncanny to the return of the repressed, in Müller's theater this framework becomes problematic, as the uncanny encounters can no longer be grasped within the framework of the repressed but instead confront us with something that the subject can no longer make sense of. What we encounter here, as I have argued, leaning on Malabou, is the indifferent subject

---

18. Aristotle, *Poetics*, 40. Emphasis in the original.

created by accident, blind to the hermeneutic dimension of this accident. In other words, Müller's theater confronts us with a slightly reworked notion of the uncanny that derives from the void as the groundless ground of his theater. It is precisely this reworked understanding of the uncanny that makes it so compelling for our present. What appears uncanny today goes beyond repression. Hyperobjects are uncanny because they can no longer be assimilated into or appropriated by the subject. They radically challenge our notion of subjectivity and confront us with the limits of our cognition.

However, anagnorisis in Müller does not lead to despair or utter (self-)surrender. On the contrary, as I described in chapter 2, it allows a sentiment of joy and ease to arise in the narrator. This is due to the acceptance of a radically new and entangled world and the willingness to practice alternative modes of meaning production. Moreover, we see an ethical dimension emerging that promises a new form of responsibility for the planet and whoever inhabits it. In all the encounters described at the end of "Der Mann im Fahrstuhl," the narrator has the ability to act, but decides not to.[19] Following Žižek, this becomes readable as the elemental ethical gesture, a "negative one, the one of blocking one's direct inclinations."[20] This is where freedom arises, according to Žižek, as this choice inserts a possibility for the future as well as for the past. It breaks with determinism and shows that we can escape our given script. It is no surprise that Malabou references this analysis by Žižek and argues that what we see here is a possibility in the absence of future.[21] In other words, the ethical dimension inherent in Müller's text is once again linked to plasticity and to the formation of a future at a time when we seem radically deprived of one. It is an ethics based not on morals but on freedom. Such an ethical dimension speaks to our present, which is shaped by the feeling of living in the end times, as

---

19. Žižek, *The Parallax View*, 202. This is reinforced by the fact that in the discussion about "The Wound Woyzeck," in which he speaks of the experience of living after the end of the world, Müller once again brings in Brecht's *Galileo* (Müller, "Ich bin ein Neger," 410).

20. Žižek, *The Parallax View*, 202. Žižek develops this in his reading of Freud's reflections on Michelangelo's *Moses*.

21. Malabou, *Plasticity at the Dusk of Writing*, 81.

it inserts possibility, freedom, and change when there seems to be a lack of future.

Monstrous Beings

The theater of the void, which moves away from representation in the form of the image and instead emphasizes the ear and all the other senses, introduces new possibilities and modes for how to make contact and how we conceive of recognition. In all the works by the theater makers discussed in this book, we experience a heightened focus on the moment of contact, on the voices and sounds that reach us, reminding us that we are embedded in an environment that cannot be limited to human agency. In Müller, what reaches us is the landscape constituted by an indeterminate past and future possibilities. In Jelinek, we are addressed by hyperobjects, such as the nuclear power plant in Fukushima, as well as the environment, which claims justice for the injustice it has suffered due to human activity. In Schlingensief, inanimate objects are revealed as having a life of their own. In Pollesch, human agency dissolves into an agency shared between human and nonhuman actors.

The importance of this moment of contact can be better understood within the framework that I suggest in this conclusion. The uncanny reveals the gruesomeness of something that seemed familiar. Following Morton, we can comprehend it as a form of strangeness and horror that cannot be removed from our lives. Instead, it is at the center of our human condition, which is, in our present, no longer limited to the human and thus demands that we speak, in fact, of a non/human condition. Morton subsequently quotes from the chorus of Sophocles's *Antigone*, calling attention to the line I discussed in the introduction: "Monstrous, a lot. But nothing more monstrous than man."[22] Indeed, this line has been repeatedly quoted in philosophy and literature to address the frightening power of

---

22. Sophocles, *Antigone*, 81. Morton actually quotes from a different translation by Martin D'Ooge: "Many are the disturbing beings in existence, but none is more disturbing than man" (Morton, *Hyperobjects*, 200).

humans that results from our ability to create, which at the same time unleashes enormous destruction.²³ The warning about human hubris is already reflected in Sophocles's play, where the chorus's line not only comments on Antigone's violation of King Creon's law but also resonates with numerous examples that the chorus gives throughout the play that praise the capabilities of human creativity while at the same time pointing to its dangers and limits.

Morton reflects on the meaning of "dreadfulness," claiming that while the ecological power of humans does indeed make them the most dreadful, this property is not limited to humans. Indeed, "all beings have a dreadful depth."²⁴ According to Morton, this results from the fact that whenever we try to fully grasp an object, it will always ultimately slip through our fingers. While this has also been true in the past, Morton is convinced that the ecological crisis we are facing right now has for the first time allowed us to fully recognize it. "The reality is that hyperobjects were already here, and slowly but surely we understood what they were already saying. They contacted us."²⁵ In other words, our uncanny encounters and our recognition of another agency that, until the moment of recognition, had appeared inanimate to us are hauntings in the form that Barad describes—hauntings not merely in the form of subjective human experiences but as the *"indeterminate wanderings of an infinity of possible configurings of spacetimematterings in their specificity."*²⁶

Jelinek's theater confronts us with such moments of recognition. Jelinek's *Epilog?* to her play on Fukushima quotes the line from *Antigone* mentioned above, yet in a clearly altered way: "But none is more disturbing than nature."²⁷ The literary scholar Ralf Schnell has pointed out that Jelinek here continues the considerations that Hegel shared in his *Encyclopedia of the Philosophical Sciences*.²⁸

---

23. Think of Hegel, who engages with this power in the second part of his *Philosophy of Nature*, or the discussion of this line in Heidegger, *Introduction to Metaphysics*, 156–76.
24. Morton, *Hyperobjects*, 200.
25. Morton, *Hyperobjects*, 201.
26. Barad, "No Small Matter," G113. Emphasis in the original.
27. Jelinek, *Epilog?* "Doch nichts ist ungeheurer als die Natur."
28. Schnell, "'Doch nichts ist ungeheurer als die Natur,'" 254–55.

Hegel considers *Antigone* to have proven his argument that man's "practical approach to Nature" is "determined by appetite, which is self-seeking." Hence, Hegel describes the relationship between man and nature as having been shaped by man's use of nature for his own advantage, "to wear her out, to wear her down, in short, to annihilate her." Yet he also points to the limits of such an approach to nature, making it clear that whatever man does, nature will counter it by unleashing its own incredible forces, such as cold, wild beasts, or water. Man, in turn, always "takes these means from Nature and uses them against herself." While this seems to describe a sovereignty of man over nature, Hegel reminds his readers that nature, "however, in her universal aspect," cannot be overcome by man in such a way, "nor can he turn her to his own purposes."[29]

Indeed, in her *Epilog?*, Jelinek presents nature as something that is dangerously alive and willing to fight back.[30] Following Morton, we can say that Jelinek shows that all beings are dreadful:[31] "The earth is a monstrosity. But many things are monstrous. I change everything else, so that what we have here is right: But nothing is more monstrous than nature. It is true that human beings are indeed monsters, but they are a speck of dirt, a nothing compared to nature."[32] The antagonistic relationship between humanity and nature[33] that Jelinek explores in her *Epilog?* is a recurrent topic in her theater. In more concrete terms, what Jelinek focuses on is the relationship between human and nonhuman, ecology, technology, and history, a relationship that is always conflictual and violent.[34]

---

29. Hegel, *Hegel's Philosophy of Nature*, 5.
30. This does not mean that Jelinek follows historical understandings of nature as durable while human action can only have limited impact. See Jonas, *Das Prinzip Verantwortung*, 19–21.
31. Morton, *Hyperobjects*, 200.
32. Jelinek, *Epilog?* Private translation by Gitta Honegger. "Die Erde ein Ungeheuer. Aber ungeheuer ist viel. Ich ändere den Rest um, damit hier das richtige steht: Doch nichts ist ungeheurer als die Natur. Der Mensch ist zwar ein Ungeheuer, aber er ist ein Dreck, ein Nichts gegen die Natur."
33. In Jelinek, the concept of "nature" is not reserved exclusively for the ecological realm but also absorbs multiple Others, such as women and the racialized othered.
34. For example, in *Das Werk* (The plant), a play that engages with the construction of a power plant in the Austrian Alps, mostly carried out by Jewish forced

She points to the danger of a human conceptualization of nature as its "Other" which needs to be conquered. While in her texts human beings exploit nature and violently shape it according to their needs (whether through factories, nuclear plants, or the expansion of ski resorts), nature continues to fight back and brings devastation in the form of floods, avalanches, hurricanes, and earthquakes. Nature does not suffer passively; it is depicted as being powerful and capable of not just fighting back but even destroying whoever counters it.

Within this conflictual relationship, Jelinek asks for responsibility. Although she is aware of the complex micro- and macrostructural entanglements that are involved, her theater is shaped by the belief that we can find and make accountable those who are responsible for the ongoing violence that we experience. Most poignantly, we find this expressed in the title of her essay *Diese Maschine ist unschuldig. Ich klage andere an* (This machine is innocent. I accuse others, 2009). In this text, Jelinek deals with the absurdity of the trial following one of the deadliest post–World War II incidents in Austria, when a fire caused by the faulty installation of a heater in a glacier lift in the Austrian village of Kaprun resulted in the deaths of 155 people in 2000. The trial ended in the acquittal of the sixteen defendants, who included the managing directors of the manufacturing company, the employees who had installed the heater, officials from the ministry of transportation, and inspectors from the Technical Inspection Association (TÜV). Their acquittal was based on the dubious interpretation of the status of the glacier lift: the heater was one that could not legally be installed in a vehicle, but because it was established that a funicular is not a vehicle, all claims of the possible misuse of the heater were dismissed. Jelinek

---

labor during the Nazi regime, Jelinek writes: "Here humans attack nature! ... Come here and look at nature as such and then look at technology, the way it vanquishes nature! And then look at humanity, how it defeats both humanity and technology, until there is nothing left." (Jelinek, *Das Werk*, 93; private translation by Gitta Honegger. "Hier greift der Mensch die Natur an! ... Kommen Sie und schauen Sie sich die Natur als solche an, und dann schauen Sie sich die Technik an, wie sie über die Natur siegt! Und dann schauen Sie sich den Menschen an, wie er über Mensch und Technik siegt, bis nichts mehr übrig ist.") This is another example of Jelinek's theater being deeply shaped by the investigation into the exploitation and destruction of human bodies, the environment, and animals due to capitalism and nationalism.

confronts and rejects such practices in her texts, revealing human hubris, capitalist greed, and stupidity to be responsible for the deaths of so many people.

Jelinek's theater provides a great example of how the theater of the void responds to our present, shaped as it is by seemingly endless cascades of catastrophes. Confronting us with the rich sounds and murmurs that belong to that void, as the realm of all that is and might yet be, this theater allows us to practice an alternative mode of meaning production. In so doing, it resists the lack of concern that not only makes it no longer possible for the subject to make sense or give meaning to catastrophes but also makes the subject into a potential aggressor. While our society is increasingly shaped by the impossibility of making sense out of the ongoing catastrophes and violent events that we face, the theater of the void counters what Malabou calls this "war on hermeneutics"[35] and invents a theatrical form in which meaning is expanded so that it arises in the mutual relationship between the material and immaterial, between living and nonliving entities.

Beginnings

Within these vast textual topologies of the theater of the void that confront us with the ruinous, contaminated landscapes of our technoscientific age, we find a future. This future arises, in the theater of the void, from the explosion, from destruction, and from the wound. As this theater shows, the violent moment does not necessarily cause an endpoint, in the sense of complete emptiness. On the contrary, it is full of movement and of possibilities that may (have) come to life.

Müller's theater will once again serve as an example of how we can find life within ruins. This time, though, let us take a closer look at his adaptation of Sophocles's *Philoktetes*. This tragedy poses the question of how to overcome conflict and hatred in order to ultimately give a future to the individual, as well as to a larger Greek

---

35. Malabou, "From Sorrow to Indifference."

community, as Odysseus orders Neoptolemus to lie to Philoctetes in order to reunite him with the Greek army in their fight against Troy. In other words, in order to have a future. In Sophocles, this future is made possible through the appearance of a deus ex machina, Hercules, who convinces Philoctetes to let go of his anger toward Odysseus and join the fight against Troy. In Müller, however, there is no longer a deus ex machina in the play to guarantee collaboration between formerly opposed individuals. While Sophocles's tragedy makes clear that, in such a desperate situation, only a god can help, Müller proposes that no such entity exists. In Müller's play, therefore, without the help of any god, the conflict is "solved" by the killing of Philoctetes, whose corpse is immediately instrumentalized by Odysseus in order to guarantee his victory in the fight against Troy. Müller's play leaves its audience with the dire vision of a future shaped by cold-blooded pragmatists who have learned how to endure and survive. As Müller explains in his letter to the director Dimiter Gotscheff,[36] Odysseus marks the "birth of archeological thinking"[37] that separates human from nature, which then leads to total destruction, symbolized here by the neutron bomb.[38] Yet, even though Müller's version seems to be deprived of any hope for an alternative or for positive change, it is precisely the vision of

---

36. See Dreyer, *Theater der Zäsur*, which demonstrates that the void is important for Dimiter Gotscheff's theater but does not take the actual process of formation or the material reality into account.

37. "Geburt des archäologischen Denkens." I discussed the shift from archeology to seismology in Müller in greater detail in chapter 1.

38. Müller, "Brief an den Regisseur der Bulgarischen Erstaufführung von 'Philoktet' am dramatischen Theater in Sofia," 268. Here, Müller's 1979 draft for another adaptation of *Philoktetes* is of interest; in this draft, unlike in other versions of this play, Philoctetes finds himself not on a deserted island but on an island densely inhabited by women. In this version, Odysseus and Neoptolemus immediately forget their task and allow themselves to be seduced by the women, while Philoctetes is eager to join the fight against Troy. Here, Heinrich Schliemann is the deus ex machina, arriving on the island by helicopter, symbolizing the birth of archeology, transforming the theater into a museum, and creating a neutron bomb, which, in the final words of the play, is "the dream weapon of archeology, the final product of humanism" ("die Traumwaffe der Archäologie, das Finalprodukt des Humanismus") (Müller, *Philoktet 1979*, 10).

the bomb that promises the possibility of new beginnings and carries the potential for a radical new future.

For Müller, the wound is the void in which new beginnings can start to form. Philoctetes suffers from a foul, gaping wound on his foot that has made him a social outcast. In his letter to Gotscheff, Müller makes it clear that this wound is not simply something that needs to be overcome. Instead, it carries the potential for utopia and for beginnings: it is the hole, the gap, that allows an opening to the always precarious space of freedom, a freedom that demands ongoing work. Finally, Müller speaks about the void as futurity, concluding: "Tragedy is left empty-handed. Its path rejects the consolation that is a deferral. It transports nothingness, the possible beginning."[39] The beginning that Müller imagines in his letter to Gotscheff ultimately allows a link to another play by Müller, *Verkommenes Ufer Medeamaterial Landschaft mit Argonauten* (*Despoiled Shore Medeamaterial Landscape with Argonauts*, 1983). In the third and last part of this play, entitled "Landscape with Argonauts," the "I" is not only reminiscent of Odysseus but also strongly resonates with the man in the elevator from *The Task* and his walk through the plains of Peru. This time, though, the walk is clearly situated in a ruinous landscape of our technoscientific age, shaped by its possible total destruction by the nuclear bomb:

> My walk through the outskirts I
> Between rubble and ruins it's growing
> THE NEW Fuckcells with district heating
> The tube vomits world into the livingroom
> Wear and tear is part of the plan The container
> Serves as a graveyard Figures among the rubble
> Natives of the concrete Parade
> Of Zombies perforated by TV spots
> In the uniforms of yesterday's morning fashion
> The youth of today ghosts of
> The dead of the war that is to happen tomorrow

---

39. Müller, "Brief an den Regisseur," 261. "Die Tragödie geht leer aus. Ihr Gang verwirft die Tröstung, die ein Aufschub ist. Er transportiert das Nichts, den möglichen Anfang."

YET WHAT REMAINS IS CREATED BY BOMBS
In the splendid mating of protein and tin
The children lay out landscapes with trash
A woman is the familiar ray of hope
BETWEEN THE THIGHS
DEATH STILL HAS HOPE.[40]

Once again, Müller presents the woman as the seductress who also bears hope. Moreover, he evokes the image of the children playing in the trash that was connected, in *The Task*, to their attempt to repair a broken hybrid of steam engine and train, which in his play is also associated with the notion of hope. While the new that starts to emerge within the rubble hints here at the endurance of capitalism and thus evokes the "zombie capitalism" that I discussed in chapter 1, citing Kohso, it also includes the opposite possibility, the possibility of a change and a beginning. Following Anna Tsing, we can speak here of a theater that sets out to find a "third nature" or a "life within ruins." In Tsing, "third nature" is added to the Hegelian and Marxist "first nature" (the prehuman) and "second nature" (artificial nature constructed by humans atop first nature or, in other words, the capitalist transformation of the environment); "third nature" describes "what manages to live despite capitalism."[41] This notion of third nature allows a link to the void, as Tsing compares it to a form of perception that is attentive to the murmurs of the void: "To even notice third nature, we must evade assumptions that the future is that singular direction ahead. Like virtual particles in a quantum field, multiple futures pop in and out of possibility; third nature emerges within such temporal polyphony."[42]

Müller's theater clearly engages with the question of how to find life in ruins. The same is true for Jelinek, Schlingensief, and Pollesch. What all four theater makers share is that they present us with a devastated world, a world in ruins. Closely related to Müller, Jelinek's textual topologies confront us with the zombie life of capitalism in a

---

40. Müller, *Despoiled Shore Medeamaterial Landscape with Argonauts*, 134.
41. Tsing, *The Mushroom at the End of the World*, viii.
42. Tsing, *The Mushroom at the End of the World*, viii.

world shaped by catastrophes that simultaneously introduce possibility. In Schlingensief, we are asked to find our way through vast spatial settings filled with piles of trash that are readable as the continuing production of waste in the ongoing overaccumulation of our neoliberal present. And yet it is within the trash that, through the emphasis on the dark and on movement, new possibilities arise and unexpected encounters can take place. In Pollesch, finally, the ruins become present through repeated references to formerly conventional ways of understanding the world that are now revealed as mere ruins, overshadowing our present which has not yet found a way to engage with our new world. In Pollesch, as in the others, the ruins do not simply signal an end but allow an opening for the void, as a realm in which the unexpected and singular can arise.

In the theater in our present, the question of the future is posed with ever more urgency. I want to point out here two works that have recently wrestled with this question and that can be seen as a continuation of the theater of the void that we find in Müller, Jelinek, Schlingensief, and Pollesch. These two works are Kevin Rittberger's *Kassandra/Prometheus: Recht auf Welt* (*Cassandra/Prometheus: Right to World*, 2019), and Florentina Holzinger's *Ophelia's Got Talent* (2022). In *Kassandra/Prometheus*, the playwright and director Kevin Rittberger returns to the famous first lines of Müller's *Hamletmaschine*: "I was Hamlet. I stood at the shore and talked with the surf BLABLA, the ruins of Europe in back of me."[43] Rittberger, attentive to the inherent futurity of Müller's theater of the void, reveals the hidden potential of these lines by reenvisioning them in terms of a life that starts to thrive amid the ruins and as a practice for beginnings: "I stand at the coast / Collect the garbage from the Waves / Re-assemblage."[44] While Rittberger primarily engages, in his theater, with modes of multispecies world-making in a postcolonial world, Florentina Holzinger thinks about futurity from a distinctly feminist perspective. In *Ophelia's Got Talent*, the stage fills up with rubble and dirt as the performance goes on so that at one point, the gigantic water basin on stage turns brownish red,

---

43. Müller, *Hamletmachine*, 53.
44. Rittberger, *Cassandra/Prometheus*.

evoking the feeling of a contaminated, poisonous environment. This is where children enter the stage. But far from there being any suggestion that they will be able to clean up the mess that the performers have produced in the past three hours, the children simply start playing with the dirt and the mess. In this work, Holzinger leads us into personal, societal, and planetary trauma and asks how to create a future from there. The future that flashes up in Holzinger's work cannot be separated from the wound. The wound becomes present on stage not only through rigorous self-discipline and acts of self-harm but also through shared personal experiences that include sexual abuse, eating disorders, and the harming of the body through medicine and therapy.[45] It is these wounds that create the void and allow Holzinger not only to make us attentive to the multiple futures and possibilities inherent in it but also to allow something like ease and joy to arise, within the ruins, between the performers and between performers and audience.

These are only two examples of a growing number of works that engage with questions of change and futurity in our technoscientific age and that connect that change to the explosion, to destruction, and to the wound. Other works are by such diverse directors, playwrights, and collectives as Julien Gosselin, Constanza Macras, Susanne Kennedy, Thomas Köck, the Otolith Group, and Toshiki Okada, who explore the groundlessness of being in our present while at the same time investigating the multiple possibilities that might arise from it. While in the past, such a groundlessness or void was often misunderstood in terms of a dystopia, this book has fleshed out another path, one that emphasizes the futurity, chance, and change that are inherent in the void. Müller saw this potential in Brecht when he pointed to a different materialism that was integral to Brecht's theater but had been hidden by his dominant Marxist dialectics. What Müller discovers and recovers in Brecht is a materialism of the aleatory that shapes the theater of the void and introduces an experience of ease, joy, and pleasure connected to the groundlessness of being in our technoscientific age. This is where the greatest potential of the theater of the void lies—in our present.

---

45. See Schopp, "Importunate Feminism."

The theater of the void is not a theater of despair but one that introduces ease and joy into our struggles for a future; joy understood not as a neoliberal desire but as labor and as the ongoing struggle for freedom and the willingness to give oneself to that struggle. As a theater that does not give up on ease, joy, and pleasure, it is a continuation of Brecht's insistence that the central quality of theater is an ease that must not be lost, because it is only that ease that allows theater to address more serious questions: "Ease makes any amount of seriousness achievable; without ease, none at all is possible."[46] Brecht wrote these lines in 1945, and he understood quite well that his praise of ease might sound shocking to his contemporaries: "It may seem almost offensive that we are sitting here, at a time when bloody wars are being fought, and discussing—but not for the purpose of escapism—the kind of theatrical issues that seem to owe their existence to our need for distraction. Tomorrow we might all be blown to bits!" But he went on to explain: "The urgency of our situation must not lead us to destroy the instrument we want to make use of.... The world is out of joint, certainly, and it will take powerful movements to set it right again. But among the various instruments that could be used for this purpose, one of them may be slight and delicate, and needs to be handled effortlessly."[47] Today, we face a world that is not only out of joint but out of scale. And yet the theater of the void introduces a future in a time of no future. It sets out to find life within the ruins. And, like the man in the elevator who suddenly finds himself on a deserted street in Peru, it does this by turning our anxious walk into a stroll. "For some time already / I had put aside fear of death, since I / Can nothing lack, if / I myself am lacking. Now / I was able to take pleasure also / In the song of every blackbird after me."[48]

---

46. Brecht, "Messingkauf, or Buying Brass," 120.
47. Brecht, "Messingkauf, or Buying Brass," 120.
48. Brecht, "When in my hospital ward....," 1071.

Bibliography

Adorno, Theodor. "Die Wunde Heine." In *Noten zur Literatur I*, 144–52. Frankfurt am Main: Suhrkamp, 1958.

Ahrens, Gerhard. "Der tote Hase und seine Bilder: Interview mit Christoph Schlingensief." *Frankfurter Rundschau*, August 22, 2005.

Alexander, Stephon. *The Jazz of Physics*. New York: Basic Books, 2016.

Alperson, Philip. "'Musical Time' and Music as an 'Art of Time.'" *The Journal of Aesthetics and Art Criticism* 38, no. 4 (1980): 407–17.

Althusser, Louis. "The Underground Current of the Materialism of the Encounter." In *Philosophy of the Encounter: Later Writings 1978–87*, edited by François Matheron and Olivier Corpet, 163–207. New York: Verso, 2006.

Annuß, Evelyn. "Christoph Schlingensiefs autobiografische Inszenierungen." In *Der Gesamtkünstler: Christoph Schlingensief*, edited by Pia Janke and Teresa Kovacs, 291–304. Vienna: Praesens Verlag, 2011.

Aristotle. *Poetics*. Translated by Malcolm Heath. London: Penguin Books, 1996.

Badiou, Alain. *Being and Event*. Translated by Oliver Feltham. London: Continuum, 2005.

Badiou, Alain. *Five Lessons on Wagner*. Translated by Susan Spitzer. New York: Verso, 2010.

Badiou, Alain. *Logics of Worlds: Being and Event*. Translated by Alberto Toscano. London: Continuum, 2009.

Badiou, Alain. *Theory of the Subject*. Translated by Bruno Bosteels. London: Continuum, 2009.

Bala, Sruti. "'Translation Is the Making of a Subject in Reparation': Elfriede Jelinek's Response to Fukushima in *Kein Licht*." *Austrian Studies* 22 (2014): 183–98.

Balme, Christopher. "Postfictional Theatre, Institutional Aesthetics, and the German Theatrical Public Sphere." *TDR: The Drama Review* 67, no. 2 (2023): 14–31.

Barad, Karen. "Diffracting Diffraction: Cutting Together-Apart." *Parallax* 20, no. 3 (2014): 168–87.

Barad, Karen. *Meeting the Universe Halfway: Quantum Physics and the Entanglement of Matter and Meaning*. Durham, NC: Duke University Press, 2007.

Barad, Karen. "No Small Matter: Mushroom Clouds, Ecologies of Nothingness, and Strange Topologies of SpaceTimeMattering." In *Art of Living on a Damaged Planet*, edited by Anna Tsing, Heather Swanson, Elaine Gan, and Nils Bubandt, G103–20. Minneapolis: University of Minnesota Press, 2017.

Barad, Karen. "On Touching the Stranger Within—The Alterity That Therefore I Am." *Poetry Project*. 2018. Accessed February 6, 2023. https://www.poetryproject.org/library/poems-texts/on-touching-the-stranger-within-the-alterity-that-therefore-i-am.

Barad, Karen. "Quantum Entanglements and Hauntological Relations of Inheritance: Dis/continuities, SpaceTime Enfoldings, and Justice-to-Come." *Derrida Today* 3, no. 2 (2010): 240–68.

Barad, Karen. "Transmaterialities: Trans*/Matter/Realities and Queer Political Imaginings." *GLQ: Journal of Lesbian and Gay Studies* 21, no. 2–3 (2015): 387–422.

Barad, Karen. "Troubling Time/s and Ecologies of Nothingness: Re-turning, Re-membering, and Facing the Incalculable." *New Formations: A Journal of Culture/Theory/Politics* 92 (2017): 56–86.

Barad, Karen. "What Flashes Up: Theological-Political-Scientific Fragments." In *Entangled Worlds: Religion, Science, and New Materialisms*, edited by Catherine Keller and Mary-Jane Rubenstein, 21–88. New York: Fordham University Press, 2017.

Barad, Karen. "What Is the Measure of Nothingness? Infinity, Virtuality, Justice." *100 Notes—100 Thoughts / 100 Notizen—100 Gedanken No. 099: Karen Barad*. dOCUMENTA 13 (2012): 4–17.

Barthes, Roland. "Diderot, Brecht, Eisenstein." In *Image—Music—Text*, 69–78. New York: Noonday Press, 1977.

Bathrick, David. *The Powers of Speech: The Politics of Culture in the GDR*. Lincoln: University of Nebraska Press, 1995.

Bathrick, David. "Robert Wilson, Heiner Müller, and the Preideological." *New German Critique* 98 (2006): 65–76.

Beier, Karin. "Dionysos und Apollon zugleich: Über die Uraufführungsinszenierung von *Kein Licht*: Karin Beier im Gespräch mit Christian Schenkermayr." *JELINEK[JAHR]BUCH: Elfriede Jelinek-Forschungszentrum* (2012): 73–79.

Benjamin, Walter. *Das Kunstwerk im Zeitalter seiner technischen Reproduzierbarkeit*. Frankfurt am Main: Suhrkamp, 1963.

Benjamin, Walter. *Über den Begriff der Geschichte*. In *Werke und Nachlaß: Kritische Gesamtausgabe*, vol. 19, edited by Gérard Raulet. Frankfurt am Main: Suhrkamp, 2010.

Benjamin, Walter. "Ursprung des deutschen Trauerspiels." In *Gesammelte Schriften, vol. 1*, edited by Rolf Tiedemann and Hermann Schweppenhäuser, 209–430. Frankfurt am Main: Suhrkamp, 1991.

Benjamin, Walter. "The Work of Art in the Age of Mechanical Reproduction." In *Illuminations*, 217–51. Translated by Harry Zohn. New York: Schocken Books, 1968.

Berka, Roman. *Schlingensiefs Animatograph: Zum Raum wird hier die Zeit*. Vienna: Springer, 2011.

Bernays, Jacob. *Grundzüge der verlorenen Abhandlung des Aristoteles über Wirkung der Tragödie*. Breslau: Eduard Trewendt, 1857.

Biesenbach, Ellen, and Franziska Schößler. "Zur Rezeption des Medea-Mythos in der zeitgenössischen Literatur: Elfriede Jelinek, Marlene Streeruwitz und Christa Wolf." *Freiburger FrauenStudien* 1 (1998): 31–59.

Brecht, Bertolt. "Als ich in weißem Krankenzimmer der Charité." In *Bertolt Brecht: Große kommentierte Berliner und Frankfurter Ausgabe: Band 15: Gedichte 5*, edited by Werner Hecht, Jan Knopf, Werner Mittenzwei, and Klaus-Detlef Müller, 300. Berlin: Suhrkamp, 1993.

Brecht, Bertolt. *Fatzer*. In *Bertolt Brecht: Große kommentierte Berliner und Frankfurter Ausgabe: Band 10: Stücke 10*, edited by Werner Hecht, Jan Knopf, Werner Mittenzwei, and Klaus-Detlef Müller, 387–529. Berlin: Suhrkamp, 1997.

Brecht, Bertolt. "Kleines Organon für das Theater." In *Bertolt Brecht: Große kommentierte Berliner und Frankfurter Ausgabe: Band 23: Schriften 3*, edited by Werner Hecht, Jan Knopf, Werner Mittenzwei, and Klaus-Detlef Müller, 65–97. Berlin: Suhrkamp, 1967.

Brecht, Bertolt. "K-Typus und P-Typus in der Dramatik." In *Bertolt Brecht: Große kommentierte Berliner und Frankfurter Ausgabe: Schriften 2*, edited by Werner Hecht, Jan Knopf, Werner Mittenzwei, and Klaus-Detlef Müller, 387–89. Berlin: Suhrkamp, 1993.

Brecht, Bertolt. *Leben des Galilei*. In *Bertolt Brecht: Große kommentierte Berliner und Frankfurter Ausgabe: Band 5: Stücke 5*, edited by Werner Hecht, Jan Knopf, Werner Mittenzwei, and Klaus-Detlef Müller, 187–290. Berlin: Suhrkamp, 1988.

Brecht, Bertolt. "Der Messingkauf." In *Bertolt Brecht: Große kommentierte Berliner und Frankfurter Ausgabe: Schriften 2*, edited by Werner Hecht, Jan Knopf, Werner Mittenzwei, and Klaus-Detlef Müller, 695–869. Berlin: Suhrkamp, 1993.

Brecht, Bertolt. "Messingkauf, or Buying Brass." In *Brecht on Performance*, edited by Tom Kuhn, Steve Giles, and Marc Silberman, 7–133. London: Bloomsbury, 2019.

Brecht, Bertolt. "Short Organon for the Theatre." In *Brecht on Theatre*, edited by Marc Silberman, Steve Giles, and Tom Kuhn, 271–308. London: Bloomsbury, 2019.

Brecht, Bertolt. "When in my hospital ward . . ." In *The Collected Poems of Bertolt Brecht*. Translated and edited by Tom Kuhn and David Constantine, 1071. New York: Liveright, 2018.

Breger, Claudia. *An Aesthetics of Narrative Performance: Translational Theater, Literature, and Film in Contemporary Germany*. Columbus: Ohio State University Press, 2012.

Breithaupt, Fritz. "History as the Delayed Integration of Phenomena." In *Benjamin's Ghosts*, edited by Gerhard Richter, 191–204. Stanford, CA: Stanford University Press, 2002.

Broad, William J. "The Terror of Threes in the Heavens and on Earth." *New York Times*, June 26, 2023.

Brown, Kate. "Marie Curie's Fingerprint: Nuclear Spelunking in the Chernobyl Zone." In *Art of Living on a Damaged Planet*, edited by Anna Tsing, Heather Swanson, Elaine Gan, and Nils Bubandt, G33–50. Minneapolis: University of Minnesota Press, 2017.

Brown, Wendy. *States of Injury: Power and Freedom in Late Modernity*. Princeton, NJ: Princeton University Press, 1995.

Bryson, Norman. *Vision and Painting: The Logic of Gaze*. London: Macmillan Press, 1983.

Canguilhem, Georges. *Vital Rationalist: Selected Writings from Georges Canguilhem*. New York: Zone Books, 1994.

Case, Sue-Ellen. *Performing Science and the Virtual*. New York: Routledge, 2007.

Chaudhuri, Una, and Shonni Enelow. *Research Theatre, Climate Change, and the Ecocide Project*. New York: Palgrave Macmillan, 2014.

Chen, Nancy N. "'Speaking Nearby': A Conversation with Trinh T. Minh-Ha." *Visual Anthropology Review* 8, no. 1 (1992): 82–91.

Clar, Peter. *"Ich bleibe, aber weg": Dekonstrutionen der AutorInnenfigur(en) bei Elfriede Jelinek*. Bielefeld: Aisthesis, 2017.

Classen, Constance, David Howes, and Anthony Synnott. *Aroma: The Cultural History of Smell*. New York: Routledge, 1994.

Combes, André. "Gegen 'die Aushöhlung von Geschichtsbewußtsein durch einen platten Begriff von Aktualität': Aspekte der Inszenierung des Zeitgemäßen bei Heiner Müller." *Germanica* 14 (1994): 134–49.

Corbin, Alain. *The Foul and the Fragrant: Odor and the French Social Imagination*. Cambridge, MA: Harvard University Press, 1988.

Cornish, Matthew. *Performing Unification: History and Nation in German Theatre after 1989*. Ann Arbor: University of Michigan Press, 2017.

Cornish, Matthew, and David Savran. "Introduction: A Dialogue on Contemporary German Theatre." *TDR: The Drama Review* 67, no. 2 (2023): 6–13.
Crockett, Clayton. *Derrida after the End of Writing: Political Theology and New Materialism*. New York: Fordham University Press, 2017.
Curtin, Adrian. *Death in Modern Theatre: Stages of Mortality*. Manchester: Manchester University Press, 2019.
Damasio, Antonio. *Feeling and Knowing: Making Minds Conscious*. New York: Pantheon Press, 2021.
Darwin, Charles. *On the Origin of Species by Means of Natural Selection; or, The Preservation of Favoured Races in the Struggle for Life*. 2nd ed. London: John Murray, 1860.
Davis, Heather, and Etienne Turpin, eds. *Art in the Anthropocene: Encounters among Aesthetics, Politics, Environments and Epistemologies*. London: Open Humanities Press, 2015.
Davis, Jack. "Who's Afraid of Kommissar Rex? Postdramatic Ecology and the Theater of the Holocaust in René Pollesch's *Cappuccetto Rosso*." In *Open Wounds: Holocaust Theater and the Legacy of George Tabori*, edited by Martin Kagel and David Z. Saltz, 125–38. Ann Arbor: University of Michigan Press, 2022.
Dax, Max. "Ich glaube an die Peinlichkeit." *Die Welt*, September 10, 2006.
Degeling, Jasmin. "Heilung durch Kunst? Schlingensiefs Reenactments der Avantgarden der Performancekunst (Ball, Brus, Beuys, Nitsch)." In *Christoph Schlingensief und die Avantgarde*, edited by Lore Knapp, Sven Lindholm, and Sarah Pogoda, 173–90. Paderborn: Wilhelm Fink, 2019.
Deleuze, Gilles, and Félix Guattari. *Anti-Oedipus. Capitalism and Schizophrenia*. Translated by Robert Hurley, Mark Seem, and Helen R. Lane. London: Penguine, 1977.
Deleuze, Gilles. *The Logic of Sense*. Translated by Mark Lester. London: The Athlone Press, 1990.
Derrida, Jacques. "No Apocalypse, Not Now (Full Speed Ahead, Seven Missiles, Seven Missives)." *Diacritics* 14, no. 2 (1984): 20–31.
Derrida, Jacques. *Specters of Marx*. New York: Routledge, 1994.
Derrida, Jacques. "A Time for Farewells: Heidegger (Read by) Hegel (Read by) Malabou." Preface to *The Future of Hegel: Plasticity, Temporality and Dialectic*, by Catherine Malabou, vii–xlvii. New York: Routledge, 2004.
Deutsch-Schreiner, Evelyn, and Katharina Pewny. "Avant-garde! Marmelade! Avant-garde! Marmelade! Schlingensief und seine Verortung in den Avantgarden." In *Der Gesamtkünstler: Christoph Schlingensief*, edited by Pia Janke and Teresa Kovacs, 236–48. Vienna: Praesens Verlag, 2011.
Diederichsen, Diedrich. "Parables of the Theatre." *Artforum* 48, no. 10 (2010): 137–40.
Dietzel, Ulrich. "Was gebraucht wird: Mehr Utopie, mehr Phantasie und mehr Freiräume für Phantasie." In *Werke 10: Gespräche 1: 1965–1987*, by Heiner

Müller, edited by Frank Hörnigk, 318–45. Frankfurt am Main: Suhrkamp, 2008.

Doane, Mary Ann. *The Emergence of Cinematic Time: Modernity, Contingency, the Archive*. Cambridge, MA: Harvard University Press, 2002.

Dorsey, John T. "The Responsibility of the Scientist in Atomic Bomb Literature." *Comparative Literature Studies* 24, no. 3 (1987): 227–90.

Dreyer, Matthias. *Theater der Zäsur: Antike Tragödie im Theater seit den 1960er Jahren*. Paderborn: Wilhelm Fink, 2014.

Dürrenmatt, Friedrich. *Die Physiker*. Zurich: Diogenes, 1998.

Eddington, Arthur Stanley. *The Nature of the Physical World*. New York: Macmillan, 1928.

Edelmann, Gregor. "Solange wir an unsere Zukunft glauben, brauchen wir uns vor unserer Vergangenheit nicht zu fürchten." In *Werke 10: Gespräche 1: 1965–1987*, by Heiner Müller, edited by Frank Hörnigk, 455–71. Frankfurt am Main: Suhrkamp, 2008.

Eichler, Jeremy. "A Hullabaloo for an Opening at Bayreuth." *New York Times*, July 27, 2004.

Eiermann, André. *Postspektakuläres Theater*. Bielefeld: transcript, 2009.

Ernst, Wolf-Dieter. "Akteur-Netzwerk Theorie und Aufführungsanalyse." In *Methoden der Theaterwissenschaft*, edited by Christopher Balme and Berenika Szymanski-Düll, 153–68. Tübingen: Narr Francke Attempo, 2020.

Felber, Silke. "Neue Theatertexte: Institutionen und Instanzen: Gespräch mit Andreas Beck, Julia Danielczyk, Amely Joanna Haag, Ute Nyssen." In *Postdramatik: Reflexion und Revision*, edited by Pia Janke and Teresa Kovacs, 413–26. Vienna: Praesens Verlag, 2015.

Felber, Silke. *Travelling Gestures: Elfriede Jelineks Theater der (Tragödien-) Durchquerung*. Vienna: mdw press, 2023.

Fenves, Peter. "Aura und Irrtum: Das Problem der Popularisierung von Benjamin bis Heidegger." *Cultural Inquiry* 13 (2017): 61–77.

Fenves, Peter. "The Problem of Popularization in Benjamin, Schrödinger, and Heidegger circa 1935." *The Germanic Review* 91, no. 2 (2016): 112–25.

Fischer-Lichte, Erika. *Ästhetik des Performativen*. Frankfurt am Main: Suhrkamp, 2004.

Fischer-Lichte, Erika. *The Transformative Power of Performance: A New Aesthetics*. Translated by Saskya Iris Jain. London: Routledge, 2008.

Fisher, Mark. *Capitalist Realism: Is There No Alternative?* Alresford: Zero Books, 2009.

Fisher, Mark. *Ghosts of My Life: Writings on Depression, Hauntology and Lost Futures*. Alresford: Zero Books, 2014.

Fleishman, Ian. *An Aesthetics of Injury: The Narrative Wound from Baudelaire to Tarantino*. Evanston, IL: Northwestern University Press, 2018.

Forrest, Tara, and Anna Teresa Scheer, eds. *Christoph Schlingensief: Art without Borders*. Bristol: Intellect, 2010.

Foucault, Michel. *Archeology of Knowledge and the Discourse on Language*. Translated by A. M. Sheridan Smith. New York: Pantheon Books, 1972.

Foucault, Michel. *The Hermeneutics of the Subject*. Translated by Graham Burchell. New York: Palgrave, 2005.

Fraleigh, Sondra. *Butoh: Metamorphic Dance and Global Alchemy*. Champaign: University of Illinois Press, 2010.

Frisch, Max. *Die Chinesische Mauer*. Frankfurt am Main: Suhrkamp, 1964.

Fukuoka, Asako. "Erzählen der unerlebten Katastrophen: Übersetzen als literarisches Modell bei Elfriede Jelinek und Autoren der zweiten Generation." *Forschungsplattform Elfriede Jelinek*. 2016. Accessed August 8, 2022. https://fpjelinek.univie.ac.at/fileadmin/user_upload/proj_ejfz/PDF-Downloads/Beitrag_Asako_Fukuoka.pdf.

Fukuoka, Asako. "Das Zitat als Mittel zur Kommunikation mit den Toten? Kommunikation mit den Toten mittels des Zitats? Fukushima in Texten von Elfriede Jelinek und Hiromi Kawakami." *Forschungsplattform Elfriede Jelinek*. 2014. Accessed August 8, 2022. https://fpjelinek.univie.ac.at/fileadmin/user_upload/proj_ejfz/PDF-Downloads/Fukuoka_Das_Zitat_als_Mittel_zur_Kommunikation.pdf.

Gabriel, Leon, and Nikolaus Müller-Schöll, eds. *Das Denken der Bühne: Szenen zwischen Theater und Philosophie*. Bielefeld: transcript, 2019.

García, Anonio, and Francisco Guillén. "The Silent Utopia: An Approach to Light and Colour in the Work of Robert Wilson." In *Expression in the Performing Arts*, edited by Inma Álvarez, Héctor J. Pérez, and Francisca Pérez-Carreño, 247–61. Cambridge: Cambridge Scholars Publishing, 2010.

Geisenhanslüke, Achim. "Schreie und Flüstern: Rene Pollesch und das politische Theater in der Postmoderne." In *Politisches Theater nach 1968, Regie, Dramatik und Organisation*, edited by Ingrid Glicher-Holtey, Dorothea Kraus, and Franziska Schößler, 254–68. Frankfurt am Main: Campus, 2006.

Ghosh, Amitav. *The Great Derangement: Climate Change and the Unthinkable*. Chicago: University of Chicago Press, 2016.

Girard, René. *Deceit, Desire, and the Novel: Self and Other in Literary Structure*. Translated by Yvonne Freccero. Baltimore: Johns Hopkins University Press, 1976.

Girard, René. "Ein gefährliches Gleichgewicht: Versuch einer Deutung des Komischen." In *Die verkannte Stimme des Realen: Eine Theorie archaischer und Moderner Mythen*, 180–201. Müchen: Hanser, 2005.

Girshausen, Theo. "Katharsis." In *Metzler Lexikon Theatertheorie*, edited by Erika Fischer-Lichte, Doris Kolesch, and Matthias Warstat, 163–70. Stuttgart: Metzler, 2005.

Goebbels, Heiner. *Aesthetics of Absence: Texts on Theatre*. London: Routledge, 2015.

Goebbels, Heiner. "Text als Landschaft: Libretto-Qualität, Auch wenn nicht gesungen wird." *Neue Zeitschrift für Musik* 157, no. 2 (1996): 34–38.

Gordon, Avery. *Ghostly Matters: Haunting and the Sociological Imagination*. Minneapolis: University of Minnesota Press, 2008.

Gunning, Tom. "Never Seen This Picture Before: Muybridge in Multiplicity." In *Muybridge and the Instantaneous Photography Movement*, edited by Phillip Prodger, 222–72. New York: Oxford University Press, 2003.

Gürtler, Christa. "Elfriede Jelineks *Wut*: Zwischen Sprech-Wut und Katharsis." In *Elfriede Jelinek: Provokationen der Kunst*, edited by Uta Degner and Christa Gürtler, 77–91. Berlin: De Gruyter, 2021.

Haas, Maximilian. "Theoretische Bemerkungen zu einer Dramaturgie der nichtmenschlichen Anderen (nach Haraway)." In *Postdramaturgien*, edited by Sandra Umathum and Jan Deck, 195–208. Berlin: Neofelis, 2020.

Haas, Robert Bartlett. *Muybridge: Man in Motion*. Berkeley: University of California Press, 1976.

Hamacher, Werner. "(The End of Art with the Mask)." In *Hegel after Derrida*, edited by Stuart Barnett, 105–30. New York: Routledge, 1998.

Haraway, Donna. *Modest_Witness@Second_Millennium. FemaleMan©_Meets_OncoMouse™*. New York: Routledge, 1997.

Haraway, Donna. *Staying with the Trouble: Making Kin in the Chthulucene*. Durham, NC: Duke University Press, 2016.

Haraway, Donna. *When Species Meet*. Minneapolis: University of Minnesota Press, 2008.

Harrasser, Karin. "Violence and the Care for Images: Doing History with Strangers." *Artistic Practices as Cultural Inquiries*. 2024. Accessed May 8, 2024. https://insert.art/ausgaben/dis-sense/violence-and-the-care-for-images/.

Haß, Ulrike. *Das Drama des Sehens: Auge, Blick und Bühnenform*. Paderborn: Wilhelm Fink, 2005.

Hecht, Gabrielle. "The Power of Nuclear Things." *Technology and Culture* 51, no. 1 (2010): 1–30.

Heeg, Günther. *Das Transkulturelle Theater*. Berlin: Theater der Zeit, 2017.

Hegel, G. W. F. *Hegel's Philosophy of Nature*. Translated by A. V. Miller. New York: Oxford University Press, 1970.

Hegel, G. W. F. *Lectures on the Philosophy of History*. Translated by J. Sibree. London: George Bell and Sons, 1881.

Hegel, G. W. F. *Phenomenology of Spirit*. Translated by A. V. Miller. New York: Oxford University Press, 1977.

Hegemann, Carl. "Alles schreit: Notizen zu Christoph Schlingensiefs PARSIFAL." In *Carl Hegemann: Plädoyer für die unglückliche Liebe: Texte über Paradoxien des Theaters 1980–2005*, edited by Sandra Umathum, 240–45. Berlin: Theater der Zeit, 2005.

Hegemann, Carl. "Sterben lernen? Christoph Schlingensiefs Beschäftigung mit dem Tod." In *Der Gesamtkünstler: Christoph Schlingensief*, edited by Pia Janke and Teresa Kovacs, 328–41. Vienna: Praesens Verlag, 2011.

Hegemann, Carl. "Werkstatt Bayreuth: Nachnotizen vom 27./28. Juli 2005." In *Carl Hegemann: Plädoyer für die unglückliche Liebe: Texte über Paradoxien des Theaters 1980–2005*, edited by Sandra Umathum, 268–72. Berlin: Theater der Zeit, 2005.

Hegenbart, Sarah. "Animatographische Editionen." In *Schlingensief-Handbuch*, edited by Teresa Kovacs, Peter Scheinpflug, and Thomas Wortmann. Stuttgart: Metzler, forthcoming.

Hegenbart, Sarah. "Psychic Interiors: Christoph Schlingensief's Animatograph." In *Art of Wagnis: Christoph Schlingensief's Crossing of Wagner and Africa*, edited by Fabian Lehmann, Nadine Siegert, and Ulf Vierke, 89–100. Vienna: Cornerhouse Publications, 2017.

Heidegger, Martin. *Being and Time*. Translated by John Macquarrie and Edward Robinson. Oxford: Basil Blackwell, 1962.

Heidegger, Martin. *Introduction to Metaphysics*. Translated by Gregory Fried and Richard Polt. New Haven, CT: Yale University Press, 2000.

Heise, Wolfgang. "Ein Gespräch zwischen Wolfgang Heise und Heiner Müller." In *Werke 10: Gespräche 1: 1965–1987*, by Heiner Müller, edited by Frank Hörnigk, 496–521. Frankfurt am Main: Suhrkamp, 2008.

Herbig, Jost. "Die Dinge haben ihre Sprache: Interview mit Joseph Beuys." *Süddeutsche Zeitung*, January 26, 1980.

Hochholdinger-Reiterer, Beate. "Spricht wer? Zwischenbilanz textanalytischer Annäherungen." In *Postdramatik: Reflexion und Revision*, edited by Pia Janke and Teresa Kovacs, 98–111. Vienna: Praesens Verlag, 2015.

Hofmann, Hans. *Search for the Real, and Other Essays*, edited by Sara T. Weeks and Bartlett Hayes. Cambridge, MA: MIT Press, 1967.

Holmberg, Arthur. *The Theatre of Robert Wilson*. Cambridge: Cambridge University Press, 1996.

Horn, Eva. *Zukunft als Katastrophe*. Frankfurt am Main: Fischer, 2014.

Hörnigk, Frank. "Zu Heiner Müllers Stück *Der Auftrag*." *Weimarer Beiträge* 27, no. 3 (1981): 114–31.

Hurley, Jessica. *Infrastructures of Apocalypse: American Literature and the Nuclear Complex*. Minneapolis: University of Minnesota Press, 2020.

Issbrücker, Volker, and Christian Hippe, eds. *Brecht und Naturwissenschaften*. Berlin: Verbrecher Verlag, 2017.

Jahnn, Henny. *Die Trümmer des Gewissens*. Hamburg: Europäische Verlagsanstalt, 1961.

James, Ian. "(Neuro)Plasticity, Epigenesis and the Void." *parrhesia* 25 (2016): 1–19.

Jameson, Fredric. *Postmodernism, or, The Cultural Logic of Late Capitalism*. Durham, NC: Duke University Press, 1991.

Janke, Pia, and Teresa Kovacs, eds. *Der Gesamtkünstler: Christoph Schlingensief*. Vienna: Praesens Verlag, 2011.

Janke, Pia, and Teresa Kovacs, eds. *Postdramatik: Reflexion und Revision*. Vienna: Praesens Verlag, 2015.

Jeannerod, Marc. *Le cerveau intime*. Paris: Odile Jacob, 2002.

Jelinek, Elfriede. *Der Einzige, sein Eigentum (Hello Darkness, My Old Friend)*. *manuskripte* 216 (2017): 51–53.

Jelinek, Elfriede. *Epilog? Elfriede Jelinek*. 2012. Accessed May 8, 2024. https://original.elfriedejelinek.com/ffukushima.html.

Jelinek, Elfriede. "Es ist Sprechen und aus." *Elfriede Jelinek*. 2013. Accessed May 8, 2024. https://original.elfriedejelinek.com/fachtung.html.

Jelinek, Elfriede. "Fremd bin ich." *Elfriede Jelinek*. 2011. Accessed May 8, 2024. https://original.elfriedejelinek.com/fmuelh11.html.

Jelinek, Elfriede. "Grußwort nach Japan." *Elfriede Jelinek*. 2012–2014. Accessed May 8, 2024. https://original.elfriedejelinek.com/fjapanfestival.html.

Jelinek, Elfriede. "Immer hinauf auf den Steg: Wie der Mensch auf die Bühne kommt." *Süddeutsche Zeitung*, June 21, 2004.

Jelinek, Elfriede. *Kein Licht*. *Elfriede Jelinek*. 2011. Accessed March 29, 2024. https://original.elfriedejelinek.com/fklicht.html.

Jelinek, Elfriede. *Kein Licht. Theater heute* 11 (2011).

Jelinek, Elfriede. *Kein Licht: Prolog? Elfriede Jelinek*. 2012–2015. Accessed May 8, 2024. https://original.elfriedejelinek.com/fkeinlicht-prolog.html.

Jelinek, Elfriede. *Nach Nora. Elfriede Jelinek*. 2013. Accessed May 8, 2024. https://original.elfriedejelinek.com/fnachnora.html.

Jelinek, Elfriede. "Das Parasitärdrama." *Elfriede Jelinek*. 2011. Accessed May 8, 2024. https://original.elfriedejelinek.com/fparasitaer.html.

Jelinek, Elfriede. "Statement für den 'Frauen im Theater-Workshop' beim jährlichen Treffen der Dramaturgischen Gesellschaft: Wien, 15.11.1987." In *Frauen im Theater: Dokumentation 1986/87: Autorinnen*, edited by Dramaturgische Gesellschaft Berlin, 98. Berlin: Self-Published, 1988.

Jelinek, Elfriede. "Textflächen." *Elfriede Jelinek*. 2013. Accessed May 8, 2024. https://original.elfriedejelinek.com/ftextf.html.

Jelinek, Elfriede. *Das Werk*. In *In den Alpen: Drei Dramen*, 89–251. Berlin: Berlin Verlag, 2002.

Jelinek, Elfriede. "Die Zeit flieht." *Elfriede Jelinek*. 1999. Accessed May 8, 2024. https://original.elfriedejelinek.com/flmarkst.html.

Jelinek, Elfriede. "Zu Japan." *profil*, March 21, 2011.

Jonas, Hans. *Das Prinzip Verantwortung: Versuch einer Ethik für die technologische Zivilisation*. Frankfurt am Main: Suhrkamp, 2020.

Kaiser, Joachim. "Es waren 100.000 Robben, die wir mit Wagner beschallt haben." *Süddeutsche Zeitung*, May 17, 2010.

Kaiser, Joachim. "Ich bin eigentlich ein metaphysisch obdachloser Metaphysiker." *Süddeutsche Zeitung*, June 25, 2004.

Kalb, Jonathan. "Samuel Beckett, Heiner Müller and Postdramatic Theater." *Samuel Beckett Today / Aujourd'hui* 11 (2001): 74–83.

"Die Katze ohne Plan." *TAZ*. December 12, 2007. Accessed March 23, 2023. https://taz.de/Foucault-und-Darwin/!5189880/.

Kershaw, Baz. *Theatre Ecology: Environments and Performance Events*. Cambridge: Cambridge University Press, 2007.

Kipphardt, Heinar. *In der Sache J. Robert Oppenheimer*. Frankfurt am Main: Suhrkamp, 1964.

Kirby, Vicki. *Quantum Anthropologies: Life at Large*. Durham, NC: Duke University Press, 2011.

Klein, Christian. "Der Auftrag: Erinnerung an eine Revolution." In *Heiner Müller-Handbuch*, edited by Hans-Thies Lehmann and Patrick Primavesi, 189–93. Stuttgart: Metzler, 2003.
Kleist, Heinrich von. "Feelings before Friedrich's Seascape." *Art Journal* 33, no. 3 (1974): 208.
Kluge, Alexander. "Anti-Oper." *Kluge Library*. Accessed January 15, 2023. https://kluge.library.cornell.edu/de/conversations/mueller/film/100/segment/1826.
Kluge, Alexander. "The Complete Version of a Baroque Invention by Christoph Schlingensief." In *Christoph Schlingensief: German Pavilion, 2011: 54th International Art Exhibition La Biennale di Venezia*, edited by Susanne Gaensheimer, 241–44. London: Sternberg Press, 2011.
Kluge, Alexander. "In erster Linie bin ich Filmemacher: Begegnung mit Christoph Schlingensief." In *Alexander Kluge: Magazin des Glücks*, edited by Sebastian Huber and Claus Philipp, 108–14. Vienna: Springer, 2007.
Kluge, Alexander. "It Is an Error, That the Dead Are Dead." *New German Critique* 73 (1998): 5–11.
Kluge, Alexander. "Parsifal verlernen." *dctp.tv*. 2022. Accessed January 15, 2023. https://www.dctp.tv/filme/alexander-kluge-parsifal-verlernen?thema=zu-parsifal.
Kluge, Alexander. "What Does Nothingness Mean? Alexander Kluge in Conversation with Oskar Negt." *Kluge Library*. Accessed January 15, 2023. https://kluge.library.cornell.edu/conversations/negt/film/2126/transcript/.
Knapp, Lore. "Radikale Autonomie und Eigenleben im Film *Tunguska: Die Kisten sind da*." In *Christoph Schlingensief und die Avantgarde*, edited by Lore Knapp, Sven Lindholm, and Sarah Pogoda, 93–110. Paderborn: Wilhelm Fink, 2019.
Knapp, Lore, Sven Lindholm, and Sarah Pogoda, eds. *Christoph Schlingensief und die Avantgarde*. Paderborn: Wilhelm Fink, 2019.
Kohso, Sabu. *Radiation and Revolution*. Durham, NC: Duke University Press, 2020.
Kovacs, Teresa. *Drama als Störung: Elfriede Jelineks Konzept des Sekundärdramas*. Bielefeld: transcript, 2016.
Kovacs, Teresa. "Flowing Space: Theater—Raum—Bewegung bei Christoph Schlingensief und Friedrich Kiesler." In *Christoph Schlingensief und die Avantgarde*, edited by Lore Knapp, Sven Lindholm, and Sarah Pogoda, 153–72. Paderborn: Wilhelm Fink, 2019.
Kovacs, Teresa. "Götterdämmerung im Ruhrgebiet: Christoph Schlingensiefs *Wagner-Rallye*." *German Studies Review* 46, no. 1 (2023): 77–96.
Kovacs, Teresa. "Postdramatik als Label? Gespräch mit Carl Hegemann, Katja Jung, Patrick Primavesi, Stefan Tigges, moderiert von Teresa Kovacs." In *Postdramatik: Reflexion und Revision*, edited by Pia Janke and Teresa Kovacs, 61–73. Vienna: Praesens Verlag, 2015.

Kovacs, Teresa. "Zwischen Bildern: Christoph Schlingensief und Werner Nekes." In *Arbeit am Bild: Christoph Schlingensief und die Tradition*, edited by Thomas Wortmann and Peter Scheinpflug, 21–42. Paderborn: Wilhelm Fink, 2022.

Kovacs, Teresa, and Monika Meister. "Fläche und Tiefenstruktur: Die leere Mitte von Geschichte in Jelineks *Rechnitz (Der Würgeengel)* und *Winterreise*." In *Postdramatik: Reflexion und Revision*, edited by Pia Janke and Teresa Kovacs, 119–29. Vienna: Praesens Verlag, 2015.

Kovacs, Teresa, and Koku Nonoa, eds. *Postdramatisches Theater als transkulturelles Theater*. Tübingen: Narr Francke Attempo, 2018.

Kracauer, Siegfried. *History: The Last Things before the Last*. New York: Oxford University Press, 1969.

Kramer, Richard E. "'The Sculptural Drama': Tennessee Williams's Plastic Theatre." *The Tennessee Williams Annual Review* 5 (2002): https://tennesseewilliamsstudies.org/journal/work.php?ID=45.

Lacoue-Labarthe, Philippe, and Jean-Luc Nancy. "Dialog über den Dialog." Translated by Ulrich Müller-Schöll. In *Politik der Vorstellung: Theater und Theorie*, edited by Joachim Gerstemier and Nikolaus Müller-Schöll, 20–42. Berlin: Theater der Zeit, 2006.

Langston, Richard. *Dark Matter: A Guide to Alexander Kluge and Oskar Negt*. New York: Verso, 2020.

Langston, Richard. "Junger und Neuer Deutscher Film." In *Schlingensief-Handbuch*, edited by Teresa Kovacs, Peter Scheinpflug, and Thomas Wortmann. Stuttgart: Metzler, forthcoming.

Langston, Richard. "Schlingensief's Peep-Show: Post-Cinematic Spectacles and the Public Space of History." In *After the Avant-Garde: Contemporary German and Austrian Experimental Film*, edited by Randall Halle and Reinhild Steingröver, 204–23. Rochester: Camden House, 2008.

Laudenbach, Peter. "Weehee, Weehee." *Tagesspiegel*, July 26, 2004.

Lawtoo, Nidesh. *The Affective Hypothesis*. Vol. 2 of *Violence and the Mimetic Unconscious*. East Lansing: Michigan State University Press, 2023.

Layne, Priscilla. "Space Is Place: Afrofuturism in Olivia Wenzel's *Mais in Deutschland und anderen Galaxien* (2015)." *German Life and Letters* 71, no. 4 (2018): 511–28.

Layne, Priscilla, and Lily Tonger-Erk, eds. *Staging Blackness: Representation of Race in German-Speaking Drama and Theatre*. Ann Arbor: University of Michigan Press, 2024.

Lee, Tanya H. "H-Bomb Guinea Pigs! Natives Suffering Decades after New Mexico Tests." *Indian Country Media Network*. 2014. Accessed February 26, 2023. https://indiancountrymedianetwork.com/news/environment/h-bomb-guinea-pigs-natives-suffering-decades-after-new-mexico-tests/.

Lehmann, Hans-Thies. "Das Denken der Tragödie." In *Ereignis Denken—TheatRealität, Performanz, Ereignis*, edited by Arno Böhler and Susanne Granzer, 33–46. Vienna: Passagen Verlag, 2009.

Lehmann, Hans-Thies. "Dramatische Form und Revolution in Georg Büchners *Dantons Tod* und Heiner Müllers *Der Auftrag*." In *Georg Büchner: Dantons Tod: Die Trauerarbeit im Schönen*, edited by Peter von Becker, 106–21. Frankfurt am Main: Syndikat, 1980.

Lehmann, Hans-Thies. "Müllers Gespenster." In *Das Politische Schreiben*, 283–300. Berlin: Theater der Zeit, 2002.

Lehmann, Hans-Thies. *Postdramatic Theatre*. Translated by Karen Jürs-Munby. London: Routledge, 2006.

Lehmann, Hans-Thies. *Postdramatisches Theater*. Berlin: Verlag der Autoren, 1999.

Lehmann, Hans-Thies. *Theater und Mythos: Die Konstitution des Subjekts im Diskurs der antiken Tragödie*. Stuttgart: Metzler, 1991.

Lehmann, Hans-Thies. "Wie politisch ist postdramatisches Theater?" In *Das Politische Schreiben*, 11–21. Berlin: Theater der Zeit, 2002.

Lehmann, Hans-Thies, Monika Meister, Karen Jürs-Munby, Pia Janke and Artur Pełka. "Für jeden Text das Theater neu erfinden." In *Postdramatik: Reflexion und Revision*, edited by Pia Janke and Teresa Kovacs, 33–45. Vienna: Praesens Verlag, 2015.

Lévi-Strauss, Claude. *The Way of the Mask*. Translated by Sylvia Modelski. Seattle: University of Washington Press, 1982.

Lücke, Bärbel. "Fukushima oder die Musik der Zeit: Zu Elfriede Jelineks Bühnenstück *Kein Licht*." *Weimarer Beiträge* 3 (2012): 325–50.

Lücke, Bärbel. *Jelineks Gespenster: Grenzgänge zwischen Politik, Philosophie und Poesie*. Vienna: Passagen Verlag, 2007.

Lynch, Thomas. *Apocalyptic Political Theology: Hegel, Taubes and Malabou*. London: Bloomsbury, 2019.

Mairhofer, Lukas. *Bertolt Brechts Interferenz mit der Quantenphysik: Das moderne Theater und die moderne Physik*. Berlin: de Gruyter, 2023.

Malabou, Catherine. "Again: 'The Wounds of the Spirit Heal, and Leave No Scars Behind.'" *Mosaic: An Interdisciplinary Critical Journal* 40, no. 2 (2007): 27–37.

Malabou, Catherine. "From Sorrow to Indifference." *World Lecture Project*. October 22, 2013. Accessed April 22, 2023. https://world-lecture-project.org/videos/B0B2C5D6-81DE-11EB-BBE1-00D861A8BA28/.

Malabou, Catherine. *The Future of Hegel: Plasticity, Temporality and Dialectic*. Translated by Lisabeth During. New York: Routledge, 2004.

Malabou, Catherine. *The Heidegger Change: On the Fantastic in Philosophy*. Translated by Peter Skafish. New York: SUNY Press, 2011.

Malabou, Catherine. *The New Wounded: From Neurosis to Brain Damage*. Translated by Steven Miller. New York: Fordham University Press, 2012.

Malabou, Catherine. *Ontology of the Accident: An Essay on Destructive Plasticity*. Translated by Carolyn Shread. Cambridge: Polity Press, 2012.

Malabou, Catherine. *Plasticity at the Dusk of Writing*. Translated by Carolyn Shread. New York: Columbia University Press, 2010.

Malabou, Catherine. *What Should We Do with Our Brain?* Translated by Sebastian Rand. New York: Fordham University Press, 2008.

Malabou, Catherine. "Whither Materialism? Althusser/Darwin." In *Plastic Materialities: Politics, Legality, and Metamorphosis in the Work of Catherine Malabou*, edited by Brenna Bhandar and Jonathan Goldberg-Hiller, 47–60. Durham, NC: Duke University Press, 2015.

Malabou, Catherine. "The Wounds of the Spirit Heal, and Leave No Scars Behind." *Mosaic* 40, no. 2 (2007): 27–37.

Malabou, Catherine, and Clayton Crockett. "Plasticity and the Future of Philosophy and Theology." *Political Theology* 11, no. 1 (2010): 15–34.

Malabou, Catherine, and Adrian Johnston. *Self and Emotional Life*. New York: Columbia University Press, 2013.

Malzacher, Florian. "Citizen of the Other Place: A Trilogy of Fear and Hope." In *Christoph Schlingensief: Art without Borders*, edited by Tara Forrest and Anna Teresa Scheer, 187–200. Bristol: Intellect, 2010.

Malzacher, Florian. *Gesellschaftsspiele: Politisches Theater heute*. Berlin: Theater der Zeit, 2020.

Marranca, Bonnie. "'Despoiled Shores': Heiner Müller's Natural History Lessons." *Performing Arts Journal* 11, no. 2 (1988): 17–24.

Marranca, Bonnie. *Ecologies of Theater*. Baltimore: Johns Hopkins University Press, 1996.

Massumi, Brian. *Ontopower: War, Powers, and the State of Perception*. Durham, NC: Duke University Press, 2015.

Masumoto, Hiroko. "Die Atombombe als literarischer Topos in der deutschsprachigen und japanischen Literatur." In *Japanisch-deutsche Diskurse zu deutschen Wissenschafts- und Kulturphänomenen*, edited by Tilman Borsche, Teruaki Takahashi, and Yoshito Takahashi, 191–205. Paderborn: Wilhelm Fink, 2016.

Mather, George, Frans Verstraten, and Stuart Anstis, eds. *The Motion Aftereffect: A Modern Perspective*. Cambridge, MA: MIT Press, 1998.

Meister, Monika. "Zirkulationen des Schmerzes. Schlingensiefs Fluxus-Oratorium *Eine Kirche der Angst vor dem Fremden in mir* und die Katharsis." In *Der Gesamtkünstler: Christoph Schlingensief*, edited by Pia Janke and Teresa Kovacs, 96–111. Vienna: Praesens Verlag, 2011.

Michalzik, Peter. "Schlingensief in Angst und Schrecken." *Frankfurter Rundschau*, July 17, 2004.

Michalzik, Peter. "Der Todestag: Interview mit Christoph Schlingensief." *Frankfurter Rundschau*, August 22, 2004.

Miéville, China. *October: The Story of the Russian Revolution*. London: Verso, 2017.

Millner, Alexandra. "Prae—Post—Next? Über Polyphonie, Partitur und Kontingenz in Theatertexten von und nach Elfriede Jelinek." In *Postdramatik: Reflexion und Revision*, edited by Pia Janke and Teresa Kovacs, 167–84. Vienna: Praesens Verlag, 2015.

Molnar, Dragana Jeremić. "Inception of Wagner's Doctrine of Regeneration Prior to the Revolution 1848–1849." *New Sound: International Journal of Music* 42 (2013): 71–85.
Moore, Jason W., ed. *Anthropocene or Capitalocene? Nature, History, and the Crisis of Capitalism*. Oakland, CA: PM Press, 2016.
Morley, Michael. "Dürrenmatt's Dialogue with Brecht: A Thematic Analysis of *Die Physiker*." *Modern Drama* 14, no. 2 (1971): 232–42.
Morton, Timothy. *Hyperobjects: Philosophy and Ecology after the End of the World*. Minneapolis: University of Minnesota Press, 2013.
Morton, Timothy, Marcus Boon, and Eric Cazdyn. *Nothing: Three Inquiries in Buddhism*. Chicago: University of Chicago Press, 2015.
Moten, Fred. *In the Break: The Aesthetics of the Black Radical Tradition*. Minnesota: University of Minnesota Press, 2003.
Müller, Heiner. "Am Anfang war . . . Ein Gespräch unter der Sprache." In *Heiner Müller: Werke 8: Schriften*, edited by Frank Hörnigk, 296–306. Frankfurt am Main: Suhrkamp, 2005.
Müller, Heiner. *Anatomie Titus Fall of Rome Ein Shakespearekommentar*. In *Shakespeare Factory 2*, 125–225. Berlin: Rotbuch, 1989.
Müller, Heiner. *Der Auftrag*. In *Heiner Müller: Werke 5: Die Stücke 3*, edited by Frank Hörnigk, 11–42. Frankfurt am Main: Suhrkamp, 2002.
Müller, Heiner. *Bildbeschreibung*. In *Heiner Müller: Werke 2: Die Prosa*, edited by Frank Hörnigk, 112–19. Frankfurt am Main: Suhrkamp, 1999.
Müller, Heiner. "Bonner Krankheit." In *Heiner Müller: Werke 8: Schriften*, edited by Frank Hörnigk, 311–14. Frankfurt am Main: Suhrkamp, 2005.
Müller, Heiner. "Brief an den Regisseur der Bulgarischen Erstaufführung von 'Philoktet' am dramatischen Theater in Sofia." In *Heiner Müller: Werke 8: Schriften*, edited by Frank Hörnigk, 259–69. Frankfurt am Main: Suhrkamp, 2005.
Müller, Heiner. *Cement*. Translated by Helen Fehervary, Sue-Ellen Case, and Marc Silberman. Supplement, *New German Critique* 16 (1979).
Müller, Heiner. *Description of a Picture/Explosion of a Memory*. Translated by Carl Weber. *Performing Arts Journal* 10, no. 1 (1986): 106–110.
Müller, Heiner. "Description of a Picture Is." Translated by Carl Weber. *Performing Arts Journal* 10, no. 1 (1986): 96–97.
Müller, Heiner. *Despoiled Shore Medeamaterial Landscape with Argonauts*. In *Hamletmachine and Other Texts for the Stage*. Translated and edited by Carl Weber, 123–35. New York: Performing Arts Journal Publications, 1984.
Müller, Heiner. "Für immer in Hollywood oder: In Deutschland wird nicht mehr geblinzelt." In *Heiner Müller: Werke 12: Gespräche 3*, edited by Frank Hörnigk, 459–75. Frankfurt am Main: Suhrkamp, 2008.
Müller, Heiner. *Grundlings Leben Friedrich von Preußen Lessings Schlaf Traum Schrei*. In *Heiner Müller: Werke 4: Stücke 2*, edited by Frank Hörnigk, 509–37. Frankfurt am Main: Suhrkamp, 2001.

Müller, Heiner. *Hamletmachine*. In *Hamletmachine and Other Texts for the Stage*. Translated and edited by Carl Weber, 49–58. New York: Performing Arts Journal Publications, 1984.

Müller, Heiner. *Die Hamletmaschine*. In: *Heiner Müller. Werke 4: Stücke 2*, edited by Frank Hörnigk, 543–554. Frankfurt am Main: Suhrkamp, 2001.

Müller, Heiner. "Ich bin ein Neger." In *Heiner Müller: Werke 10: Gespräche 1: 1965–1987*, edited by Frank Hörnigk, 386–439. Frankfurt am Main: Suhrkamp, 2008.

Müller, Heiner. "I Do Not Believe in a Harmony between Theatre and Literature." In *Heiner Müller: Werke 8: Schriften*, edited by Frank Hörnigk, 170–71. Frankfurt am Main: Suhrkamp, 2005.

Müller, Heiner. "Der Mann im Fahrstuhl." In *Heiner Müller: Werke 2: Die Prosa*, edited by Frank Hörnigk, 104–10. Frankfurt am Main: Suhrkamp, 1999.

Müller, Heiner. *Mauser*. In *Heiner Müller Reader*. Translated and edited by Carl Weber, 93–107. Baltimore: Johns Hopkins University Press, 2001.

Müller, Heiner. *Philoctetes*. In *Three Plays: Philoctetes, The Horatian, Mauser*. Translated by Nathaniel McBride, 27–67. London: Seagull, 2019.

Müller, Heiner. *Philoktet*. In *Heiner Müller: Werke 3: Die Stücke 1*, edited by Frank Hörnigk, 289–327. Frankfurt am Main: Suhrkamp, 1999.

Müller, Heiner. 2002. *Philoktet 1979: Drama mit Ballett (Entwurf)*. In *Heiner Müller: Werke 5: Die Stücke 3*, edited by Frank Hörnigk, 9–10. Frankfurt am Main: Suhrkamp, 2002.

Müller, Heiner. *Die Schlacht*. In *Heiner Müller: Werke 4: Stücke 2*, edited by Frank Hörnigk, 469–82. Frankfurt am Main: Suhrkamp, 2001.

Müller, Heiner. *The Task*. In *Hamletmachine and Other Texts for the Stage*. Translated and edited by Carl Weber, 81–101. New York: Performing Arts Journal Publications, 1984.

Müller, Heiner. "Der Weltuntergang ist zu einem modischen Problem geworden." In *Heiner Müller: Werke 10: Gespräche 1: 1965–1987*, edited by Frank Hörnigk, 364–74. Frankfurt am Main: Suhrkamp, 2008.

Müller, Heiner. "The Wound Woyzeck." In *Heiner Müller Reader*. Translated and edited by Carl Weber, 108–11. Baltimore: Johns Hopkins University Press, 2001.

Müller, Heiner. "Die Wunde Woyzeck." In *Heiner Müller: Werke 8: Schriften*, edited by Frank Hörnigk, 281–83. Frankfurt am Main: Suhrkamp, 2005.

Müller, Klaus-Detlef. "Brechts *Leben des Galilei* und die Folgen: Der Physiker als Gegenstand literarischer Phantasie." In *"Scientia poetica" Literatur und Naturwissenschaft*, edited by Norbert Elsner and Werner Frick, 379–402. Göttingen: Wallstein Verlag, 2004.

Müller-Schöll, Nikolaus. "Arbeit am Gelände (des Theaters): Heiner Müller als politischer Dramaturg." In *Heiner Müllers KüstenLANDSCHAFTEN: Grenzen—Tod—Störung*, edited by Till Nitschmann and Florian Vaßen, 57–83. Bielefeld: transcript, 2021.

Müller-Schöll, Nikolaus. "Denken auf der Bühne: Derrida, Forsythe, Chétouane." In *Mnema: Derrida zum Andenken*, edited by Hans-Joachim Lenger and Georg Christoph Tholen, 187–208. Bielefeld: transcript, 2007.

Müller-Schöll, Nikolaus. *Das Theater des "konstruktiven Defaitismus."* Frankfurt am Main: Vittorio Klostermann, 2002.

Müller-Schöll, Nikolaus. "'. . . die Wolken still / Sprachlos die Winde': Heiner Müllers Schweigen." *theatercombinat*. 2004. Accessed March 6, 2023. http://www.theatercombinat.com/projekte/mauser/mauserNms.html.

Murphy, Michelle. *Sick Building Syndrome and the Problem of Uncertainty: Environmental Politics, Technoscience, and Women Workers*. Durham, NC: Duke University Press, 2006.

Nancy, Jean-Luc. *After Fukushima: The Equivalence of Catastrophes*. New York: Fordham University Press, 2015.

Nancy, Jean-Luc. "The Existence of the World Is Always Unexpected: Jean-Luc Nancy in Conversation with John Paul Ricco." In *Art in the Anthropocene: Encounters among Aesthetics, Politics, Environments and Epistemologies*, edited by Heather Davis and Etienne Turpin, 85–92. London: Open Humanities Press, 2015.

Nekes, Werner. "Whatever Happens between the Pictures: A Lecture by Werner Nekes; Edited and with an Introduction by David S. Lenfest." *Afterimage* 5, no. 5 (1977): 7–13.

Nietzsche, Friedrich. *The Birth of Tragedy and Other Writings*. Translated by Ronald Speirs. Edited by Raymond Geuss and Ronald Speirs. Cambridge: Cambridge University Press, 1999.

Nietzsche, Friedrich. *Menschliches, Allzumenschliches I und II*. Munich: de Gruyter, 1999.

Nixon, Rob. *Slow Violence and the Environmentalism of the Poor*. Cambridge, MA: Harvard University Press, 2011.

No Light (Kein Licht). Rowohlt Theaterverlag. Publisher's thumbnail description of the play. Accessed March 23, 2023. https://www.rowohlt-theaterverlag.de/foreign-rights/play/kein-licht-1687.

Partridge, Damani. *Blackness as a Universal Claim: Holocaust Heritage, Noncitizen Futures, and Black Power in Berlin*. Oakland: University of California Press, 2022.

Pełka, Artur. *Das Spektakel der Gewalt—die Gewalt des Spektakels: Angriff und Flucht in deutschsprachigen Theatertexten zwischen 9/11 und Flüchtlingsdrama*. Bielefeld: transcript, 2016.

Pewny, Katharina. *Das Drama des Prekären*. Bielefeld: transcript, 2011.

"DIE PILOTEN: 10 Jahre TALK 2000: Gründung der Ersten Animatographischen Gesellschaft." *Akademie der Künste*. 2007. Accessed March 23, 2023. https://www.adk.de/de/aktuell/veranstaltungen/i_2007/DIE-PILOTEN-10-Jahre-TALK-2000.htm.

Pitts-Taylor, Victoria. "The Plastic Brain: Neoliberalism and the Neuronal Self." *Health* 14, no. 6 (2010): 635–52.

Pohlmann, Jens. *The Creation of an Avant-Garde Brand: Heiner Müller's Self-Presentation in the German Public Sphere.* Oxford: Peter Lang, 2023.

Pohlmann, Jens. "Heiner Müller's Cooperation with the 'Institution of Art'—An Analysis of His Performance at the Büchnerpreis Award Ceremony." *Monatshefte* 113, no. 2 (2021): 208–29.

Pollesch, René. "Dialektisches Theater Now!" In *Liebe ist kälter als das Kapital*, 301–5. Reinbek bei Hamburg: Rowohlt, 2005.

Pollesch, René. "Ich würde gern in der U-Bahn schreien." In *Liebe ist kälter als das Kapital*, 319–26. Reinbek bei Hamburg: Rowohlt, 2005.

Pollesch, René. "Der Ort, an dem Wirklichkeit anders vorkommt." In *Liebe ist kälter als das Kapital*, 313–8. Reinbek bei Hamburg: Rowohlt, 2005.

Pollesch, René. *Der Schnittchenkauf: 2011–2012.* Berlin: Galerie Buchholz, 2012.

Pollesch, René, and Frank M. Raddatz. "Die Probleme der Anderen: René Pollesch im Gespräch über Brecht, das Normale als Konstruktion und die Theoriefähigkeit des Alltags." *Theater der Zeit* 2 (2007): 22–26.

Poulet, Jacques. "Es lebe der Widerspruch!—Den Widerspruch leben!" In *Heiner Müller: Werke 10: Gespräche 1: 1965–1987*, edited by Frank Hörnigk, 746–61. Frankfurt am Main: Suhrkamp, 2008.

"Pressemitteilung Schlingensiefs Animatograph Island Edition—House of Obsession." *Christoph Schlingensief.* 2005. Accessed March 23, 2023. https://www.schlingensief.com/projekt.php?id=t052.

Primavesi, Patrick. "Theater als Labor und Experiment." In *Experimente in den Künsten: Transmediale Erkundungen in Literatur, Theater, Film, Musik und bildender Kunst*, edited by Stefanie Kreuzer, 131–62. Bielefeld: transcript, 2012.

Puchner, Martin. *The Drama of Ideas: Platonic Provocations in Theater and Philosophy.* New York: Oxford University Press, 2010.

Raddatz, Frank M. "Abenteuer Gaia: Nietzsches und Brechts Theatersysteme im Licht des Anthropozäns." *Lettre International* 138 (2022): 102–10.

Raddatz, Frank M. *Dämonen unterm Roten Stern: Zur Geschichtsphilosophie und Ästhetik Heiner Müllers.* Stuttgart: Metzler, 1991.

Raddatz, Frank M. *Das Drama des Anthropozäns.* Berlin: Theater der Zeit, 2021.

Raddatz, Frank M. "Ich wünsche mir Brecht in der Peep-Show." In *Heiner Müller: Werke 11: Gespräche 2: 1987–1991*, edited by Frank Hörnigk, 313–31. Frankfurt am Main: Suhrkamp, 2008.

Rancière, Jacques. *The Emancipated Spectator.* Translated by Gregory Elliott. New York: Verso, 2008.

Rancière, Jacques. *The Ignorant Schoolmaster: Five Lessons in Intellectual Emancipation.* Translated by Kristin Ross. Stanford, CA: Stanford University Press, 1991.

Reinarz, Jonathan. *Past Scents: Historical Perspectives on Smell.* Champaign: University of Illinois Press, 2014.

Riegel, Hans Peter. *Beuys: Die Biographie.* Berlin: Aufbau, 2013.

Rilke, Rainer Maria. *Duineser Elegien*. Leipzig: Insel, 1923.
Rilke, Rainer Maria. *Duino Elegies & The Sonnets to Orpheus*. Translated by Stephen Mitchell. New York: Vintage, 2009.
Rittberger, Kevin. *Cassandra/Prometheus:Right to World*. Translated by Jack Davis. Unpublished manuscript prepared for *Diffractive World-Making: Theatre & Science Beyond the Capitalocene* conference organized by Teresa Kovacs and Kevin Rittberger. Indiana University Bloomington, November 10–12, 2022.
Roach, Joseph. *The Player's Passion: Studies in the Science of Acting*. Ann Arbor: University of Michigan Press, 1993.
Robinson, Dylan. *Hungry Listening: Resonant Theory for Indigenous Sound Studies*. Minneapolis: University of Minnesota Press, 2020.
Roesner, David. "From the Spirit of Music: Dramaturgy and Play in Contemporary German Theatre." *TDR: The Drama Review* 67, no. 2 (2023): 105–23.
Rokem, Freddie. *TheaterDenken: Begegnungen und Konstellationen zwischen Philosophen und Theatermachern*. Berlin: Neofelis, 2017.
Roselt, Jens. *Phänomenologie des Theaters*. Munich: Wilhelm Fink, 2008.
Rosenthal, Mark. "Joseph Beuys: Staging Sculpture." In *Joseph Beuys: Actions, Vitrines, Environments*, edited by Mark Rosenthal, 10–135. London: Other Distribution, 2004.
Sarasin, Philipp. *Darwin und Foucault*. Frankfurt am Main: Suhrkamp, 2009.
Schade, Julia. "Hold Your Breath Against Time: Zum Denken einer Widerständigkeit der Zeit bei William Kentridge." In *Das Denken der Bühne: Szenen zwischen Theater und Philosophie*, edited by Leon Gabriel and Nikolaus Müller-Schöll, 201–14. Bielefeld, transcript, 2019.
Schaub, Mirjam. "Sich in den Weltzusammenhang hineindrehen: Schlingensiefs Animatograph, mit Aristoteles und Hegel gelesen." In *Der Gesamtkünstler: Christoph Schlingensief*, edited by Pia Janke and Teresa Kovacs, 182–95. Vienna: Praesens Verlag, 2011.
Schiller, Friedrich. "Die Schaubühne als moralische Anstalt betrachtet." 1784. Reprinted in *Sämtliche Werke, vol. 11*, edited by Eduard von der Hellen, 91–101. Tübingen: Cotta, 1904.
Schiller, Friedrich. "Theater Considered as a Moral Institution." Translated by John Sigerson and John Chambless. *The Schiller Institute*. Accessed April 18, 2024. https://archive.schillerinstitute.com/transl/schil_theatremoral.html.
Schlaich, Frieder. *Interviewfilm—Christoph Schlingensief*. Berlin: Filmgalerie 451, 2004. DVD, 77 min.
Schlingensief, Christoph. *The African Twintowers*. Berlin: Filmgalerie 451, 2005. DVD, 399 min.
Schlingensief, Christoph. *Ich weiß, Ich war's*. Köln: Kiepenhauer & Witsch, 2012.
Schlingensief, Christoph. "*Kaprow City*, Program Notes." *Kaprow City*. Program booklet. Volksbühne am Rosa-Luxemburg-Platz, Berlin, 2006.

Schlingensief, Christoph. *Eine Kirche der Angst vor dem Fremden in Mir*. Program booklet. Ruhrtriennale, 2008.

Schlingensief, Christoph. "Die Kunst ist." *Invitrust Stiftung Operndorf Afrika*. 2009. Accessed October 23, 2023. https://www.invitrust.org/stiftung-operndorf-afrika/.

Schlingensief, Christoph. *Mea Culpa*. Vienna: Hoanzl, 2009. DVD, 120 min.

Schlingensief, Christoph. *So schön wie hier kanns im Himmel gar nicht sein*. Köln: Kiepenhauer and Witsch, 2009.

Schlingensief, Christoph. "We Will Not Redeem." *Operndorf Afrika*. 2010. Accessed October 23, 2023. https://www.operndorf-afrika.com/en/about/about-us/.

Schlingensief, Christoph. "Wir sind zwar nicht gut, aber wir sind da." In *Schlingensief! Notruf für Deutschland*, edited by Julia Lochte and Wilfried Schulz, 12–39. Hamburg: Rotbuch Verlag, 1998.

"Schlingensief-Installation in der Burg." *ORF Wien*. 2006. Accessed March 23, 2023. https://wiev1.orf.at/stories/83132.

Schmidt, Hannah. "Gedankenstromlogorrhoe?" *Terzwerk*. 2017. Accessed August 10, 2022. https://www.terzwerk.de/text/.

Schnell, Ralf. "'Doch nichts ist ungeheurer als die Natur'—Transkulturalität und Universalität bei Elfriede Jelinek." In *Postdramatisches Theater als Transkulturelles Theater*, edited by Teresa Kovacs and Koku Nonoa, 253–61. Tübingen: Narr Francke Attempo, 2018.

Schönsee, Rebecca. "Strahlende Geiselhaft: Jelineks Lärmblendung *Kein Licht*." *Studia austriaca* 26 (2018): 45–74.

Schopp, Caroline. "Importunate Feminism." *Texte zur Kunst*. 2023. Accessed October 1, 2023. https://www.textezurkunst.de/en/131/caroline-lillian-schopp-florentina-holzinger-importunate-feminism/#id6.

Schößler, Franziska. "Intermedialität und das 'Fremde in mir': Christoph Schlingensiefs ReadyMadeOper *Mea Culpa*." In *Der Gesamtkünstler: Christoph Schlingensief*, edited by Pia Janke and Teresa Kovacs, 117–34. Vienna: Praesens Verlag, 2011.

Schößler, Franziska. "Die Sehnsucht nach Wirklichkeit und ihre ästhetische Form: (Dokumentar-)Dramen und Anlassstücke nach 1989." *Zeitschrift für Deutsche Philologie* 131 (2012): 79–94.

Schulz, Genia. *Heiner Müller*. Stuttgart: Metzler, 1980.

Schütte, Uwe. "Brückenschlag, Familienalbum und Traum/a-Material—Zur Rolle der Prosa im Werk von Heiner Müller." *Euphorion* 100 (2006): 461–88.

Schwab, Gabriele. *Radioactive Ghosts*. Minneapolis: University of Minnesota Press, 2020.

Seidensticker, Bernd. "Philologisch-literarische Einleitung." In *Das griechische Satyrspiel*, edited by Ralf Krumeich, Nikolaus Pechstein, and Bernd Seidensticker, 1–40. Darmstadt: Wissenschaftliche Buchgesellschaft, 1999.

Serres, Michel. *Genesis*. Translated by Geneviève James and James Nielson. Ann Arbor: University of Michigan Press, 1995.

Serres, Michel. *The Five Senses: A Philosophy of Mingled Bodies.* Translated by Margaret Sankey and Peter Cowley. New York: Bloomsbury, 2016.
Serres, Michel. *Musique.* Paris: Pommier, 2011.
Serres, Michel. *The Parasite.* Translated by Lawrence R. Schehr. Minneapolis: University of Minnesota Press, 2007.
Serres, Michel, and Bruno Latour. *Conversations on Science, Culture, and Time.* Translated by Roxanne Lapidus. Ann Arbor: University of Michigan Press, 1995.
Shepherd-Barr, Kirsten E., ed. *Cambridge Companion to Theatre and Science.* Cambridge: Cambridge University Press, 2020.
Sieg, Katrin. *Choreographing the Global in European Cinema and Theater.* New York: Palgrave, 2008.
Solnit, Rebecca. *Savage Dreams: A Journey into the Hidden Wars of the American West.* Berkeley: University of California Press, 1994.
Sonderegger, Ruth. "Adorno geht in das Theater von René Pollesch und fragt nach Kulturkritik heute." *Zeitschrift für Ästhetik und Allgemeine Kunstwissenschaft* 48, no. 2 (2003): 175–93.
Sophocles. *Antigone.* In *Hölderlin's Sophocles.* Translated by David Constantine, 69–112. Hexham: Bloodaxe Books, 2001.
Sophocles. *The Ichneutae of Sophocles.* Edited and translated by Richard Johnson Walker. London: Burns and Oates, 1919.
Sophocles. *Philoktetes.* In *The Complete Plays of Sophocles.* Translated by Robert Bragg and James Scully, 191–282. New York: Harper Collins, 2011.
Spahn, Claus. "Das Bayreuther Hühnermassaker." *Die Zeit,* July 29, 2004.
Spinoza. *Ethics: Proved in Geometrical Order.* Translated by Michael Silverthorne. Edited by Matthew J. Kisner. Cambridge: Cambridge University Press, 2018.
Spivak, Gayatri. "Can the Subaltern Speak?" In *Marxism and the Interpretation of Culture,* edited by Cary Nelson and Lawrence Grossberg, 271–313. Champaign: University of Illinois Press, 1988.
Stegemann, Bernd. *Kritik des Theaters.* Berlin: Theater der Zeit, 2013.
Stegemann, Bernd. *Lob des Realismus.* Berlin: Theater der Zeit, 2015.
Stein, Gertrude. *Lectures in America.* Boston: Beacon Press, 1985.
Sterne, Jonathan. *The Audible Past: Cultural Origins of Sound Reproduction.* Durham, NC: Duke University Press, 2003.
Stoever, Jennifer Lynn. *The Sonic Color Line: Race and the Cultural Politics of Listening.* New York: New York University Press, 2016.
Storch, Wolfgang. "Die Bildenden Künste." In *Heiner Müller Handbuch,* edited by Hans-Thies Lehmann and Patrick Primavesi, 113–21. Stuttgart: Metzler, 2003.
Szondi, Peter. *Theory of the Modern Drama.* Translated by Michael Hays. Cambridge: Polity Press, 1987.
Teraoka, Arlene Akiko. "Der Auftrag und Die Maßnahme: Models of Revolution in Heiner Müller und Bertolt Brecht." *The German Quarterly* 59, no. 1 (1986): 65–84.

Thiele, Rita. "Glücklich ist, wer vergisst? Eine E-Mail-Korrespondenz zwischen Elfriede Jelinek und Rita Thiele." In *Das Werk/Im Bus/Ein Sturz*. Cologne: Program Booklet Schauspiel Köln, 2010.

Thiele, Rita. "'Nicht einmal ein Wort rührt uns an': Über *Kein Licht* von Elfriede Jelinek." *JELINEK[JAHR]BUCH: Elfriede Jelinek-Forschungszentrum* (2012): 63–72.

Tiedemann, Kathrin. "Das Deutsche scheut das Triviale." *Theater der Zeit* 6 (1994): 34–39.

Tigges, Stefan, ed. *Dramatische Transformationen*. Bielefeld: transcript, 2007.

Tisdall, Caroline. *Joseph Beuys*. New York: Guggenheim Museum, 1979.

Truffaut, François. *Hitchcock*. New York: Simon and Schuster Paperbacks, 1984.

Tsing, Anna. *The Mushroom at the End of the World*. Princeton, NJ: Princeton University Press, 2015.

Ullrich, Calvin D. "The Future of Nothingness: Plastic Apocalypticism or an Insistent Messianic?" *Stellenbosch Theological Journal* 8, no. 1 (2022): 1–24.

Vahanian, Noëlle. "A Conversation with Catherine Malabou." *JCRT* 9, no. 1 (2008): 1–13.

van Daele, Eva. "The Absence of Traditional Characters in Philippe Manoury's Thinkspiel *Kein Licht*. (2011/2012/2017)." *Jelinetz*. 2018. Accessed August 10, 2022. https://jelinetz2.files.wordpress.com/2018/07/eva-van-daele.pdf.

Vanden Heuvel, Mike. "Good Vibrations: Avant-Garde Theatre and Ethereal Aesthetics from Kandinsky to Futurism." In *Vibratory Modernism*, edited by Anthony Enns and Shelley Trower. New York: Palgrave Macmillan, 2013.

Vaßen, Florian. "Bildbeschreibung." In *Heiner Müller Handbuch*, edited by Hans-Thies Lehmann and Patrick Primavesi, 197–200. Stuttgart: Metzler, 2003.

Viala, Jean. *Butoh: Shades of Darkness*. Tokyo: Shufunotomo, 1988.

Vogel, Juliane. "Ich möchte seicht sein: Flächenkonzepte in Texten Elfriede Jelineks." In *Lob der Oberfläche*, edited by Juliane Vogel and Thomas Eder, 9–18. Munich: Wilhelm Fink, 2010.

Vogel, Juliane, and Thomas Eder, eds. *Lob der Oberfläche*. Munich: Wilhelm Fink, 2010.

Vogel, Sabine. "Christoph Schlingensief: Burgtheater Wien." *Artforum* 44, no. 9 (2006): 302.

von Graevenitz, Antje. "Erlösungskunst oder Befreiungspolitik: Wagner und Beuys." In *Unsere Wagner: Joseph Beuys, Heiner Müller, Karlheinz Stockhausen, Hans Jürgen Syberberg: Essays*, edited by Gabriele Förg, 11–49. Frankfurt am Main: Fischer, 1984.

Wark, McKenzie. *Molecular Red: Theory for the Anthropocene*. New York: Verso, 2016.

Weber, Carl. "The Pressure of Experience." In *Hamletmachine and Other Texts for the Stage*. Translated and edited by Carl Weber, 13–30. New York: Performing Arts Journal Publications, 1984.

Werner, Hendrik. "Verwaltungsakte produzieren keine Erfahrungen." In *Heiner Müller: Werke 12: Gespräche 3: 1991–1995*, edited by Frank Hörnigk, 712–33. Frankfurt am Main: Suhrkamp, 2008.
Wilson, Edward O. *In Search of Nature*. Washington, DC: Island, 1996.
Wirth, Andrzej. "Realität auf dem Theater als ästhetische Utopie oder: Wandlungen des Theaters im Umfeld der Medien." *Gießener Universitätsblätter* 2 (1987): 83–93.
Wittstock, Uwe. "Der Weltuntergang ist zu einem modischen Problem geworden." In *Heiner Müller: Werke 10: Gespräche 1: 1965–1987*, edited by Frank Hörnigk, 364–74. Frankfurt am Main: Suhrkamp, 2008.
Žižek, Slavoj. *Less Than Nothing: Hegel and the Shadow of Dialectical Materialism*. London: Verso, 2012.
Žižek, Slavoj. *The Parallax View*. Cambridge, MA: MIT Press, 2006.
Žižek, Slavoj, and Mladen Dolar. *Opera's Second Death*. New York: Routledge, 2002.
Zuckmayer, Carl. *Das kalte Licht*. Frankfurt am Main: Fischer, 1955.
Zupančič, Alenka. *The Shortest Shadow: Nietzsche's Philosophy of the Two*. Cambridge, MA: MIT Press, 2003.

Index

accident, unexpected, 28, 31–32, 38, 46–50, 54–58, 74, 101, 143, 155–57, 209. *See also* possibility; unpredictability
alienation *(Verfremdung)*, 25, 67
Althusser, Louis, 8n15, 19, 23
anagnorisis, 17, 35, 204–5, 207–9
Anthropocene, 15, 24, 205n12, 206. *See also* technoscientific age
anticipation, 31, 47–49, 55, 79–80, 83, 101. *See also* hope
apocalypse, 37, 41, 43–44, 59, 79, 86, 88, 115, 173n6, 203. *See also* catastrophe; end times
Aristotle, *Poetics*, 131–32, 182, 207–8
Artaud, Antonin, 4, 25
atomic time, 83–90
atomic warfare: bombing of Hiroshima and Nagasaki, 5, 9, 40, 59, 106n2, 116. *See also* catastrophe; nuclear threat
audience, 2, 12, 22, 25, 58, 121; activation of, 192; co-constitution of theater with, 192–200; identification with characters, 131–32, 134, 175 (*see also* empathy); spatial arrangements and, 139, 145–46, 151, 154, 157, 171–75, 182–83, 186. *See also* catharsis; emotion; hearing; senses; visual image and gaze
aura, 116–17
avant-garde, 4, 24–25, 154, 158, 166n55, 168–69

Badiou, Alain, 18, 47n37, 155–56, 169
Barad, Karen, 2n2, 10n20, 10n21, 29, 33, 45n31, 65, 106n2, 115, 196, 204, 211; agential realism, 52n55, 198–99; double-slit experiment, 34,

Barad, Karen (*continued*)
  53n56, 175, 188–92; on quantum physics and the void, 16, 18, 20–22, 116n25, 122, 127–29; on "space-timematterings," 21–22, 52n55, 90, 119, 211; on time and space in quantum age, 84–85, 88, 90, 116, 119
Barthes, Roland, 64–65
Beckett, Samuel, 3, 4n3, 136n68
becoming: chaos as, 126–27; film and, 146–48; music and, 124; nothingness and, 124–25; ongoing process of, 34, 190–200; potential for, 17, 22, 28, 34, 42, 142, 146, 155, 164 (*see also* void). *See also* change; creation; metamorphosis; plasticity; spacetimematterings; transformation; world-making
beginnings, 37, 46, 205, 214–20
Benjamin, Walter, 52n55, 55, 66, 72–73, 75, 75n15, 85, 91n56, 109, 116–17
betrayal, 72, 95–97
Beuys, Joseph, 159–65
biology, 9, 18, 27–29, 32, 34, 176–83; evolution, 66, 172–73, 180–81 (*see also* Darwin); neurobiology, 99, 135n66, 148. *See also* human-nonhuman, relationship between; neuroscience
Bohr, Niels, 189–91
boundaries, 11, 124, 139–40, 151, 188–89, 191, 198–99
Brecht, Bertolt, 4, 9, 12, 17, 24–26, 59–64, 75, 87n49, 109, 134n63, 171–72, 182, 193, 200, 219, 220; "Als ich in weißem Krankenzimmer der Charité," 59–60, 62–63, 75, 94; *Der Messingkauf*, 34, 174; *Die Maßnahme*, 75, 95n71; *Fatzer*, 39–40; *Life of Galileo*, 42, 59, 75, 94, 209n19
Büchner, Georg, 46; *Woyzeck*, 38, 55–57
Bulletin of the Atomic Scientists, 87. *See also* Doomsday Clock

Canguilhem, Georges, 20
capitalism, 26–27, 38–42, 106n2; time and, 84, 89–90, 92, 114–15; violence of, 108, 122, 214; zombie life of, 41–42, 217
catastrophe, 2–3, 5, 17, 27–28, 33–34, 40–42, 45n30, 63, 73, 87–88, 106–9, 136, 173, 202–3, 214, 218. *See also* apocalypse; atomic warfare; climate change; death; destruction; end times; explosion; Fukushima nuclear disaster; global warming; nuclear threat; ruins; tragedy
catharsis, 17, 25, 33, 130–37, 164, 208. *See also* emotion
cerebrality/cerebral subject, 50, 60, 96, 163
change, 35–37, 47–49, 90, 96, 163–67, 181. *See also* becoming; ease, joy, and pleasure; explosion; metamorphosis; mutability; plasticity; revolution; transformation
chaos, 4, 11, 111, 116, 120–30. *See also* void
cinematic principles. *See* film
climate change, 35, 43–45, 202, 211. *See also* catastrophe; global warming
co-constitution, 90, 148, 190–200, 204. *See also* entanglement
Cold War, 39, 88, 106n2, 201
colonialism/imperialism, 26–27, 37, 75, 106n2; atomic clocks and, 84; time and, 84, 89–90, 92, 114–15; violence of, 108, 122
complementarity principle, 190–91
contingency, 8, 18, 49, 56, 142, 168, 180, 188. *See also* possibility
creation, 142, 155–56, 158, 193–96. *See also* becoming
cuts, 50, 55–56, 61, 80–81, 198; filmic, 80, 141, 145, 169. *See also* wound

Damasio, Antonio, 65, 99n87, 135n66
dark phase, in film, 147–54
Darwin, Charles, 8n15, 10n20, 19–20, 34, 48, 174–75, 180–83, 190

Index   247

D-*Dramatik* (Darwin-type theater), 174–75, 182, 195
death, 37, 79, 93; of art, 167–69; freedom and, 169 (*see also* freedom); plasticity and, 46 (*see also* plasticity); possible endings, 168–69; as transformation, 161–62, 167 (*see also* transformation). *See also* life and death, relationship between
decomposition, 33, 139–40, 159, 166
deconstruction, 5, 18, 31, 61, 81, 169
Derrida, Jacques, 18–19, 39, 44, 48, 51n51, 52n55, 61
destruction, 37, 79, 86–87, 97–98, 148, 155, 168, 169, 214–15. *See also* catastrophe; explosion; nuclear threat; ruins; wound
destructive plasticity, 31, 49–52, 73, 92, 135–36, 164. *See also* plasticity
detection, 40, 45, 57, 64, 65, 204, 208. *See also* observation; perception
determination, 31, 56, 101; boundaries and, 189–90; contingency and, 168, 180; Newtonian physics, 188; observation and, 174–75. *See also* indeterminacy; observation; predetermination
determinism, 48–50, 63, 93
dialectical theater, 8, 26, 31, 200
dialectics, 18, 19n47, 59, 61, 87n49, 133
didactic plays, 17, 34, 75, 171, 193
difference, 49, 58, 62, 76, 85, 92, 99, 107, 175, 177–78, 189, 191, 196, 200
diffraction, 175, 177–78; in double-split experiment, 185; as queer phenomenon, 188–89; of space, 116, 148; of time, 85, 87n49, 89, 90, 116, 118, 148
Dionysian theater, 24–25
dis/affection, 130–31, 134–37. *See also* indifference
disappearance, 33, 39, 95, 99, 115, 118–19, 123, 150, 166–67, 193, 195

disruption, 158–59; of time and space, 32, 40, 43, 71–92, 128, 151. *See also* rupture
Doomsday Clock, 27n76, 45n31, 84, 87–88
doppelgänger, 76, 80, 94–95, 99–100
double-slit experiment, 34, 53n56, 184–85, 188–92
Dürrenmatt, Friedrich, 42
dystopia, 219

ease, joy, and pleasure, 32, 35, 60, 62, 79, 93–96, 98n83, 99, 169, 209, 219–20
Eddington, Arthur Stanley, 117
Edison, Thomas, 145
emotion, 33, 77, 130–37, 173, 182. *See also* catharsis; dis/affection; indifference
empathy, 25–26, 131–32, 134, 174–75, 182, 195
emptiness, 2, 4n4, 17–18, 20, 33, 55n64, 69, 102n93, 103n95, 124, 127, 147, 214. *See also* nothingness; void
end times, 32, 86–89, 114–15, 202–3. *See also* apocalypse; catastrophe
entanglement, 112–18, 123–24, 128, 148, 154, 163, 174–75, 179, 190–91, 198–200. *See also* co-constitution
ephemerality, 115, 119, 166–67
ethics, 209
evolution, 66, 172–73, 180–81. *See also* Darwin
exclusion, 133, 174–75, 190–91, 198–200
existence. *See* non/existence
existentialist drama, 3
experimental theater, 2–5, 24–26. *See also* postdramatic theater; theater of the void
explosion, 46, 53–58, 63–70, 92, 96, 99–101, 159, 164, 165, 168, 169, 202, 214. *See also* change; destruction
extinction, 27–28

film: dark phase, 147–54; failure and, 144–45, 155; materiality of, 141–42, 155–59; superimposition of images, 140, 146–47, 150–54
Fischer-Lichte, Erika, 6n7
Fisher, Mark, 39
fluctuation, 11–12, 17, 35, 102n93, 142, 148, 150, 158, 163, 188. *See also* quantum fluctuation
forgetting, 34, 96, 148, 215n38
Foucault, Michel, 49, 178n15, 180
fourth wall, 172. *See also* audience
fragmentation, 57–58, 151, 154, 178
freedom, 35, 38, 43, 47, 49, 53, 93, 96, 98n83, 163–64, 167, 169, 173, 209–10, 216, 220
Freud, Sigmund, 50–52, 76, 95, 209n20
Friedrich, Caspar David, 56–57, 80
Frisch, Max, 42
Fukushima nuclear disaster, 10, 32, 41, 106–8, 111–12, 115, 122. *See also* catastrophe
futurity, 66; absent, 66; catastrophe and violence, 108, 202–3, 214; groundlessness and, 205; haunting and, 119 (*see also* haunting); plasticity and, 209 (*see also* plasticity); void and, 2–3, 17, 31, 34–38, 72, 214–20; wound and, 214, 216, 219. *See also* becoming; hope; possibility; time

Galileo, 26
Gesamtkunstwerk (total work of art), 17, 25, 34, 139n1, 142, 164–66
Ghosh, Amitav, 35, 204–5, 207–8
ghostliness, 72–73, 172. *See also* haunting
Girard, René, 109, 131–34
Global South, 75, 89–90, 92, 97
global warming, 27, 44–45, 202–7, 211. *See also* catastrophe; climate change
Godard, Jean-Luc, 149–50
Goebbels, Heiner, 3, 73n5, 102–3
Gotscheff, Dimiter, 3, 69, 102, 215–16
Greek theater, ancient, 2, 7, 25, 164

groundlessness, 16, 35, 70, 127, 205, 209, 219. *See also* fluctuation; void

Haraway, Donna, 9n20, 29, 175, 176–79, 187, 189
hare: Schlingensief's film on, 139–41, 159–66, 169; symbolism of, 159–60, 165–66
haunting: music and quantum physics, 112, 119; quantum fluctuation and, 21–22; uncanny encounters and, 211; void and, 20. *See also* void
hauntology, 22, 32, 39–40
healing, 25–26, 31, 47n37, 58–63, 161–64, 167, 169
hearing, 14. *See also* sound
Hecht, Gabrielle, 43
Hegel, G. W. F., 8, 18, 48n41, 59, 61, 133, 211–12, 211n23, 217
Heidegger, Martin, 109, 115n24, 211n23
history and historiography, 16, 46, 50, 52–53, 55, 72–75, 85, 100, 212; of film, 144–46; German, 37, 151, 154; as seismology, 31, 66–68; as time, 89. *See also* futurity; time
Hitchcock, Alfred, 195
Hölderlin, Friedrich, 4, 24
Holzinger, Florentina, 3, 218–19
hope, 37, 46, 54, 73, 79, 90, 95, 97–99, 120–21, 181, 217
human-nonhuman, relationship between, 176–79, 200, 205–6, 210, 212–14
Hurley, Jessica, 43–44
hyperobjects, 15n40, 44n27, 203–6, 209–11

identity, 53–54. *See also* subjectivity
illness, 161–62, 168–69
indeterminacy, 16–22, 45n30, 72, 85, 110–11, 122, 127, 142, 174, 180–82, 188–93, 196, 200, 210–11. *See also* determination
indifference, 32, 37–38, 50, 77, 99–100, 135–36, 173, 182, 208–9. *See also* dis/affection; emotion

Jahnn, Hans Henny, 42
Jelinek, Elfriede, 1, 3, 16–17, 21, 28–30, 29n79, 32–33, 58, 103–37, 173, 197, 210, 217; *Abraumhalde*, 10n22; *Das Werk*, 212n34; *Diese Maschine ist unschuldig*, 213; *Epilog?*, 107, 211–14; "Grußwort nach Japan," 11; *Kein Licht*, 10–11, 32–33, 105–37; *Kein Licht: Prolog?*, 107; *Wut*, 134
joy. *See* ease, joy, and pleasure

K-Dramatik (type of theater), 174
Kipphardt, Heinar, 42
Kleist, Heinrich von, 56–57, 80, 186
Kluge, Alexander, 66–67, 139n3, 141n7, 142n9, 144n17, 147n24, 165
knowledge: language and, 124–27. *See also* anagnorisis
Kohso, Sabu, 40–41, 106n2, 217
Kracauer, Siegfried, 67

landscape, 64
language, 68, 134; deconstruction of, 5; knowledge and, 124–27; as sound, 102–3, 106. *See also Textflächen* (text surfaces)
Latour, Bruno, 124
Lehmann, Hans-Thies, 5–9
Lessing, Gotthold Ephraim, 10n22, 131–33
Lévi-Strauss, Claude, 57–58
life and death, relationship between, 10–17, 20–21, 33–34, 106, 111, 115, 124, 127–30, 140, 148, 154, 165–67. *See also* death; fluctuation; haunting; non/existence; void
linear time: disruption of, 72, 89; end of, 114–15 (*see also* end times). *See also* time

MacGuffin, theory of, 195
Malabou, Catherine, 8n15, 29, 163, 208–9, 214; on Darwin, 19–20, 34, 48, 180n23; on destructive plasticity, 31, 49–52, 92, 135–36; metamorphosis and subjectivity, 32; on plasticity, 31, 36–37, 46, 48–54, 57, 85, 100, 178n15; on regeneration, 60–62, 167; void and, 18–20, 22–23, 98; on war against meaning, 41n19
Malzacher, Florian, 206
Marey, Étienne-Jules, 146
materialism, 8, 19, 76n18, 98n83; of aleatory, 8, 19, 219; historical, 55
materiality, 119, 181; of film, 141–42, 155–59
meaninglessness, 65n90, 87, 93, 126, 137, 195–96
meaning-making, 16n41, 68, 79, 102, 134; alternative modes of, 209, 214; anagnorisis and, 208; cerebral subject and, 50; experimental conditions and, 191; negative feelings and, 136–37; noise and, 122–27; possibility and, 147, 154, 157, 177, 180; void and, 110–11, 121–29 (*see also* void); war against, 41n19
messianism, 51n51, 52n55, 55, 70, 75, 75n15
metamorphosis, 25, 32, 50–54, 74, 76, 81, 91–100, 103, 140, 159–64. *See also* becoming; change; plasticity; transformation
metaphysics, 17, 51n51, 62, 64, 167, 176, 189, 191, 198
militarism, 26–27, 39, 106n2; time and, 84, 89–90, 92, 114–15; violence of, 108, 122
monstrous beings, 210–14
Morton, Timothy, 15n40, 18, 35, 44n27, 203–5, 210–12
"motor scheme" of writing, 40, 80n30
movement, 156–64, 169
Müller, Heiner, 3, 4n3, 16–17, 28–33, 64–66, 68–70, 96, 97n77, 173, 197, 201, 210, 219; *Anatomie Titus Fall of Rome*, 66; *Der Auftrag* /"Der Mann im Fahrstuhl," 32, 50, 55n63, 70–103, 135n67, 208–9, 216–17, 220; *Description of a Picture*, 12–16, 57, 63, 65, 74, 101–4; *Despoiled Shore*, 40, 57; *Die Hamletmaschine*, 85–86, 218; *Die Schlacht*, 87n49,

250   Index

Müller, Heiner (*continued*) 94n65; "Für immer in Hollywood," 36; *Germania Tod in Berlin*, 94n65; *Grundlings Leben*, 57; *Mauser*, 54; Sophocles's *Philoctetes*, adaptation of, 214–16; *Verkommenes Ufer Medeamaterial Landschaft mit Argonauten*, 216–17; "The Wound Woyzeck," 31, 37–41, 45–58, 94n65, 97n78, 140n6, 202–3, 209n19
music, 64, 110–19, 123–24, 127
mutability, 16, 19, 174, 180–81, 188, 190. *See also* change; metamorphosis; plasticity; transformation
Muybridge, Eadweard, 146

Nancy, Jean-Luc, 9n15, 41n19, 108n8
nationalism, 39, 108, 114, 213n34
natural selection, 19–20, 22. *See also* evolution
negative possibility, 51–54. *See also* possibility
Nekes, Werner, 141nn7–8, 144n17, 147
neoliberalism, 6, 8, 15n40, 165n51, 173, 218, 220
neuroscience, 29, 49, 65, 99–100, 135, 148
New German Cinema, 142n9
Newtonian physics, 20, 32, 75, 89–90, 154, 170, 187–89, 191
Nietzsche, Friedrich, 4, 24–26, 46, 96n76
noise, 122–27. *See also* sound
non/existence, 10, 20–21, 126–28, 151, 163. *See also* life and death, relationship between
nothingness, 3, 120–30; darkness and, 150; theories of, 17–18. *See also* emptiness; void
nuclear threat, 13, 16n41, 23, 27–28, 31, 35–45, 201–3, 215–16; mundane and sublime, 43–45, 202. *See also* catastrophe; Doomsday Clock; Fukushima nuclear disaster; radiation

observation, 14, 56, 64, 117, 155, 157, 197–99; scientific modes of, 25–26, 174–75, 190–92. *See also* detection; perception
Odysseus, 96, 98
ontoepistemology, 175, 188

past. *See* haunting; history and historiography; time
Paul, Robert W., 145n19
P-Dramatik (type of theater), 174
perception, 45, 56–57, 65, 80, 101, 112, 113, 204, 207. *See also* detection; observation; sound; visual image and gaze
performative approach, 189–91
physics. *See* Newtonian physics; quantum physics
plasticity, 38, 45–58, 81, 103, 148; change and, 48, 96 (*see also* change); Darwin and, 181; death and, 46; destructive, 31, 49–52, 73, 92, 135–36, 164; fragmentation and, 154; freedom and, 96 (*see also* freedom); futurity and, 209; healing and, 62, 162 (*see also* healing); Malabou on, 31, 36–37, 46, 48–54, 57, 85, 92, 100, 135–36, 178n15; movement and, 158; musical, 156; as progressive possibility, 100, 168; theater of the void and, 38; wound and, 49–50, 57. *See also* becoming
pleasure. *See* ease, joy, and pleasure
Pollesch, René, 3, 9n20, 16–17, 28–29, 28n77, 58, 104, 170–200, 173n6, 210, 217, 218; *Cappuccetto Rosso*, 176, 177; *Carol Reed*, 195; *Der Schnittchenkauf*, 34, 174, 180–81; *(Life on earth can be sweet) Donna*, 176; *Passing*, 176; *Probleme Probleme Probleme*, 34, 170–71, 183–87
possibility: catastrophe and, 218; death and, 168–69; destruction and, 155; explosion and, 168; meaning-making and, 147, 154, 157, 177, 180; negative, 51–54; progressive, plasticity as, 100, 168 (*see also*

plasticity); unanticipated accidents and, 155–57 (*see also* accident, unexpected); violence and, 214; void and, 210, 217. *See also* contingency
postdramatic theater, 5–9, 196, 205
postmodernism, 178, 196, 199, 205
posttraumatic subjectivity, 32, 50, 53, 60, 99–100, 136–37
potential. *See* becoming; possibility; void
predetermination, 19, 174, 181
present: void and, 202–14. *See also* time
proscenium stage, 14n36, 102
psychoanalysis, 75, 163

quantum fluctuation, 21–22, 127
quantum physics, 9, 18, 20–22, 27, 29, 83; double-slit experiment, 34, 53n56, 184–85, 188–92; Müller and, 32, 75, 80; Pollesch and, 28–29, 34, 172, 175, 177, 183–93; time and space in, 84–85, 88, 90, 116, 119
queerness, 34, 175, 183, 188, 191–92

Raddatz, Frank M., 24–26, 62, 206
radiation, 113–14, 119
R-Dramatik (representational-type theater), 174
realism, 52n55, 196–200
rebirth, 160, 164, 167. *See also* resurrection
recognition, 27, 35, 51, 76, 78, 100, 204–5, 207–11. *See also* anagnorisis
reconciliation, 8, 38, 123
redemption, 31, 33, 47, 99, 140, 142, 160, 166. *See also* salvation
regeneration, 23, 31, 38, 60–63, 98, 164, 167
rehearsal, 28n77, 29, 149, 168, 186–87, 193–94
representation, 11, 14–15, 17, 33, 57, 63–65, 81, 110–11, 162, 176, 196; geometry and, 64–65, 89. *See also* senses; sound; visual image and gaze
representational theater, 4, 10–17, 63–65, 110–11, 162–63, 174, 176–77, 196–200

resurrection, 13, 34, 46, 58, 61, 94, 156, 160, 167. *See also* rebirth
revolution, 37, 71–77, 82, 87, 89–91, 95–98, 159, 164. *See also* change
rhythm, 15, 25–26, 102, 126
Rilke, Rainer Maria, 109, 122–23
Rittberger, Kevin, 3, 9n20, 218
rotating stage, 33, 141, 144, 155–57
ruins, 214–20
rupture, 23, 28, 31, 43, 53, 79, 101, 140, 202. *See also* disruption; tragedy

salvation, 31, 33, 38, 47, 54, 58, 60, 99, 140, 142. *See also* redemption
sampling, 178
Sarasin, Philipp, 180
scale, 15–17, 107–8
Schiller, Friedrich, 109, 178–79
Schlingensief, Christoph, 3, 16–17, 28–29, 33–34, 58, 80n32, 104, 138–69, 171n4, 173, 192, 193, 197, 210, 217, 218; *The African Twintowers,* 142–44, 151; Animatograph, 33, 141, 144–46, 151–54, 156–58, 161, 169; "Animatographic Editions," 140n5, 143n13, 144–46, 151–54, 168; *Area 7: Matthäusexpedition,* 151–54; *Bitte liebt Österreich,* 145–46; *Chance 2000,* 161n43; *Diana II,* 146; *Die 120 Tage von Bottrop,* 142; *Die Piloten,* 146n21; *Eine Kirche der Angst vor dem Fremden in mir,* 140n5, 162, 168–69; hare film, 139–41, 159–66, 169; *Kaprow City,* 145, 146; *Kunst und Gemüse, A. Hipler,* 161; *Mea Culpa,* 138, 140n5, 149–50, 165n51, 169; *Menu total,* 149; Opera Village Africa in Burkina Faso, 158, 160n42, 168; *Sterben Lernen,* 167–69; *Tunguska,* 155; Wagner's *Flying Dutchman,* staging of, 149; Wagner's *Parsifal,* staging at Bayreuth, 33–34, 47n37, 139–41, 155–57, 159–69
Schwab, Gabriele, 40

science: entanglement with capitalism, militarism, and imperialism, 26–27, 106n2, 108; theater and, 2–3, 17–18; tragedy and, 25. *See also* biology; neuroscience; Newtonian physics; nuclear threat; observation; quantum physics; seismology; technoscientific age

science fiction, 176–77, 205

seismology, 31, 53, 107n3; history as, 66–68

Self and Other, 173, 177–78, 189, 200. *See also* subjectivity

senses, 14–15, 25, 63–67, 107, 210. *See also* sound; visual image and gaze

Serres, Michel, 122, 124, 126–27

silence, 69–70, 102; "speaking silence," 21, 127, 129

singularity, 22–23, 34, 51, 84, 103, 121, 142, 155, 182–93, 217–18

slow violence, 13, 27, 38

Sophocles, 109; *Antigone*, 2, 10–11, 205, 210–12; *Ichneutae*, 124, 128–29; *Philoctetes* (or *Philoktetes*), 47, 214–16

sound, 14, 15n38, 21, 25–26, 32–33, 63–64, 102–3, 105–11, 127. *See also* music; noise; silence

space: diffraction of, 116, 148; disruption of, 32, 40, 43, 71–92; empty, 4n4 (*see also* emptiness); ghostly, 112; landscape, 64; music and, 116; reconfiguration of, 16n41, 151–54. *See also* topology

spacetimematterings, 21–22, 52n55, 90, 119, 211. *See also* becoming; haunting

Spinoza, 135

subjectivity, 46; disaffected, 130–31, 134–37; hyperobjects and, 209; indifference and, 32, 37–38, 99–100; metamorphosis and, 32, 50–54, 76–77, 91–100; posttraumatic, 32, 50, 53, 60, 99–100, 136–37; through destruction and transformation, 92, 96, 99–100, 148. *See also* cerebrality/cerebral subject; indifference; Self and Other; transsubjectivation

superimposition of images, 140, 146–47, 150–54

synthesis, 57–58, 154

Szondi, Peter, 7–8

technoscientific age, 2–3, 9, 13–17, 26–35, 80, 106n2, 200, 204; use of term, 15n39. *See also* nuclear threat; quantum physics; science

teleology, 8, 17–18, 19n47, 20, 23, 72, 74, 90, 156

Textflächen (text surfaces), 108–9; *Sprachflächen* (language surfaces), 108n10

theater of the void: concept of the void and, 2–5, 16–17 (*see also* void); overview of, 28–35; principles of, 37–70; science and, 9, 13–16, 28–29, 204. *See also* Jelinek; Müller; Pollesch; Schlingensief

time: audience and, 172; diffraction of, 85, 87n49, 89, 90, 116, 118, 148; disruption of, 32, 40, 43, 71–92, 128, 151; entangled with capitalism, militarism, nationalism, and imperialism, 84, 89–90, 92, 114–15; linear, 72, 89, 114–15; music and, 115–16; quantum age and, 81–92. *See also* futurity; history and historiography

topology, 16, 76, 89, 107

tragedy, 2, 17, 25, 131, 164, 173. *See also* catastrophe; rupture

transformation, 25, 46, 140; death as, 161–62, 167; hare as symbol of, 159–60; rotating stage and, 141; wound and, 161–64. *See also* becoming; change; metamorphosis; plasticity

transsubjectivation, 49, 92, 99, 178n15

trauma, 32, 50, 60, 100, 135n66, 163, 219. *See also* posttraumatic subjectivity; wound

Tsing, Anna, 203n3, 217

uncanny encounters, 35, 150, 203–4, 207–11. *See also* fluctuation; haunting

uncertainty, 48, 78, 80, 172, 185; uncertainty principle, 191n39

unpredictability, 20, 23, 31, 34, 55, 98, 121, 156, 193. *See also* accident, unexpected

Verschränkung (entanglement), 112–18, 123–24, 128, 148, 154, 163, 174–75, 179, 190–91, 198–200

violence, 37; catastrophe and, 108, 202–3, 214; catharsis and, 133–34; of colonialism, capitalism, imperialism, and militarism, 108, 122, 214; possibility and, 214; resistance and, 86; slow, 13, 27, 38; transformation and, 159

visual image and gaze, 14, 81, 101, 102, 106–7, 110; explosion of, 63–70; quantum physics and, 197–98; wound as limit of, 159–64. *See also* representation

void: chaos, 4, 11, 111, 116, 120–30; concept of, 2–5, 16–17, 28–35; destructive plasticity and, 31 (*see also* plasticity); futurity and, 2–3, 17, 31, 34–38, 72, 214–20 (*see also* ease, joy, and pleasure); ground zero and, 2, 101; haunting and, 20 (*see also* haunting); meaning and, 110–11, 121–29 (*see also* meaning-making); ontology of, 190; present and, 202–14; as radical potential, 17–24, 38, 142, 147, 173, 193, 196; and relationship between life and death, 10–17, 20–21, 33–34, 106, 127–30; sensing and, 14–15, 21, 25, 63–67, 70, 122, 128; teleology and, 17–18; third nature and, 217. *See also* accident, unexpected; becoming; beginnings; catastrophe; change; creation; emptiness; fluctuation; groundlessness; metamorphosis; nothingness; nuclear threat; possibility; singularity; theater of the void; transformation; wound

Wagner, Richard, 4, 24–25, 47, 140, 156; *Gesamtkunstwerk* (total work of art), 142, 164–66. *See also* Schlingensief, Christoph

world-making, 180, 196–200. *See also* becoming

wound: futurity and, 214, 216, 219; healing and transformation, 61, 63, 161–64 (*see also* healing; transformation); as limit of image, 159–64; narrative, 80n30; open, 31, 33, 46–47, 58; plasticity and, 49–50, 57 (*see also* plasticity); as productive force, 140. *See also* trauma

zombie capitalism, 41–42, 217
Zuckmayer, Carl, 42

www.ingramcontent.com/pod-product-compliance
Lightning Source LLC
Chambersburg PA
CBHW030534230426
43665CB00010B/885